THE IOWA STATE UNIVERSITY PRESS SERIES
IN THE HISTORY
OF TECHNOLOGY AND SCIENCE

HAMILTON CRAVENS
Series Editor

BOOKS IN THE
IOWA STATE UNIVERSITY PRESS SERIES
IN THE HISTORY OF TECHNOLOGY AND SCIENCE

Christiaan Huygens' *The Pendulum Clock*
or Geometrical Demonstrations Concerning
the Motion of Pendula as Applied to Clocks

> Translated with Notes by Richard J. Blackwell
> Introduction by H. J. M. Bos

The History of Modern Science:
A Guide to the Second Scientific Revolution, 1800–1950

> by Stephen G. Brush

John B. Jervis:
An American Engineering Pioneer

> by F. Daniel Larkin

JOHN B. JERVIS

John B. Jervis

An American Engineering Pioneer

F. DANIEL LARKIN

IOWA STATE UNIVERSITY PRESS / AMES

To my father, Francis M. Larkin,
and to the memory of my mother, Frances E. Larkin,
who aided and encouraged my study of history.

F. Daniel Larkin is Professor of History at State University College, Oneonta, New York.

Frontispiece: John B. Jervis; probably taken in the 1870s. Courtesy Rome Historical Society.

Maps by Susan E. Zeigler

Library of Congress Cataloging-in-Publication Data

Larkin, F. Daniel, 1938–
   John B. Jervis, an American engineering pioneer / F. Daniel Larkin.—1st ed.
     p. cm.
   Includes bibliographical references.
   ISBN 0–8138–0355–1 (alk. paper)
   1. Jervis, John B. (John Bloomfield), 1795–1885. 2. Civil engineers—United States—Biography. I. Title.
TA140.J46L37   1990
624′.092—dc20
   [B]   89–26953

CONTENTS

Series Editor's Introduction, ix
Preface, xi
Acknowledgments, xv
Prologue, xvii

1. **Axeman to Engineer,** 3

2. **The Delaware and Hudson Canal,** 16

3. **A New Challenge,** 35

4. **Canaling Again,** 52

5. **A Different Kind of Waterway,** 61

6. **The Douglass Affair,** 81

7. **Not Only an Engineer,** 95

8. **The Last Eastern Engineering Projects,** 106

9. **To the Mississippi and Beyond,** 120

Epilogue, 145
Notes, 155
Bibliography, 179
Index, 187

SERIES EDITOR'S INTRODUCTION

F. Daniel Larkin's *John B. Jervis: An American Engineering Pioneer* is the third volume published in the Iowa State University Press Series in the History of Technology and Science. Under the general editorship of Hamilton Cravens, the series operates in conjunction with the Center for Historical Studies of Technology and Science at Iowa State University. Larkin's volume follows Richard J. Blackwell's translation of Christiaan Huygen's *The Pendulum Clock* and Stephen G. Brush's *The History of Modern Science: A Guide to the Second Scientific Revolution, 1800–1950.* It is also a series first. *John B. Jervis* is the initial monograph in the series, the traditional instrument through which historians long have communicated research results.

The term "traditional" also serves this volume in another sense. What is striking about Larkin's book is not its methodological innovation or its sophisticated interpretive framework but rather its simplicity. In some ways, it is a throwback to an era in American history historiography in which scholarly works had heroes and villains and where historical figures were lionized or despised. In our present jaded age Larkin's reverence for Jervis is refreshing.

To be sure, Larkin has compelling reasons to be enchanted with his subject. Jervis was an early nineteenth-century American builder/manager *par excellence.* His career began with the Erie Canal and continued into the 1880s. He was involved with early American railroads, made several crucial technical innovations, and managed an early trunk line. Jervis was also significant for who he knew. His relationships to other builders/managers/designers were legion. Indeed, the American Society of Civil Engineers acknowledged Jervis's myriad contributions by making him that organization's first honorary member.

Larkin focuses on Jervis's building career, devoting less attention to his manufacturing interests and his explicit role in molding professional engineering societies. In that sense, Larkin contributes most directly to the debate initiated in Daniel H. Calhoun's *The American Civil Engineer: Origins and Conflict* (Cambridge: Massachusetts Institute of Technology Press, 1960) and expanded by Alfred D. Chandler, Jr. in his *The Visible Hand: The Managerial Revolution In American Business* (Cambridge: Belknap Press, 1977). This debate accentuates the importance of early- and mid-nineteenth century builders/managers/designers not simply for their own time, but for future generations, as those persons who helped begin our time. Readers not comfortable with terms of that debate will still recognize *John B. Jervis* as informative, providing much information for skeptics to fashion their own conceptions. Within the confines of his approach and interests, Larkin presents an exceedingly thorough book.

ALAN I MARCUS
Director, Center for History Studies of Technology and
Science, and Professor of History, Iowa State University

PREFACE

PROBABLY not many railroad passengers ever stop to consider that a simple truck mechanism keeps a high-speed locomotive from derailing on a curve. The swivel truck guides or leads the engine, enabling it to negotiate the curved section of the track while maintaining its momentum. The swivel truck is a simple machine, indeed, but without it the rapid spread of railroads across America's rugged terrain would have been slowed considerably. Think of the expense that would have been involved in constructing the straight, well-ballasted, English-type roads over the vast American landscape.

Over a century and a half ago, an American engineer did consider expense as a factor, as well as high-speed safety. John B. Jervis adapted railroad locomotives to the varied American landscape by replacing the forward rigid driving wheels with the swivel truck.

The forward truck on locomotives, like many of Jervis's innovations, had a profound effect on railway expansion and was but one of Jervis's many contributions to the development of engineering technology in the United States. As a civil engineer, Jervis was principally involved in building and/or managing three canals, seven railroads, and two major urban water systems, not to mention the numerous additional projects on which he acted as consultant. He was actively engaged in civil engineering for fifty of his eighty-nine years. During his last twenty years, although involved in a manufacturing enterprise, he continued to remain abreast of the engineering profession that he had helped to create.

Jervis not only worked to establish engineering as a profession in the United States, but he contributed to it through his inventive spirit. In conjunction with the Delaware and Hudson Canal, Jervis was responsible for constructing the first railroad in North America that was built for use with steam locomotives; he also developed of an air convoy system for braking loaded vehicles on downgrades on that railroad. On another railroad project, Jervis applied the movable forward truck to steam locomotives. While building the Chenango Canal, Jervis invented a gauge to measure rainfall and runoff so he could check the feasibility of a reservoir system to feed the canal. His work on the Croton Aqueduct produced, among other improvements, the use of a reverse curve spillway and stilling basin as part of the Croton Dam. The movable truck, the rain gauge, and the spillway and stilling basin all became models for future engineers and builders.

Until the 1970s, only two works had been published in this century that contained an appreciable amount of material on Jervis. The first was an article by J. K. Finch titled "John Bloomfield Jervis, Civil Engineer," published in the *Transactions of the Newcomen Society* (1931). The second was Nelson M. Blake's *Water for the Cities* (1956), in which Blake included information on Jervis in conjunction with the latter's work on the Croton Aqueduct. Jervis had been mentioned in other general histories, engineering histories, and transportation studies, but seldom had he been given more than one or two sentences. Much of this material on Jervis was repetitive and, in some cases, lacking in accuracy.

During the 1970s, Jervis's achievements became more widely recognized. First, a large portion of the Jervis manuscript collection was microfilmed and therefore made more readily available to historians. In addition, Elting B. Morison included a chapter on Jervis in his short history *From Know-How to Nowhere: The Development of American Technology* (1974); the chapter was titled "The Works of John B. Jervis." Morison and Finch provide thoughtful analyses of Jervis as a civil engineer. However, both works are brief and were not meant to fill the role of a formal biography.

Finally, Neal FitzSimons, a civil engineer, edited the Jervis "autobiography," which Jervis had titled "Fact and Circumstances in the Life of John B. Jervis." FitzSimons's book, which he titled *The Reminiscences of John B. Jervis, Engineer of the Old Croton* (1971), is of special value because of the editorial notes that explain technical terms in Jervis's original work. The *Reminiscences* contains some of Jervis's views on his many projects, especially the important Croton Aqueduct, but it is far from a complete autobiography. The title that FitzSimons chose accurately describes what Jervis had written, which is much more complete in regard to his pre-1850 years than for the period after 1850.

But, even with Jervis's emergence in the 1970s from nearly total obscurity, he still did not receive proper recognition. Edward K. Spann in his otherwise informative *The New Metropolis: New York City, 1840–1857,* opens Chapter Six by praising the Croton Aqueduct as the city's "greatest civil triumph." The author explains the importance of the Croton in ushering in a "new era of civic order, beauty, cleanliness, health, and security," but he omits mention of the person who built it. Carl

Condit's history of railroads in the New York City area, titled *The Port of New York* and published a year before Spann's book, at least credits Jervis with the Croton Aqueduct, the Hudson River Railroad, and even with the design of the Mohawk and Hudson's "DeWitt Clinton." Condit does not elaborate on Jervis's role relative to the two engineering projects and, in the opinion of this author, Condit should have given Jervis credit for the locomotive "Experiment" instead of the "DeWitt Clinton," whose four-fixed-wheel design had been in common use previously. But at least Jervis is included in Condit's book. Mention of him is missing from Robert Albion's acclaimed history, *The Rise of New York Port,* published in 1939. Here again, however, Albion's omission of Jervis and his important contributions to New York City's expansion is not surprising, given Jervis's lack of notoriety in the 1930s. The most recent references to Jervis and his works are in David Freeman Hawke's *Nuts and Bolts of the Past* (1988). However, the parts of the book that relate to Jervis contain many errors, so the information is not reliable.

There are many aspects of Jervis's life and character that influenced his engineering career but have largely been ignored. For example, he was deeply religious and guided by Calvinistic principles. Jervis regularly contributed to the support of his church and of Christianity in general. A Jacksonian Democrat, Jervis was swayed to Barnburner free-soilism in the 1840s, and he was the Softshell Democratic candidate for the post of State Engineer and Surveyor in 1855. Because of the split in the Democratic Party, Jervis was unsuccessful in his bid for office. The following year, his continued commitment to the free-soil cause resulted in the publication of a series of letters titled *Freedom and the Union* under the pen name "Hampden." It was then that Jervis switched to the newly organized Republican Party, or, as he referred to it, the Democratic Republican Party. He remained a Republican for the rest of his life.

In addition to his brief venture into politics, Jervis was extensively involved in banking, real estate, and business. His investment in banks began relatively early in his career, as did his speculation in real estate. Jervis often purchased property near the projects on which he was employed. Apparently, his real estate investments were profitable. Jervis's venture into industry came late in his career, after he had passed age seventy. In 1868, after building and managing several midwestern railroads, Jervis helped organize the Rome Merchant Iron Works. He remained influential in the company until his death in 1885. His interest in banking and business can be seen in his pamphlet, *Currency and Public Debt of the United States* (1868), and in his two books, *Railway Property* (1861) and *The Question of Labour and Capital* (1877). Actually the two books were as much an outgrowth of his philosophy on life as they were manifestations of his ideas on business and engineering.

Many of Jervis's pursuits in areas other than engineering came after 1850. They followed the completion of his period of learning and maturation in his chosen field. In Jervis's field, it was the Erie, the Delaware and Hudson, and the Chenango canals; the Mohawk and Hudson, the Saratoga and Schenectady, and the Hudson River railroads; and that most significant work, the Croton Aqueduct, that produced John B. Jervis, Civil Engineer.

ACKNOWLEDGMENTS

IT IS MOST DIFFICULT to recognize everyone who graciously assisted me in preparing this book. Those listed below deserve particular attention; without their help, I would not have completed the Jervis story.

Carole Fowler, Director; William Dillon, Director (retired); Keith Kinna, Assistant Director; and all the members of the Jervis Public Library staff provided me with access to the Jervis collection and to the facilities of the library in general. Indeed, their support and encouragement made this book possible, and words cannot suffice to express my debt of gratitude to them.

Neal FitzSimons of Washington, D.C., editor of the Jervis *Reminiscences,* gave advice on sources and helped me to better understand the basic terminology of civil engineering. Herbert R. Hands, Manager, Historical Activities, American Society of Civil Engineers, New York, New York, extended to me the hospitality of the Society and provided me with useful data and information. Peter Osborne of the Port Jervis Historical Society, Port Jervis, New York, supplied information on the Delaware and Hudson Canal and on Russell Lord in particular.

Eilene E. Moeri, Special Collections Librarian at Hobart and William Smith Colleges, Geneva, New York, contributed much appreciated assistance relative to David Bates Douglass. Alan C. Aimone, Chief, Special Collections, United States Military Academy Library, West Point, New York, provided me with advice on sources and with astute observations about the Hudson River Railroad's impact on the Hudson River. The personnel at the following institutions all contributed their time and talent in patiently assisting me with the seemingly endless search for pertinent information: the United States Military Academy Library at West Point; the New York State Archives, Albany, New York; the New York State Library, Albany, New York; the State University

College Library, Oneonta, New York; the Cornell University Library Regional History Collection, Ithaca, New York; the University of Massachusetts at Amherst Library; the Vassar College Library, Poughkeepsie, New York; the New York Public Library Manuscript Division, New York City; the Port Jervis Public Library, Port Jervis, New York; the Library of Congress, Washington, D.C.; the Albany Institute of History and Art, Albany, New York; the Erie Canal Museum, Syracuse, New York; the Rome Historical Society, Rome, New York; the Erie County Historical Society, Buffalo, New York; and the New-York Historical Society Library, New York City, New York.

Phyllis Bowerman, formerly of Oneonta, New York, and Candace Sweet of Gilbertsville, New York, deserve special thanks for suffering through the manuscript, type character by type character, and learning more about Jervis than, I am certain, they ever desired to know.

Patrick Reynolds of Rome, New York, provided me with the excellent pictures of the Jervis engineering drawings, and photographer Judith Rhein of Goshen, New York, contributed her superb work on the structures of the Delaware and Hudson Canal. To both of these artists, my sincere appreciation.

Professor Ivan Steen of the State University at Albany, New York, urged me to research the Jervis collection, and Professor (emeritus) David Ellis, Hamilton College, Clinton, New York, advised me to persist in the publication of the completed work.

Finally, a special acknowledgment is due Professor Robert Wesser of the State University at Albany. He read major portions of the manuscript, commented on and critiqued them, and provided me with the guidance and encouragement necessary to complete the initial study. He deserves to share in the credit for bringing Jervis to life. To you, Bob, a very sincere thanks.

And to everyone involved in this project, my most genuine gratitude.

PROLOGUE

THE FORCES that interacted to create Jervis the engineer appeared well before he obtained his first job as an axeman with an engineering party on the Erie Canal. The influence of both religion and education produced an individual who was well infused with the principles of Calvinism. A belief in the perfect wisdom of God, a devotion to work, and a feeling that it was necessary to persevere in the execution of a job, no matter how menial, was the code by which Jervis lived and worked.

While learning to be a civil engineer, Jervis was careful not to do anything that might suggest to his superiors a lack of interest in his work, and he persisted in gaining knowledge from those in the survey parties who possessed engineering skills. He was quick to learn from observation as well as from any written material he could acquire.

In this regard, Jervis was assisted by two persons who had a particularly important impact on his life. His uncle, John Bloomfield, was as close to Jervis as anyone. He provided Jervis with useful books during his young nephew's apprentice period, and he gave the student engineer sound advice on a wide variety of subjects. The other person who influenced Jervis, particularly during the latter's developmental period as an engineer, was Benjamin Wright.

The benefit Jervis derived from his contact with Wright, the "Father of American Civil Engineering," was considerable. That Jervis happened to live in Rome, New York, at the time when Erie Canal construction began there and that he was introduced to Wright, the chief engineer of the canal, were crucial to Jervis's career as an engineer. Wright had the necessary contacts to help the young man's advancement, and he was able to provide Jervis with advice on engineering problems. Jervis owed to Wright not only his position on the Delaware and Hudson Canal, but also his ultimate appointment as chief engineer of that project. Once in a decision-making position, it was easier for Jervis to begin making important contributions to American engineering.

All of Jervis's major innovations in the fields of engineering and mechanics were made during the years of the New York projects. Jervis introduced new methods or machines on every assignment, from the original Erie Canal to the Hudson River Railroad. Not all of these represented significant contributions to engineering, but all demonstrated Jervis's desire to achieve a simple solution to a potentially complex problem.

The first important example of Jervis's overcoming a difficult obstacle through the use of a relatively simple method was the construction of the "gravity railroad" as part of the Delaware and Hudson Canal. The problem was to move freight through an area that posed difficult problems in canal building. Jervis's solution indicated his willingness to rely on rail transportation and, in doing so, to go beyond what Wright and others had recommended. Not only were stationary steam engines to be used, but Jervis attempted to use the steam locomotive, a machine practically untried in the United States. A more timid individual might not have done this, but Jervis had, as usual, made many calculations to show that the plan would work. The theory was sound, but because Jervis's instructions were not followed to the letter, the locomotive was a failure. When Jervis had another opportunity to build a railroad and to choose between horse power and steam power, he chose the latter. This time the engine was built to his specifications, and it was a success.

Jervis's first major mechanical innovation was the moveable forward truck for a railway locomotive. It was another example of a simple solution, this time to the problem of running a locomotive at rapid speed over railroads with uneven roadbeds and many curves. Jervis's replacement of the locomotive's forward fixed wheels with a four-wheeled swivel truck was so simple that his colleague Horatio Allen felt it would not work. The locomotive would run, Allen believed, but it would not be able to develop enough traction. Allen's solution to the same problem was much more complex than Jervis's; because of this, it neither performed well nor gained the acceptance that Jervis's truck locomotive did.[1] Jervis's contribution of the forward truck was a great advancement in railroading, and it was perhaps his most important innovation. But for Jervis, it was one of many.

During the New York years, Jervis not only produced advancements in railroading, but also in the building of waterways. Here, as in his railroad projects, Jervis demonstrated his willingness to experiment and his ability to reduce the complex to the simple. The measurement of rainfall and runoff on the Chenango Canal resulted from Jervis's refusal to accept other experts' calculations of the amount of rain water that could be collected in reservoirs. Jervis developed a more efficient method of measurement and proved previous calculations to be in error. Several new engineering developments came out of the Croton waterworks as well. They, like the rain gauge of the Chenango, resulted from Jervis's attempt to find new methods to deal with construction problems.

In his approach to various problems, Jervis's tendency to find simple solutions also resulted from his desire to keep costs at a minimum. An example of this was the high bridge over the Harlem River with its novel hollow wall design. The plan meant that less stone was needed to build the huge bridge and thus that the great cost of the structure was reduced.

The high bridge, although Jervis's most spectacular work on the Croton, was not the structure that was most copied. That structure was the Croton Dam, which was a milestone in dam building that incorporated features which became standard in dam construction. The chief problem with building the dam was to find a way to break the force of the water falling over the spillway. Again Jervis's solution was remarkably simple. The spillway—which was built in the shape of a reverse curve to gradually turn the vertical drop of the water—and the use of a stilling basin—which slowed the water at the base of the dam—became common in dam design.

The uncomplicated, graceful lines of the dam were repeated by Jervis in other aqueduct structures. The best example is the facade of the distributing reservoir. Jervis decided on a plain Egyptian facing for that Croton structure, which would be most in the public eye. In selecting the Egyptian style, Jervis acted contrary to most architects of the 1840s. By then the more elaborate, complicated Gothic style was coming into vogue. Jervis used a functional design form because to do otherwise would have not been in accord with his building philosophy and because Gothic architecture would have been too ostentatious for the "general style of the work."[2] Jervis derived a great deal of satisfaction from his engineering works. This might account for his willingness and even desire to avoid ornate monuments to his professional ability.

Jervis's engineering talents were much in demand and resulted in an uninterrupted work schedule from one project to another. This gave the false impression that Jervis cared for little beyond the field of engineering. In fact, Jervis's interests were as multifaceted as the man himself. Possessing a naturally inquisitive mind, he was involved in and well versed in a variety of activities, and he approached his many other interests with the same intensity as he did engineering. But engineering was his preoccupation, and his devotion to it made Jervis, by the mid–nineteenth century, "the most famous engineer of the day."[3]

JOHN B. JERVIS

Axeman to Engineer

IN 1798, Timothy Jervis, his wife, Phebe, and their three-year-old son, John, made the 300-mile journey from Huntington, Long Island, to Oneida County in central New York.[1] Instead of living on the land they had recently purchased, the Jervises located at nearby Fort Stanwix so Timothy could pursue his carpenter trade.[2]

The fort, which had been built in 1758 as a frontier outpost during the French and Indian War, was occupied by the patriot army at the beginning of the American Revolution and used to defend the western end of the Mohawk Valley. By the time the Jervises arrived at the small community that surrounded the fort, the fort itself had outlived its usefulness. Yet scarcely more than two decades had passed since its small garrison had successfully stood for three weeks against a larger British force and had saved the valley.

The post-Revolutionary growth of the Fort Stanwix settlement was aided significantly by its location. Between the fort and Albany, which was about 100 miles to the east, the Mohawk River carved a deep, narrow cut through the Appalachian Mountains on its way to its junction with the Hudson River a few miles north of Albany. The Mohawk Valley was the only water-level route through the Appalachians. Not only did this route connect with New York City by way of the Hudson, but it also provided a gateway to the West for land-hungry New Englanders. Even before the war with England officially ended in 1783, the Yankees began to seek the open land in the Fort Stanwix area and beyond.

By the time the Jervises arrived in the village, the influx of New Englanders had turned into a large-scale "invasion," swelling the population of Fort Stanwix and the surrounding countryside. Among the New Englanders who had settled near Fort Stanwix was Benjamin Wright. The Jervis family's location at Fort Stanwix, or Rome as it was becoming known, and the fact that Wright lived nearby, profoundly shaped the destiny of young John Bloomfield Jervis.

After remaining in the village for seven years, Timothy Jervis moved his family to a farm he had purchased on the outskirts of the community. There, in addition to farming, Jervis operated a sawmill.[3] His eldest child, John, helped with the farm work and the lumbering.

At age fifteen, John Bloomfield Jervis discontinued his formal education and, for the next seven years, remained on the farm to aid his father. Jervis later recalled that he thought of continuing his education beyond the common school, but "my father was not able to help me, and in fact he needed the service I could render him."[4] Also, about the time John Jervis finished common school, his father was experiencing financial difficulties. Although Timothy Jervis's holdings were valuable as farmland, apparently the property was heavily mortgaged.[5]

John B. Jervis completed his common school education by 1810. The following year, at age sixteen, he became a member of the First Congregational Society of Rome.[6] Jervis remained deeply attached to his religion for the remainder of his life. The influence of the church plus the impact of the common school were powerful factors in shaping Jervis's philosophy towards work and his behavior patterns in general.

Throughout New England and particularly in places that were intellectual and social extensions of New England, such as early nineteenth century Rome, the *New England Primer* and other school books in use reflected Calvinistic values.[7] Since Jervis's schooling was a steady rote of these texts, supported by the sermons of his Yale-trained minister, it makes sense that the admonitions of the "Protestant Ethic" became deeply instilled in the future engineer. If his lifestyle and writings are an example, perhaps these admonitions affected Jervis even more than they did many of his contemporaries.

Jervis's writing is filled with his beliefs and advice in regard to God, the work ethic, thrift, proper morals, and devotion to one's profession. Jervis was faithful to his beliefs throughout his life. His disdain for idleness was obvious. He savored every moment as one that could and would be used for some form of industry. Jervis's emphasis on thrift was manifested in his writings as well as in his manner of living. After commenting on the evils of misusing wages and on the benefits of saving, Jervis, in *The Question of Labour and Capital* (1877), reduced the chief reason for the inequality of wealth to the existence of "two classes of men—the thrifty and the unthrifty."[8] Numerous examples of personal frugality were cited in his autobiographical sketches. The rapid retirement of the mortgage on his father's farm during the early stages of Jervis's career, when his earnings were still relatively low, was but one illustration. Assertions of the benefits of high moral character are found frequently throughout Jervis's works. Advice on the subject appeared most pointedly in *The Question of Labour and Capital,* where entire sections were devoted to the importance of morality in life.[9] In an earlier work on railroads, Jervis combined moral rectitude with professionalism.[10] His faith in the values acquired from his education and religion remained with him as the key to success and the good life.

Jervis's proclivity in this direction was strong to the end. Seven years before his death, he recommended the study of the scriptures in order to discover the "rules for the defining and enforcing industry, prudence, and frugality in affairs—uprightness in all business intercourse; purity and forbearance in manners, and the courtesy, kindness and fellow feeling that make happiness for the individual and for society, and lay the foundation of civil liberty."[11] The effects the *New England Primer,* the common school textbooks, and the church had on Jervis's career were evident throughout his life.

In addition, there is no question that the prevalent political, economic, and social currents influenced Jervis during his first two decades. The victory and widespread acceptance of Jeffersonian republicanism over the British aristocratic system associated with the Federalist opposition undoubtedly had an impact on the young man. His readings and alert nature also made him aware of an emerging economic thinking in which nineteenth century Americans pursued money not solely to amass it, but more because of what it meant. Money was a symbol of their own energies. It served as proof of an individual's achievements. But, as with their New England forebearers, money was not simply to be stockpiled for its own intrinsic pleasure, but rather to be used for the common benefit to build a stronger, more viable nation. The vibrant society of the early nineteenth century America into which Jervis came of age was one in which a John B. Jervis was almost certain to become a perfect example.

With the early education of the young man completed, such as it was, it now was up to a major event to change the farmer to an axeman and finally to an engineer. The building of the Erie Canal provided the next phase in the education of the future master builder of waterways and railroads.

The War of 1812 did more than confirm the status of the United States as an independent nation. Among the outcomes of the conflict was an emphasis on the need for internal transportation improvements. Communication between the coastal cities and the interior was slow and woefully inadequate. In 1812, rivers were still the fastest, cheapest, and in many areas virtually the only means of moving bulk freight without the transportation costs outstripping the value of the goods being shipped. However, even in New York State, with its unique water-level route through the Appalachians, the war proved that the Mohawk River was not a dependable trade route. Spring floods and low water in the summer meant that the river's transportation value was questionable during certain times of the year. In any case, upstream freight rates averaged four times higher than downstream rates, making shipments into the interior costly even by river. Transportation of goods by land was almost prohibitively expensive. At the outbreak of the war, land transportation costs per ton mile were five times greater than the cost of moving freight upstream and twenty-four times the cost of floating goods downstream.

During the decade before the war, New York began to discuss the possibility of a canal between its fjord-like Hudson River and the Great Lakes. Surveys were conducted and costs estimated, but the war's outbreak interrupted canal planning activity. Yet the military shipments between New York City and frontier bases further proved the existing system could not handle the demand. Immediately after the war, agitation for canals began again. Under the influential leadership of future governor DeWitt Clinton, the canal bill cleared the legislature in 1816. Not only would the state underwrite the cost of the Erie Canal, a 365-mile-long ditch from Albany to Lake Erie, but a second canal would be dug simultaneously to connect the Hudson River above Albany with Lake Champlain. The canal era was about to boom. Both New York State and national expansion would benefit immeasurably from the projects.

On July 4, 1817, the ceremonial first spadeful of earth for the construction of the Erie Canal was turned near Wood Creek in the town of Rome. Rome resident Benjamin Wright was appointed chief engineer of the middle section of the Erie project. Wright was a friend of Jervis's father, and he called on the elder Jervis to obtain axemen for an engineering party that was surveying the canal line through a cedar swamp south of Rome. Since Timothy Jervis was interested in submitting a bid to construct a section of the canal, he felt that his son John could both obtain useful first-hand information as an axeman and earn some money.[12] The younger Jervis agreed and went to work on the canal.

The building of the Erie Canal coincided with the emergence of the era of the "common man" and its associated ideas about the role of individuals in the political process and the economy. Small wonder it was deemed in keeping with the equal-rights-for-all approach, not the least of which was the emphasis on equality of economic opportunity, to give virtually anyone who desired it an option to bid on a construction contract. New York's ambitious canal undertakings meant a virtually unprecedented input of hard money into the state's economy. The state ended up spending nearly four times as much on the original Erie Canal as it contributed towards defending itself in the second war with England. Of course, not only did the awarding of contracts for the construction of short sections of the canal reflect the spirit of the new economic liberalism, but it was politically wise. The project was by no means as widely supported in 1817 as it was in 1825. By then its success accounted for much of its popularity. In the early years of construction, it made sense beyond simply an attempt at democratization to involve as many potential supporters as possible to ensure the canal's completion.

To achieve this and allow for almost any person to benefit from the work, contracts were let for sections as short as a quarter of a mile in length. Contractors who won the bids were expected to furnish the necessary equipment. Although the state often advanced money to the contractors for the purchase of supplies, it was not directly involved in the actual canal construction. As the independent contractors were responsible for completing their assigned portions of the canal, it was also up to them to hire laborers. The workers were largely recruited along the route of the canal. Contrary to a continuing misconception, most canal workers were not immigrant Irish. Approximately three-fourths of them were native to the United States.[13]

While there was no lack of contractors and laborers to build the Erie and Champlain canals, there was a lack of engineers to lay out the route and to assist and inspect construction. The "engineers" hired by the Canal Commission at the start of construction were, for the most part, surveyors. But, as Daniel Calhoun noted in his work on the origins of civil engineering in America, the "conversion of surveyors into engineers left unfilled an implicit need for some way to recruit engineers without wrenching men abruptly from one occupation to another."[14]

One approach to this problem was the development of a hierarchy of engineers, which began rudimentarily in 1817. By 1819, the process had become refined to the point that the canal commissioners reported that the portion of the canal under construction had been divided into five parts. Each part was under an assistant engineer "who had previously learnt the use of the levelling instrument; an accurate method of designating the dimensions of the canal, upon every variety of surface; the general principles necessary to ensure the best construction; and the nature of the stipulations contained in the several contracts."[15]

The report also described the field work of the assistants as that of staking out the "width of the grubbing and clearing, of the excavation or embankment, and of the mucking from under the banks." They set pegs, marked the depth and width of the canal and the height and slope of the banks, watched "that no work should be done unfaithfully," and dealt with "all unforeseen obstructions." It was from the ranks of the assistants that principal engineers, the next level in the hierarchy, were drawn. Each principal had responsibility for a significant distance or division of the canal.[16]

Jervis described the process of "making" an engineer, starting with the very basic job of axeman, in his *Reminiscences*. Although Jervis wrote the description several decades later, his recollections accurately coincided with those related by another young axeman who also learned his engineering skills on the Erie Canal. William C. Young was a contemporary of Jervis who worked on sections of the canal west of Jervis's region. Young was Jervis's principal assistant on the Saratoga and Schenectady Railroad. Young left a more detailed picture of an engineering party than did Jervis, and it corroborates that of his one-time boss. The accounts left by Jervis and Young are rare vignettes of the "classrooms" of the Erie Canal engineering "school."[17]

In addition to clearing the way for the survey, the task of an axeman was to cut stakes and pegs used in marking the line of the canal. Jervis described himself, when he started work, as being "of slender frame rarely weighing over one hundred and twenty-five pounds."[18] Evidently he had some difficulty in pushing through the thick brush of the cedar swamp; however, he approached his job zealously since his "main ambition was to satisfy the chief of the party."[19] The engineer in charge of the party was Nathan Roberts. According to Jervis, Roberts was a very stern, exacting person[20] and was regarded by the members of the party "with a reverence that did not allow familiarity."[21]

Jervis's advancement from axeman to targetman (rodman), the next level of rank in a survey party, provides additional insight into his character. The targetman carried a 10½-foot-long, rodlike instrument, called a target, that was used to assist the surveyor in calculating changes in elevation levels. The *Reminiscences* reveal that during moments of leisure, Jervis watched the targetmen, discreetly questioned them about their job, and in time was allowed to examine the target itself. In addition to the knowledge Jervis gained about the tasks of the targetmen and the use of the target, he discovered that the position of targetman was regarded as the first step towards learning the science of engineering.[22] At the close of the 1817 work season, Jervis felt he had a sufficient grasp of the duties of a targetman to approach Nathan Roberts about the possibility of employment for the following season. Much to his surprise, the party chief approved his request and informed Jervis that the pay would be twelve dollars per month.[23] Thus, in the spring of 1818,

Jervis eagerly undertook the first significant job that led to his becoming an engineer.

"Learn to love the path to the shop, better than the path from it," advised John B. Jervis in 1877.[24] He lived by this maxim. As a targetman in the party of Nathan Roberts, Jervis pursued his work with diligence and used every available opportunity to study the instrument for which he was responsible. The Roberts party was assigned a survey of thirty-six miles from Geddesburg (Syracuse) to Montezuma on the Seneca River. Jervis later wrote of the difficulties the party encountered, ranging from snow in April to swarms of mosquitoes as the season advanced.[25] Jervis endeared himself to his principal by his constant readiness to perform any kind of work involved in the survey. He later related that there were instances when engineer Roberts required his targetmen to perform duties regarded as those of axemen. Many targetmen looked upon this as an infringement on their dignity. But Jervis thought no honest labor was degrading and performed additional assignments with the same speed and diligence as his regular work.[26] Roberts, impressed with the industriousness of young Jervis, gave him instructions in the use of levelling instruments and in the computations involved in ascertaining levels. By the time his work with the Roberts party was completed, Jervis had acquired an elementary knowledge of levels and of the plotting of lines and profiles on maps.[27]

Upon his return to Rome in July 1818, Jervis was assigned to a party whose principal engineer was David S. Bates. The crew was charged with surveying approximately seventeen miles of the canal line in Madison and Onondaga counties. It was a small party and required only one targetman.[28] Bates, a land surveyor of many talents, was limited in his surveying skill to two-dimensional measurements. As a result, Jervis's career received an additional boost. He later wrote, "as my experience in handling levelling instruments was greater than his, he [Bates] very readily allowed me to run his levels."[29] Jervis became familiar with the use of levelling instruments and the calculations that were required in computing the work. He admitted in his later writings that since the terrain in the section to which he was assigned was quite level, mathematical skill was not needed. Jervis reasoned that although he received no extra compensation for his work with the levels, he gained valuable knowledge and his situation was "favorably advanced."[30]

The Bates party concluded work for the 1818 season in December, after which it returned to Rome and was disbanded. Instead of being released from employment on the canal, Jervis was assigned the task of supervising the weighing of stone for locks. Stone was weighed as a method of determining payment to the quarry owners. He spent the

Fig. 1.1. Benjamin Wright, 1770–1842. Photo courtesy American Society of Civil Engineers.

winter months of 1819 on location near Syracuse. About the first of April, he completed his job as weighman and returned to Rome.[31]

At the opening of the work season in the spring of 1819, Jervis was promoted again, this time to his first engineering position. Since David Bates was given more extensive duties on another portion of the canal, Wright appointed Jervis to head Bates's old division. Jervis, age twenty-three, was made a resident engineer at a salary of one dollar and twenty-five cents per day plus fifty cents for expenses.[32] Although happy to be an engineer, Jervis was disappointed with his part of the canal, since it had few mechanical structures: "a few wood trunk aqueducts, waste weirs, and bridges, and small stone culverts." The section contained no locks, so Jervis could not increase his knowledge and experience relative to these structures.[33] He complained that many of the wooden structures were, at that time, more the product of craftsmen than engineers. By way of illustration, he cited the instance of Benjamin Wright calling upon a Mr. Cady, a Chittenango carpenter, for the plans of a wooden trunk aqueduct. The Cady plan was adopted for nearly all the wooden trunk aqueducts on the canal.[34]

While a resident engineer, Jervis became better acquainted with Canvass White, Benjamin Wright's principal assistant. He referred to White as "having had the most strict Engineering mind of any of this time." In his opinion, Wright and White "worked remarkably harmonious[ly] together and made a better service to the canal than either could have done alone."[35]

The section of the Erie Canal under Jervis's charge was completed along with the rest of the middle section at the end of the 1819 work season. Jervis returned to Rome in time to witness the run of the *Chief Engineer* in October 1819. The boat, named in honor of Benjamin Wright, was the first on the Erie Canal.[36] The following month, Jervis was named as surveyor in a party led by his former superior, David Bates, who had been selected to conduct a survey of the Oneida and Oswego rivers. Upon completion of the month-long task, Jervis went to Bates's home in Mexico, Oswego County, because the party chief had requested Jervis's aid in preparing the map of the survey.

After finishing the map, Jervis returned to Rome by way of Constantia, a small village on the north shore of Oneida Lake. There he visited his uncle, John Bloomfield, and used his uncle's library.[37] Jervis was constantly striving to improve his knowledge in order to gain advancement. Not one to waste valuable time, Jervis spent the winter of 1820 familiarizing himself with mechanical engineering and studies of canals, waterworks, and bridges, using as his chief source the *Edinburgh Encyclopaedia* that he had borrowed from John Bloomfield.

Jervis was less than enthusiastic with his next assignment, which was largely one of maintenance and improvement on the completed middle section of the Erie Canal. He felt that work on new sections would add more to his engineering experience. He was also of the opinion that the better positions had gone to those with political and social influence. But Jervis repressed expressions of bitterness and vowed to devote himself to any assignment, no matter what his personal feelings might be. His autobiographical sketches describe his attitude toward the job at hand, however unsatisfactory it was. "It was for me to do my work so well that my chief would not like to spare me,"[38] he later professed.

Apparently this approach had its rewards. In the spring of 1821, Jervis was notified that he had been assigned the position of resident engineer for seventeen miles of canal, extending from Anthony's Nose (between Canajoharie and Fonda) to Amsterdam. He was pleased with the assignment and was determined "that no effort of mine should be

wanting to give satisfaction, and at the same time improve my knowledge of engineering."[39] Jervis was elated because the assignment was
much more difficult and challenging than the previous one on the middle
section of the canal. There were many more mechanical structures, especially locks, due to the varied terrain.[40] The surface of the middle section
was comparatively level, while the eastern portion paralleled the Mohawk River, making it necessary to construct the ditch along abrupt side
hills and, in many places, to protect it from the floods of the Mohawk.
Under the circumstances, Jervis found it necessary to learn additional
methods of computation to calculate the rises and falls in elevation. He
was instructed by the man whose engineering ability he so highly respected, Canvass White.[41]

Work on the eastern section of the canal presented Jervis with the
occasion to give his superiors suggestions on hydraulic engineering. Initially, he was cautious and apprehensive in making any recommendations relative to the work.[42] His first opportunity resulted from his observations of the method of crossing large streams. When it was
necessary to build the canal across streams whose beds were close to, or
the same level as, the canal bottom, it became common practice to cross
them by means of dams and guard locks. Under these circumstances,
aqueducts could not be used because there was not enough clearance to
allow for the passage of the streams under the canal. Dams and guard
locks were not always a completely satisfactory method since, in times of
high water, sand and gravel were washed downstream and into the boat
channel. In one particular case, Jervis observed that although the stream
bed and the canal bottom were at the same level, there was a sufficient
fall in the level of the Mohawk River (into which the streams flowed) to
permit high water in the streams to run off. The greatest problem was to
contain the movement of stream gravel. The solution involved the use of
an aqueduct. Free passage of water and the containment of gravel beneath the aqueduct was ensured by the construction of a plank spillway
between the aqueduct abutments.[43] Jervis approached his superiors with
the idea "with hesitating caution." He asked to be allowed to build such a
structure to give his plan a trial. His request was granted and "the result
was completely satisfactory and gave me [Jervis] confidence to exercise
judgment more freely than I had ventured to do previously. Subsequently the same plan was adopted for other streams."[44]

Jervis's duties on the canal in 1822 were the same as his work in
1821. Departure from the routine came at the end of the regular work
season with his retention to help with the settlement of contractors'
accounts. In the construction of the Erie Canal, some detail "in all contracts was omitted in the rates provided for in the specified items of

contract and left to be adjusted by the chief engineer."[45] During Benjamin Wright's tours of the canal, the discussions between Wright and the contractors were rarely recorded. As a result, the chief engineer had to depend on the records of the resident engineers. Jervis, as a resident engineer, kept careful notes. This coincided with his orderly approach to his work and, for that matter, his manner of living. Lack of such records gave rise to contract extras and "most contracts had more-or-less extra claims as it was by no means rare for ingenious contractors to swell these claims to large amounts."[46]

The case of *Marvin Crosby* v. *John B. Jervis* very likely was an example of such fraudulent practice on the part of contractors. Marvin Crosby was a subcontractor on a section of the Erie Canal located in the town of Charleston, Montgomery County. In 1822 he brought suit against resident engineer Jervis for the recovery of $400 worth of canal work that allegedly had been done. Apparently the meticulous Jervis was able to furnish proof to the contrary, because the judgment was in his favor.[47] Jervis's characteristic attention to detail prompted the chief engineer to remark that in any dispute on his division, Jervis simply "pulls out his papers"[48] and helps to solve the matter.

Jervis's careful record-keeping caused him to be recognized not only by Benjamin Wright, but also by Henry Seymour, the canal commissioner on the eastern portion of the canal. At the close of the 1822 season, Seymour congratulated Jervis on the fact that his records had saved the state of New York $30,000. This recognition greatly pleased the young resident engineer, and later Jervis could not resist the temptation to use the event as an example to young people.[49] After assuring his readers that he was simply doing his job and not looking for any particular favor from his superiors, Jervis explained his purpose in including the account about the praise of his work. It was "for the benefit of young men, that they may see the course that gives the highest satisfaction is most sure to contribute to advancement. The whole is in a nutshell—a steady, resolute, discreet and upright purpose is the basis of all worth, for any profession."[50]

In addition to the notes Jervis kept on the contracts, he also recorded the computations he made as part of his engineering work on the canal. Canvass White had directed each resident engineer to keep such records. Jervis, of course, followed the instructions and was informed by his delighted superiors that he was possibly the only resident engineer that had complied with White's directions.[51]

The coming of spring 1823 brought with it another promotion for Jervis. He was appointed superintendent of fifty miles of the eastern section, approximately one-seventh of the entire canal.[52] He shared his

duties with Dr. John Martineau, the resident engineer for the section
between Amsterdam and Schenectady.[53] Jervis was pleased with the position as it gave him the opportunity to observe the canal in actual operation.

Since the work was new, the canal and its structures frequently
failed and needed almost constant attention. Leaks and breaks in the
canal banks frequently occurred. They were particularly prevalent after
the water was let into the canal at the beginning of each season of
operation. The action of the frost on the earthen banks tended to cause ˋ
the banks to heave and weaken. When the canal was filled to its operating depth of four feet, the water pressure plus the displacement of water
by the boats caused leaks and sometimes major breaks. Breaks in the
canal banks almost always resulted in closing the affected portion of the
canal until the bank was repaired. Canal engineers, Jervis included, regularly experimented with various kinds of soils, particularly clays, in
efforts to determine the best substance to seal the leaks. Tests were also
made with stone, wood, and a combination of both to find rapid
methods of closing the breaks. Traffic was so heavy on the canal that it
was crucial to keep interruptions as brief as possible.

In addition to the knowledge that he acquired about repairs, Jervis
also gained valuable experience in the construction and operation of
locks and culverts, knowledge that would be used in future canal construction and the building of railroads.[54] Jervis retained his position as
superintending engineer until March 1825. During his final year he was
in sole charge of the division, because Dr. Martineau had left at the close
of navigation in 1823.[55] Jervis's income for the year ending March 1825
was $1,000.[56] His salary had increased by more than $300 per work
season since his initial appointment as an engineer.

By 1824, there was an increased demand for civil engineers in the
United States.[57] Benjamin Wright had already accepted the position of
chief engineer on the Delaware and Hudson Canal and was devoting
only a portion of his time to the Erie project. Canvass White left the Erie
for work on canals in neighboring states. Jervis felt the time had arrived
for him to seek new opportunities too. Henry Seymour attempted to
persuade him to remain on the Erie as superintendent and included an
increase in salary as part of the inducement, but Jervis remained steadfast in his decision to leave.[58] He had no particular job in mind, but felt
certain of getting a position, since "both Judge Wright and Canvass
White had intimated prospects for employment on new works if I [Jer-
vis] concluded to leave my superintendency on the Erie canal."[59] Jervis's
confidence was rewarded; the interim between jobs was a brief one.

The Erie Canal, in the words of one urban historian, was the

"Mother of Cities."[60] This appropriate sobriquet could be altered to apply as well to the American engineering profession. By the time of its completion, New York's new waterway added as many civil engineers to the national total as had previously existed.[61] Included among the new professionals was John Jervis.

The commencement of the Erie Canal construction in Rome was extremely important to Jervis's career. It provided him with an opportunity for employment and brought him into contact with those who could aid him in obtaining an education in engineering. Upon completion of the canal Jervis emerged, at age thirty, not among the first rank of American engineers, but certainly on the junior level of the profession. His skill was acquired largely by observing his superiors and by repeated application of the new knowledge.

Jervis supplemented his field training by studying whatever technical books could be obtained from the engineers in charge of construction. Obviously he possessed considerable native intelligence. This was necessary for a man who had only an elementary education to grasp the fundamentals of civil engineering, however rudimentary they may have been at that time. To his intelligence, Jervis added determination and perseverance. Throughout his writings, he frequently acclaimed the importance of these two traits. His own career serves as his best testimonial.

2

The Delaware and Hudson Canal

JERVIS'S GROWING DISSATISFACTION with the nature of his work on the Erie Canal resulted in a search for more challenging employment. Although his first job after leaving the Erie was, initially, simply another canal, it turned out to be much more. Jervis was hired to assist Benjamin Wright on the Delaware and Hudson. After serving two years under his mentor, Jervis succeeded Wright as the canal's chief engineer. It was in this position that he had the opportunity to plan and direct the construction of one of the first railroads in the United States and the first one to use a locomotive engine. Where the terrain along the railroad's route was too steep to permit traction, Jervis designed a "gravity railroad" to overcome the problem. The second railroad to be built in the United States, the gravity railroad provided a method by which the terrain itself was changed from a transportation obstacle to an aid in the movement of goods.

Late in the winter of 1825, Jervis left Albany via Hudson River steamboat for New York City. This was very likely his first experience with steam transportation. It was also his first of many visits to the metropolis to whose development he would contribute so much. New York City in 1825 was the largest city in the nation, just as New York State—with its more than 1,500,000 people—was the largest state. In 1820, the state had surpassed Virginia to gain that title. New York City's 166,000 inhabitants put it well ahead of Philadelphia, its former population rival. When Jervis first arrived there, the city's growth was still exploding. By mid-century, it would be well past the half-million mark.

But New York's growth was not limited to a population increase. Its superb harbor made it the nation's premier port, outstripping its closest rivals—Boston, Philadelphia, and Baltimore. The completion of the Erie Canal in October 1825 established a link to the hinterlands that could never be seriously challenged by any of the coastal contenders. The new channel of cheap transportation came at just the proper time to bring raw material to feed the growing industrial appetite of city and state. New York was one of the leaders of the emerging industrial revolution. Its abundant, swift-flowing streams and its vast hardwood forests could power industry's growth. Its rapidly expanding population could provide the needed labor. And its reserve of merchant capital could provide the seed money for infant industries.

By 1825, New York City was an established money center. Its first bank opened in the 1790s. Insurance companies appeared to underwrite the city's maritime activities. New York's coffee houses and mercantile exchanges were the scene of numerous joint investment ventures. This was not the least of the reasons that the Wurtz brothers of Philadelphia brought their coal to the Tontine Coffee House on Wall Street to demonstrate its fuel value and to seek financing for their planned canal to get the coal to urban markets. Their home city, Philadelphia, was the location of the mighty Second Bank of the United States, but its demise in 1836 helped New York City's rise to financial supremacy.

To add to the reasons for New York City's predominance was its political strength. By 1825, New York State had been, for 20 of the past 24 years, the vice-presidential end of the successful Virginia–New York political axis. All three New Yorkers who had held the vice-presidency after 1801 were down-staters with strong New York City political and entrepreneurial connections. Although in 1798 the state capitol was moved 140 miles up the Hudson to Albany, New York City remained the state's unofficial capitol.

So it was little wonder that the Wurtz brothers came to New York to seek support for their project; that the Mohawk and Hudson Railroad was directed from New York City instead of Albany; that the Poughkeepsie capitalists that spearheaded the campaign to build the Hudson River Railroad sought an imprimatur from their counterparts in New York City; and that so many midwestern railroads in the 1840s and 1850s had their headquarters in New York City.

It was to this expanding metropolitan magnet at the mouth of the Hudson that Jervis, who in Rome in 1817 had been in the right place at the right time, was in 1825 wisely attracted to the next right place, New York City.

The purpose of Jervis's trip to New York City was a meeting with his former chief, Benjamin Wright, who previously had mentioned to Jervis that he could secure a position for him. Their conversation resulted in Wright's recommending Jervis to the board of managers of the Delaware and Hudson Company.[1]

The company had been chartered in 1823 under the leadership of the two Philadelphia merchants, William and Maurice Wurts. They owned coal lands in northeastern Pennsylvania, and they faced the problem of transporting the anthracite from the mines to the Hudson River and New York City. Hence, the purpose of the company was to raise money to finance the construction of a canal to connect the coal fields with the Hudson River.[2]

Benjamin Wright had been chosen as chief engineer for the project. It was upon his recommendation that Jervis was selected for the post of principal assistant engineer on March 12, less than two weeks after Jervis left the Erie project.[3] Although the final decisions on matters of importance were made by Wright, the responsibility of organizing the engineering force and constructing the canal was left entirely to Jervis.[4]

Nearly two years before Jervis was chosen as Wright's assistant, there had been a preliminary survey of the canal route by John T. Sullivan of Massachusetts, acting under Wright's instructions.[5] Immediately after Jervis's appointment, Wright ordered him to make a second and more detailed survey of the route. Jervis was assisted in his task by John B. Mills, Sullivan's assistant in the previous survey. The two engineers left Kingston, New York, in mid-March 1825 and commenced their eight-day, 105-mile journey through rough wilderness terrain to the junction of the Dyberry Creek and Lackawaxen River in northeastern Pennsylvania.[6] Upon the completion of the survey, Jervis submitted a report in which he accepted much of the earlier Sullivan plan with two significant changes.

Sullivan had suggested constructing a regular canal from the Hudson River to the Delaware River. After reaching the valley of the Delaware, the waterway was to consist of a system of slack-water navigation, utilizing the Delaware and Lackawaxen Rivers.[7] Jervis accepted the proposal of a canal from the Hudson River to the valley of the Delaware, but he felt that Sullivan's slack-water navigation was unacceptable because of " . . . the rapid fall in the rivers, and their great rise in time of floods, requiring large expense in dams, guard locks, and guard banks to protect the navigation."[8] He felt a canal could be built for the same amount of money and that it would provide more reliable navigation. Another reason behind the alteration of the Sullivan plan may have been Jervis's awareness of the certainty of conflict with the lumber raftsmen on the Delaware if the nine dams that the earlier plan called for were constructed.[9]

The second deviation from the Sullivan plan was in connection with the Pennsylvania section of the canal. Originally, the idea was to end the canal at Keenes Pond, seven miles west of the junction of the Dyberry and Lackawaxen and to construct a short railroad from Keenes Pond to the coal fields at Carbondale. Jervis approved of the railroad, but he felt that Sullivan had stopped short of what seemed the logical eastern terminus for the railroad. While a canal could have been constructed from the Dyberry junction to Keenes Pond, thirty locks of ten feet each would have been required. In the interest of economy, both in construction and operation, Jervis extended the planned railroad the additional seven miles to the confluence of the Dyberry and the Lackawaxen. The site was the future location of Honesdale, Pennsylvania.[10] Jervis submitted his report to Wright, after which he made a second trip along the proposed route accompanied by the chief engineer. Although Wright agreed with the construction of an independent canal through the Delaware Valley, he withheld judgment on the extension of the railroad from Keenes Pond to Honesdale. Eventually Wright accepted Jervis's recommendation for the extension of the railroad.[11]

The approval by the chief engineer of Jervis's plans left the way open for the beginning of canal construction. On July 13, 1825, contracts were let for seventeen miles of canal. An appropriate groundbreaking ceremony was held on that date at Mamakating, New York, with Philip Hone, first president of the Delaware and Hudson Company, delivering the address.[12]

Jervis was not impressed with the celebration and felt the ceremony was a great deal of fuss. However, he was decidedly moved by another ceremony related to the construction of the canal that took place later the same year. A group of people assembled at a place known as Carpenters Point, New York in the Delaware Valley near the junction of the states of New York, New Jersey, and Pennsylvania. In honor of the canal's principal assistant engineer, the assembly renamed the place Port Jervis, an act that was obviously very flattering to John B. Jervis.[13] Port Jervis, Wurtsboro, and Honesdale were among villages on the canal route that were named for persons connected with the canal.

The Delaware and Hudson Canal was divided into two parts for construction and operation. The actual canal from the Hudson River at Eddyville (a "suburb" of Kingston), New York, to Honesdale, Pennsylvania, was one section, and the railroad from Honesdale to Carbondale was the other. Much of the work on the canal took place while Jervis was principal assistant engineer. Except for the difficulty of building through the rugged terrain of the Delaware Valley, work on the canal was routine and presented little in the way of new experience to Jervis.

Perhaps the single most significant occurrence during the 1825–1827 period of canal construction related more directly to Jervis the man than to Jervis the engineer. This occurrence stemmed from the project

Fig. 2.1. The Aqueduct Bridge was built by John Roebling in the late 1840s to carry the D&H Canal across the Delaware River. It replaced the original Jervis bridge. Photo by Judith Rhein.

and provides much insight into a seldom-revealed side of Jervis. This was perhaps the only time in his life that Jervis indicated open dissatisfaction with his duties to his superior. In addition, he accused his superior of neglect of duty and, at the same time, possibly demonstrated a lack of confidence in his own judgment.

On September 30, 1826, Benjamin Wright submitted a report on the railroad to the president and board of managers of the Delaware and Hudson Company. It was a supplement to the report he had submitted a year earlier and was based on the Jervis survey. Wright's 1825 report to the company's managers had been purposely evasive about the Pennsylvania end of the canal and the length of the railroad. This was not because Wright was against crossing the Moosic Mountains with a short railroad instead of a canal, since he had previously concurred with Sullivan in this respect.[14] Apparently Wright's indecision was due to his lingering skepticism about the operation of the railroad. When Wright finally did accept Jervis's recommendations for doubling the length of the railroad, he again advised caution in terms of the kind of railroad that should be built. "Above all," wrote Wright to the managers, "it must be suited to the intelligence and capability of the user." In other words, it should be simple to operate and maintain.

Wright also reminded the board that " . . . we have no experience in this country of Railways."[15] Wright was so concerned with railroad reliability that he advised that a road thirty feet wide be constructed for at least a quarter of the distance from Carbondale to Honesdale. Once completed, ten feet of the road could be taken for the construction of the railroad, leaving an emergency wagon route twenty feet wide.[16]

The remainder of the report was filled with technical data necessary for the construction of the railroad. Wright included everything from the calculation of costs to the description of the track construction and the "self moving machines" that would pull the load up the inclined planes. What he failed to mention in his report was the name of John B. Jervis.

Wright's failure to make reference to his principal assistant caused him to come under fire from his former student and friend, who was a strong proponent of the railroad and who desired to be recognized by the board of managers. Recognition could lead to advancement, and it was for advancement that Jervis had left his secure, but relatively obscure position on the Erie Canal.

It took a little more than a month after Jervis read the chief engineer's report for him to make Wright aware of his dismay over the omission of his name from the document. This was a delicate matter, and Jervis characteristically was reticent. However, the necessity for decisions on some lock contracts provided him with an opening. Jervis

Fig. 2.2. Jervis stone aqueduct (built c. 1826), showing canal bed. Photo by Judith Rhein.

refused to make decisions about the letting of the lock contracts. It is difficult to say whether this reluctance stemmed from his anger at being omitted from the railroad report or whether it was due to his own lack of confidence. In any case, he appealed to Wright to leave New York City and take personal charge of the situation.

Wright replied that he felt it would be unproductive to come to the construction site since the recent loss of his son rendered him "unfit for thinking." Wright then suggested that, if possible, Jervis "put off the settlement of [the] lock contracts (I know they are very unpleasant duties) and I will join you as soon as I can and take a share of the odium which will be put upon us whether we do right or otherwise."[17] Apparently Wright considered decisions on awarding contracts unpleasant because decisions had to be made favoring some contractors over others.

Jervis's reply was most revealing. After the usual attention to business, Jervis began to admonish Wright for Wright's absence from the project. Jervis defended his action by stating his willingness to accept any responsibility that was properly his, but he said he felt that because Wright was in charge it was up to him to bear most of the responsibility. "I think it due to myself," wrote Jervis, "and certainly the contractors have a right to expect it."[18]

Jervis's real concern was brought out in the final portion of his letter. He was fearful of making a decision since a wrong decision might injure his chances of advancement should Wright resign. When Jervis was appointed to his position, it was more or less understood that Wright would not remain as chief more than a year or two. This prompted Jervis to accept the assistant's position. Hence in his letter rebuking Wright, Jervis complained, "I am much inclined to the belief that the Delaware and Hudson will rather be an injury than a benefit to me." He added that it was too late for second thoughts, but if "I have failed to obtain what I mainly had in view it has not been in consequence of any delinquency on my part."[19] After this atypical outburst of self-defense, Jervis concluded in a perfunctory manner that above all he desired to "do the right thing" and not "shirk his duty."[20] But the fact remains that he was so disturbed at the thought of having to make a decision that might block his advancement, he actually expressed adverse feelings to a superior.

Wright's reply, although generally conciliatory, was stern and to the point. After initially explaining his reasons for not being in Kingston (he had already done so in a previous letter), Wright reminded Jervis that he had never attempted to shun responsibility, "particularly that worst and most unpleasant of duties the adjustment of accounts."[21] Wright then reaffirmed his friendship with Jervis but also noted the feeling of coldness that had been developing on Jervis's part. Wright felt that he had done nothing to deserve these feelings. He explained to Jervis some of the reasons for his remaining as chief engineer and reassured Jervis that when he did resign he would recommend Jervis for the position. "I know very well that you can perform all the duties of Chief Engineer," Wright wrote, "and if it [the recommendation] fails you will only have to charge yourself with the blame."²² As evasive as Jervis was in much of his correspondence, Wright was very direct. He left his principal assistant with the unmistakable warning that upon their next meeting "if you shall continue to possess the same feeling — the cold distant and reserved uncommunicative manner which has been exhibited toward me our meeting will be very illy [*sic*] calculated to adjust accounts."²³

That Jervis's chief concern was over the status of his reputation was reaffirmed in his reply to Wright's letter of December 14. "You were acquainted with my object — that is — the acquisition of reputation," he reminded Wright. To this he added, undoubtedly out of respect for the chief and for his position, "I expected to appear as second [subordinate] not willing to jeopardize the reputation I have by a rash attempt to advance it."²⁴ In reference to his letter of November 23, Jervis speculated that Wright had misunderstood his purpose. He reiterated that he was not dissatisfied with his subordinate position. "I deprecate the idea of wishing to supplant (if it were in my power) any person and particularly the man I esteem my friend," Jervis insisted. "Nothing could be more repugnant to my feelings than an open difficulty between us," he stated; then he added "with this view I extremely regretted the indirect severity of your letter."²⁵

Even though Jervis apparently regretted the altercation with Wright, his quest for personal advancement overcame his usual caution in matters of this nature. He was smarting over the omission of his name from "every document" although he contended that he had done all in his power to gather the basic material for them — "it may be I expected too much."²⁶

Jervis had stepped out of character and made his point. Clearly, he desired to emerge from Wright's shadow. Wright also clarified his own feelings. The chief would step down when he felt the time was right for the company and when his designated successor was ready to make important decisions. Wright's feelings in this respect were not lost on Jervis. Jervis's letter of December 16 informed the chief engineer that the lock contracts in question had been analyzed in detail, "and only wants your advice and opinion to close them." Then Jervis, returning to true form, closed this final letter of this unusual correspondence with his superior on a note of conciliation. It was signed, "with sentiments of respect I am as ever your friend—J. B. J."[27]

Three months later, Benjamin Wright resigned as chief engineer of the Delaware and Hudson Company. Jervis's temporary lack of self-confidence had not altered the decision that the more experienced Wright had originally made, based on his knowledge of Jervis's talents as an engineer. So, true to his word, he recommended Jervis for the position, and Jervis's promotion was quickly approved by the board of managers.

Within a month of his appointment as chief engineer, Jervis was directed to survey and locate a railroad route from the end of the canal at Honesdale to the coal mines at Carbondale.[28] Jervis devoted the summer of 1827 to the task of gathering data on railroad construction techniques, rail material, grades and friction, and kinds of motive power. Jervis studied the terrain between Honesdale and Carbondale to determine where inclined planes would be needed and how much of the route could be relatively level track. He relied on English experience with railroads and studied the available works of British engineers and builders as he prepared his report to the company directors. In July he traveled to Boston to observe the Quincy Railroad, one of the few in the United States at the time.[29]

On October 22, Jervis submitted to the Delaware and Hudson board of managers a long, detailed report on railroad construction that, though largely technical, did not neglect financial considerations.[30] Its significance lies in its pioneering nature. Jervis had little to rely on as a basis for study. English railroads did not have the problem of rough terrain that faced Jervis. Other than the Quincy Railroad, the only American railroad that might have been a model was the nine-mile gravity railroad at Mauch Chunk, Pennsylvania. The Mauch Chunk Railroad was under construction in 1827, hence Jervis could not observe its operation. In any case, this railroad did not include the use of locomotives in its plan.

In his search to determine the kind of railroad that would best meet the needs of the Delaware and Hudson Company, Jervis considered the feasibility of the single-rail railroad. In 1827 there were engineers who felt that this would be the most likely railroad form to be adopted universally.[31] Jervis studied the works of English engineers with regard to the reduction of friction through the use of the single rail. The Englishmen were not in agreement on the subject, and Jervis tended to side with those who felt that the use of the single rail produced no substantial reduction of friction on the axle. Hence, Jervis concluded that it had not yet been proved that the single-rail railroad was valuable for saving power.[32] Jervis also considered whether a single rail would reduce construction costs: it had been asserted that the single rail would require only half of the expense of the double-rail road. He noted a small savings in terms of rail construction, but this would be more than offset by the greater expense in excavation because of the need for deeper and wider cuttings in both sides of the track to accommodate single-rail carriages. These considerations caused Jervis to recommend the construction of a double rail for the Carbondale line.[33] The rails would consist of timber stringers set four feet, three inches apart and capped with iron plates.

Jervis cited the advantage of both cast and rolled iron plates. Each had points to recommend it and, according to the chief engineer, " . . . in view of the comparative advantages I see but little ground for a choice: I am however inclined to give preference to rolled iron." The fact that the Quincy line had plates of rolled iron may have influenced his decision.[34]

The proposed railroad route included the 900-foot ascent from Carbondale to the summit level, a distance of slightly more than three miles. The climb was divided into five inclined planes,[35] varying in length from 120 feet to 205 feet, with an inclination averaging one foot in twelve feet.[36] Since Jervis had recommended railroad cars or carriages with a 2½-ton capacity and a gross weight of approximately 3 tons,[37] the use of horses to draw the cars up the inclines was out of the question. Therefore, Jervis decided to use thirty-five horsepower, high pressure, stationary steam engines. The estimated cost of the five engines that would be required, plus that of providing a water source for their operation, was $24,500.[38]

Jervis considered the idea of using ropes between the carriages and the stationary engines. Ropes were in use in England under similar circumstances; however, their use as a method of conducting power was entirely dependent on friction. Jervis preferred chains that could be worked over fluted sheave (cog) wheels, thus eliminating any slippage. Also, he believed chains to have superior durability over rope,[39] a belief that later proved to be a miscalculation.

Jervis's uncertainty about ropes versus chains on the inclined planes was in keeping with the logical and considerable concern over grades and their effect on friction and/or traction. Nicholas Wood, the noted English engineer, was among those who discussed the problem. He maintained that the adhesion between the wheels of a vehicle and the rails could be calculated as ⅕ of the total weight of the vehicle travelling on rails in their "worst state," that is, under conditions that produced the least amount of friction. Wood's "worst state" was an imaginary midpoint between the two optimums, which he defined as rails that were either completely dry and clean or thoroughly wet and clean. In either case, the absence of foreign material such as dirt or mud on the rails was deemed best to achieve the most traction.[40]

Col. S. H. Long, one of the Army engineers assigned to the Baltimore and Ohio Railroad project, included a section on adhesion between wheels and rails in his pocket *Railroad Manual* of 1829. Long referred to Wood but disagreed with him; Long felt that the $\frac{1}{25}$ weight proportion was "too small for our present purpose." Long felt "$\frac{1}{20}$ of the entire load, (which is nearly equal to its tendency to descend on a plane whose inclination is 3 degrees) is a more accurate expression for the adhesion of the wheels in all states of the road and weather, frost and snow excepted."[41] Long also expressed his thoughts on loads descending inclined planes: "When the tendency in the direction of a plane, exceeds the adhesion of the wheels, the descent of the load must be regulated by stationary brakes. When the tendency as above exceeds the friction of the carriage and is less than the adhesion of the wheels, the descent may be regulated by brakes or convoys attached to carriages."[42] Jervis miscalculated in deciding to use chains on inclined planes, but his ideas for the brakes or "pneumatic" convoys were similar to Long's, although Jervis's ideas had been stated years earlier than those of the Army engineer.

Motive power for the descending planes to Honesdale was provided by gravity. The speed of the loaded cars travelling down the planes was decreased by having them pull empty cars up the plane. However, further braking mechanisms were needed to slow the loaded cars. In addition to the brakes on the individual carriages that were needed for final stopping, Jervis invented a pneumatic convoy that consisted of "eight sails [blades] to be attached to two vertical shafts: the motion to be communicated by a spur wheel on the shaft of the engine sheave, driving a pinion on each of the sail shafts."[43] The machinery for the pneumatic convoy, or fan wheel, was very simple to construct and operate, but, according to its inventor, " . . . must be inclosed in a building with suitable doors to admit free circulation of air but to prevent irregularity caused by the wind."[44]

After determining the power requirements for the inclined planes, Jervis discussed in his report the kind of power he felt would be appropriate for the eight level or near-level sections of the railroad. For the five sections less than a mile in length, Jervis recommended the use of horse power. He decided locomotive engines would be the most efficient form of power on the three remaining levels.[45]

Before making his decision about the locomotive engines, Jervis had reviewed data on adhesion tests conducted by the English engineers Nicholas Wood and Thomas Tredgold. Trials in England showed that the fine bituminous coal dust worked against good adhesion between the engine wheels and the rails. Jervis felt this would not be a problem on the Carbondale Railroad, since the road would carry anthracite coal. He even went so far as to compare the difference in precipitation and its relative effect on traction. Jervis reasoned that the hard rains of Pennsylvania would be more effective than the misty rains of England in washing coal dust from rails.[46] Thus, after figuring friction, speed, and load, Jervis determined that seven locomotive engines would be required, with the engines plus their tender weighing between 6¼ and 6½ tons.[47]

The remainder of the report involved cost estimates. The conclusion was that the total cost of transportation on the railroad would be 1⁸∕₁₀ cents per ton mile. This was "very little in excess of the cost of transportation on a canal, with a medium quantity of lockage."[48]

Jervis echoed Wright when he stated that he recognized that the proposed railroad might have problems from the lack of experienced men and might be prone to occasional mechanical failure. However, he closed the report by writing optimistically that he looked forward to the completion of the proposed railroad "with unequivocal confidence of success. Its successful accomplishment will form a new era in the internal improvement of our country: high dividing ridges or mountains will essentially loose [sic] their formidable character and no longer be considered as presenting insurmountable obstacles to any reasonable project to promote easy internal communication."[49]

The completed report was submitted to the board of managers who, in turn, sent it to Professor James Renwick of Columbia University, a consultant for the company.[50] Renwick supported the Jervis report, but questioned the use of water power on one of the inclined planes.[51] Apparently Jervis had intended the use of steam power on all the planes and had advised the board of his error almost simultaneously with their receipt of Renwick's comments.[52] The Delaware and Hudson directors also sent a copy of the report on the Carbondale Railroad to Benjamin Wright. In his reply, Wright's "only objection (and perhaps that is groundless) to the plan adopted by Mr. Jervis is the great number of changes or the shifting of power from horse to steam and from steam to gravitation."[53] After considering the reports from Renwick and Wright, the board instructed Jervis to proceed with the railroad along the lines of the October plan.[54]

In terms of the future of John B. Jervis, the portion of the Carbondale Railroad that was a failure was as significant as that which was a success. The actual construction of the line itself was completed with few problems. However, the track proved to be inadequate to handle the locomotive engines, which were built larger than Jervis's specifications.

A succinct account of the inability to use the locomotive on the railroad appeared in an 1877 *New York Times* article. Although meant to commemorate the Stourbridge Lion, the first locomotive "that ever turned a driving wheel on a railroad track in America,"[55] it was less than complimentary about the construction of the railroad. It claimed that as soon as the locomotive was placed on the track it was obvious that the rails would not bear the weight. The article criticized the lack of properly seasoned timber rails, which resulted in warping, and claimed that the track curves had not been properly laid out. As the track left the canal docks in Honesdale, it was constructed so as to present a curve of "threatening radius" for a locomotive with fixed (unable to swivel) wheels.[56] "Although the locomotive as a locomotive was a perfect success," the article noted, "the railroad was not calculated to stand its use."[57]

The *Times* article served to illustrate and perpetuate a half century of controversy over the subject of the Stourbridge Lion and the railroad. To Jervis, one of the two principal men involved in the controversy, there was little doubt as to reasons for the failure of the Lion. Jervis's reaction to the *Times* article was that it was "calculated to perpetuate the erroneous impression as to several facts of the case and has induced me to make some corrections."[58] The corrections appeared in the Jervis autobiography, and they showed that the chief engineer was not responsible for the failure. It should come as no surprise that other available evidence relating to the events also supports the Jervis version.

As chief engineer of the Delaware and Hudson Company, Jervis was responsible for the performance of the gravity railroad, and for any equipment used by that railroad. In this sense, Jervis could be considered at fault for the ultimate failure of the first steam locomotive. However, he did not personally arrange for the purchase of the engine. This was done by the company's representative in England, Horatio Allen, a young Columbia graduate who had been a resident engineer on the canal.

A late-1827 trip to England to observe the construction and operation of English railroads resulted in Allen's being named by the company as its agent. As such, he was instructed to purchase four English locomotives for use on the new railroad. Jervis was notified of Allen's arrival in England by a letter dated February 24, 1828, that began, "I am at length in the land of railroads and in the atmosphere of coal smoke."[59]

Allen wasted little time in arranging a meeting with Robert Stephenson, a locomotive builder "considered the expert of the kingdom on

D & H 13764   I W WROT STL WLS   BLT 9·51   L 53FT 2IN   SPRG D 3

Fig. 2.3. Replica of Stourbridge Lion, showing its size relative to that of a modern railroad flatcar. Photo by author.

steam engines."[60] However, by the end of March he had yet to conclude arrangements for a purchase. Allen had been occupied with observing English railroads and had sent Jervis detailed descriptions of the Liverpool and Manchester line and the Stockton and Darlington road.[61] But Allen's lack of action on the locomotives caused Jervis to become impatient. "I look with great anxiety for your letter on the question of locomotive engines," Jervis wrote in a gentle reminder to Allen, "but do not wish to be understood as nagging you forward to a hasty decision on the matter."[62]

Horatio Allen finally arranged for the purchase of four locomotives; by July 1828, contracts had been signed with Foster, Rastrick and Company for the Stourbridge Lion, the Delaware, and the Hudson. Robert Stephenson and Company would build a fourth engine, the America, also known as the Pride of Newcastle.[63] The four engines arrived in New York at various intervals between mid-January and mid-September 1829.[64] Upon their arrival, the first two, the America and the Stourbridge Lion, were placed on blocks and tested at the Abeel and Dunscomb Foundry and the West Point Foundry respectively[65] — with the tests proving them to be in operating order. They remained in New York City on public display for about six weeks.[66]

Prior to their shipment to Honesdale, Allen contacted Jervis from New York City with advice about placing the engines on the gravity railroad. "I agree with you in thinking it best to put the 'Pride of New-castle' on the Summit plane," he wrote; then he advised, "the other engine (the Lion) had better be placed at the head of the canal and the remaining two (if they ever arrive) taken to their place of labour before they are put up."[67]

Three weeks after he received Allen's letter, Jervis hired the ship *Congress* at a cost of seventy-five dollars to carry two locomotives and eighty pairs of railroad car wheels to Rondout, where they were shipped via canal boat to the head of the railroad.[68] The fate of the America remains a mystery. There is no evidence of its arrival in Honesdale.[69] The Stourbridge Lion did arrive and was tested. The test results revealed what was to become the center of the controversy between Allen, the locomotive buyer, and Jervis, the railroad builder. The chief engineer's earlier suspicions were confirmed; the engine was too heavy.

As early as 1827, Jervis specified that the weight of the locomotive and carriage [tender] should not exceed 6½ tons.[70] Deducting 1200 to 1500 pounds for the weight of the carriage,[71] an engine weight of between 5 and 5½ tons would be the maximum that the road would bear. Jervis planned for a weight of one ton per wheel for both the wheels of the locomotive and those of the loaded carriages.[72] To adhere to this weight distribution, Jervis originally proposed an engine of six wheels. It was felt that this would also provide more "tractile power" (tractive force) for the engine.[73]

Jervis then had second thoughts on the matter. He doubted whether six wheels mounted on a single frame would work well on a curved railway. He expressed his doubts to Allen in a letter dated April 23, 1828, informing him that the most the railroad would carry on four wheels was 5½ tons.[74] The only locomotive that was tested considerably exceeded the recommended limit. The Stourbridge Lion weighed seven tons as constructed. To this could be added an additional ton in fuel and boiler water.[75] Since the engine exceeded the maximum load capacity of the railroad by fifty percent, it is not surprising that it could not be used in regular service.

According to most sources, the trial run of the Lion was on August 8, 1829. A letter from Jervis to Delaware and Hudson president John Bolton indicates that the engine initially was tested two days earlier. The chief engineer reported, "we have had the Lion on the road from the Basin to about half across [and] at this point one of the capts [iron cap] began to fail and we run [*sic*] her back a little."[76] The engine "stood on the road all right" but "it will be necessary to give additional support to the bridge [trestle]."[77]

Jervis also advised Bolton of the events of the second test on August 8th. Optimistically, he wrote, "the Locomotive will I think fully answer our expectations when we get the road firm enough to bear it. So far I think all the difficulties discovered can be easily remedied."[78] But the next run of the Lion on September 9th confirmed Jervis's initial calculations about locomotive weights.[79] Resident engineer James Archbald examined the effect the locomotive had on the rails and reported that the locomotive impressed the iron plate into the wood. Clearly the Lion could not be used on the gravity railroad.[80]

In reflecting in his autobiography on the running of the Lion, Jervis wrote, "the experiment was a great loss to the company and to me a very serious disappointment. It was clear the agent [Horatio Allen] had not carried out my instructions."[81] However, Jervis "did not feel disposed to make severe criticism of the agent" since "it was a day in which the subject of locomotives was in its infancy and [Jervis] considered the builders had misled [Allen]."[82]

But Jervis did comment on the *New York Times* articles of 1877 and other accounts praising Allen for his bravery in operating the locomotive in the trial run of the Lion. Jervis felt it unreasonable to attribute failure to the "railway instead of the locomotive; and with all to give credit to the man who ran the engine on trial, for his courage in a case in which no special courage would have been called for if the agent had executed his mission according to instructions."[83]

Apparently Jervis was disturbed by the notoriety Allen received for his role in the operation of the nation's first locomotive. Allen's name continues to appear in connection with the event much more frequently than does Jervis's. Jervis, acutely aware of this a half century after the trials, explained why he had demurred from greater acclaim of his role in the event. "Having myself all preliminary responsibility of procuring the locomotives," Jervis stated, "I was the first to introduce on this continent a locomotive engine. Whatever honor might be attached to this (and I think it would be equal the honor of acting as the first man to run it), I did not think it worthwhile to assert."[84] His reason for remaining in the background was the failure of the trial runs, hence it is understandable that "under the circumstances [Jervis] was in no spirit to assume the honor of introducing the first locomotive."[85]

In spite of what Jervis termed Allen's failure, the two men remained on friendly terms. Allen spent his summers visiting Jervis while the former was employed on the Charleston and Hamburg Railroad and the latter was building the Mohawk and Hudson, and Allen was Jervis's principal assistant on the Croton Aqueduct project. For most of the remainder of the nineteenth century, they lived lives that in many ways were parallel.

Whether or not Jervis should be faulted for the failure of the Lion is debatable. But no account of the gravity railroad is complete without mention of a failure on the part of the line's mechanism that was installed solely on the recommendation of the chief engineer. After the experience with the Stourbridge Lion, the gravity railroad was powered entirely by stationary steam engines. The coal wagons were pulled up the inclines by chains, as Jervis had suggested in his 1827 report. Within three months of the opening of the road, it was obvious that the chains were not satisfactory. Coal wagons could be wrecked by the failure of any one of the 180,000 links, and the chains broke so regularly that it became necessary to keep blacksmith forges near the planes to hasten repair.[86]

The company managers began to consider the use of ropes as an alternative to chains. "If the objections to endless ropes cannot be obviated," manager Rufus L. Lord wrote to Jervis, "can you not have two chains on the descending planes, so that when one breaks, the other will hold the waggons [sic]."[87] Lord told Jervis that he saw nothing standing in the way of complete success except the breaking of chains.[88]

By early 1830, Jervis was forced to adopt the use of ropes, on the board of managers' decision. While Jervis admitted that ropes would be safer, he apparently felt impelled to defend his original recommendation in favor of chains,[89] claiming that the frequent breakage in the chains was due to flaws in the manufacture. He maintained that "we have not found a broken link but was either badly welded or had a flaw in the iron."[90] Jervis insisted the tension was not sufficient to break the chain had the links been made properly.[91] In any case, by the time Jervis left the Delaware and Hudson service, ropes had entirely replaced chains on the inclined planes. The ropes were satisfactory in their operation, the initial reservations of the chief engineer notwithstanding.[92]

John B. Jervis resigned his position as chief engineer of the Delaware and Hudson Company in May, 1830.[93] He continued with the company in an advisory capacity until the spring of 1831, during which time he was engaged as chief engineer of the Mohawk and Hudson Railroad. Upon his recommendation, two of his assistants were appointed superintending engineers on the Delaware and Hudson works: James Archbald for the railway and Russel F. Lord for the canal.[94] The high regard Jervis had for these men is shown in unusual praise in his final report to the board of managers. According to the report, the former chief engineer took pleasure in leaving the work in the hands of Archbald and Lord, whose "integrity, sound practical judgment, and untiring assiduity are important requisites for men managing such works."[95]

Thus, Jervis's first position as chief engineer came to a successful end. He had demonstrated his engineering ability in directing the building of a canal that was as well designed and built as any in existence in the United States. The canal made a major contribution to steam transportation and the industrial growth of New York City. By 1858 it was estimated that more than two million tons of coal were shipped to the New York City area, "mostly over the Delaware and Raritan, the Morris, and the Delaware and Hudson canals."[96]

When presented with a construction problem other than that of hydraulics, Jervis extended himself beyond his early training and designed a gravity railroad. He showed his willingness to innovate in the use of a steam locomotive. Although the locomotive itself was a failure, the railroad properly performed the function for which it was built. The experience Jervis gained from the trial of the locomotive and from the Delaware and Hudson project in general was invaluable to his future employment.

The British-built locomotives that Jervis ordered through Allen for the Delaware and Hudson Company were the first locomotives in North America.[97] Although the Stourbridge Lion, the only one tested on rails, failed its test, it was the fault of the track not poor engine performance. But subsequent British imports of the same short wheel base design and lacking a forward swivel truck were subject to excessive rocking and derailing on the uneven American tracks. Locomotives such as the Robert Fulton, built by the Stephenson works in 1831 for the Mohawk and Hudson Railroad, were unsatisfactory because "the consequence of low steam pressure and a small boiler and cylinders, prevented it from hauling a paying load over the steep grades and rough track" of the American railroad.[98] But, of course, the early British engines were built mainly for use on the railroads of England, which "were models of a civil engineering enterprise with carefully graded roadbeds, substantial tracks, and grand viaducts and tunnels to overcome natural obstacles."[99]

Although some of the earliest American railroads were built to the British design, this design soon proved impractical for American conditions. In Britain, where "capital was plentiful, distances short, and traffic density high, the British could afford to build splendid railways."[100] In the United States, the opposite was true in almost all cases. Where the British spent $179,000 per mile on their early railroads, American roads were built for approximately one-sixth that amount. But this was done partly by allowing the line of track to follow the contours of the land

and avoid major topographic obstacles. As a result, curves and grades were the rule, not the exception, on early American railroads. Often, as these roads pushed through the Appalachians, the curves were very sharp and the grades quite steep. Curves of a 1,000-foot radius were common, as were grades of thirty to fifty feet per mile. When a ravine was encountered that was too steep to build through or if a creek or river had to be crossed, cheap wooden trestles were often used instead of the well-built stone viaducts that were the practice in England.[101]

Finally, the way in which American track was built evolved into a less expensive form. Although American roads, including Jervis's next project, used stone blocks instead of wooden cross ties at first, the rails were made of wood with thin straps of iron fastened on top of the wooden rails or stringers. Soon the stone block method was abandoned for the cheaper and faster wooden cross ties to form a base for the rails. Little attention was given to proper grading and ballast, and often the ties simply rested upon the ground. The winter frost heaving and the spring rains had the imagined effect on the roadbed, and the level and parallelism of American railroads varied sharply from season to season and even from day to day. It was those differences of American railroad construction from that of the British that led to Jervis's major contribution to railroading.

3

A New Challenge

THE DECADES OF THE 1820s, 1830s, and 1840s were a time when the nation's transportation system was transformed from road and river routes to those of canals and railroads. The spectacular success of New York's Erie and Champlain canals, completed by the middle of the twenties, brought on a flourish of digging in an attempt to duplicate or outstrip New York's achievement.

A canal was constructed from Philadelphia to the Ohio River at Pittsburgh. Even though its route took it across mountains almost four times as high as the land the Erie Canal crossed, producing a construction cost of double that of the Erie, the Pennsylvanians were optimistic of its success. From Georgetown next to the nation's capital, laborers on the Chesapeake and Ohio Canal slowly dug their way towards the mountains of western Maryland. Michigan, Ohio, Indiana, and Illinois built canals to the point of bankruptcy, a condition augmented by the Depression of 1837. And in the home state of the mighty "hellespont of the West," New Yorkers were digging furiously to connect all parts of their state with the Erie main line. Excluding the Champlain, no less than eight lateral canals running from the northern and southern tiers sought succor from the flow of Erie commerce. A ninth canal, Jervis's Delaware and Hudson, tied northeastern Pennsylvania to the Hudson River and transported the fuel for factories, steamboats, and the railroads.

The first railroads using steam power arrived by 1830. The Best Friend of Charleston was in service on the Charleston and Hamburg line, followed successively by locomotive power on the Baltimore and Ohio and then the Mohawk and Hudson railroads. Within six months of the running of the Mohawk and Hudson's DeWitt Clinton between Albany and Schenectady in August 1831, twenty-five railroads had applied for corporate charters in New York State alone. By 1840, twenty-two of the then twenty-six states had railroads. The top three in terms of total mileage were Pennsylvania with 754, New York with 374, and Massachusetts with 301 miles.[1]

One result of the transportation facility construction boom was the incessant demand for skilled civil engineers. Those that were graduates of the Erie Canal "school" or the United States Military Academy at West Point were practically the only domestic engineers with the necessary skills to fulfill the need. Relatively few in terms of the demand, those who had acquired a reputation were almost constantly sought for their engineering skills. They tended to move from project to project with an eye towards what would most enhance their reputations. The junior level of engineers did the same thing since they were attempting to build a reputation. Jervis was no exception, and he frequently was quite open in revealing his goal of upward mobility when he accepted or rejected positions, although the lure of a new challenge seemed to be equally important to Jervis as enhancing his reputation. Perhaps it was even more so.

The disappointing performance of the Stourbridge Lion failed to dampen the enthusiasm for railroads of either of the two principals involved in the Lion's purchase and importation. Horatio Allen was appointed chief engineer of the South Carolina Railroad and, the test of the Lion notwithstanding, he recommended to the company directors that the road be constructed for locomotive power.[2] The first two locomotives built in the United States for actual use on a railroad were placed in service on Allen's Charleston and Hamburg line. Both were produced by the West Point Foundry in New York City.[3] The third engine built by this company was both the third used in regular service on an American railroad and the first used in New York State. The engine was the DeWitt Clinton. The railroad, the Mohawk and Hudson, was the first of several successful lines built by John B. Jervis.

Jervis was offered the position of principal engineer in March 1830. James Renwick, secretary of the Mohawk and Hudson Company, informed him that the terms of employment provided an annual salary of $2,000 in return for which Jervis would contribute at least one-half time in alternating months for the first year (May 1830–May 1831).[4] Jervis readily accepted the offer,[5] which was more than twice the salary paid to Peter Fleming, the first principal engineer. Fleming left the Mohawk and Hudson in 1829 after three years as engineering chief.[6]

Well before Jervis was hired by the Mohawk and Hudson Company and even before he conducted the tests of the Stourbridge Lion on the Delaware and Hudson's short railroad, construction on another railroad had been started. On July 4, 1828, ceremonies marked the beginning of a project to link Baltimore with the Ohio River. The merchants and city fathers of the Chesapeake Bay city hoped to tap the increasing western trade with a rail link. Although the project was pushed ahead rapidly at first, progress eventually bogged down for a variety of reasons.

The first thirteen miles of Baltimore and Ohio track were opened from Baltimore to Ellicott's Mills in May 1830.[7] The motive power for the road was horses, and not until June 1831 was a locomotive delivered for service on the railroad. This was only about a month before the DeWitt Clinton started running on the Mohawk and Hudson.

The initial use of horse power instead of locomotives was only one of the many differences between the Baltimore and Ohio and the Mohawk and Hudson. The Baltimore and Ohio was constructed to move passengers as well as freight. But the movement of goods was its chief purpose: in 1836, the railroad owned nearly twenty-five times more freight cars than passenger cars.[8] Baltimore traders had no Hudson River–Erie Canal transportation corridor on which to cheaply ship freight to and from the west as did the merchants of New York City. Also, the Baltimore and Ohio was a partly privately financed venture, whereas the State of New York built the Erie Canal. The Mohawk and Hudson Railroad was built chiefly to move people between the Hudson River and Erie Canal. The promoters of the road did not have a distant terminal goal in mind, but simply wanted to offer a faster, more direct link between Albany and Schenectady than the slower canal travel or somewhat slower and perhaps less comfortable stagecoaches.

Another difference between the Baltimore and Ohio and the Mohawk and Hudson was their respective engineering departments. Jervis was chief engineer of the latter road, and he organized his own engineering department. As chief engineer, he laid out the route of the road and supervised its construction. This was not so simply and easily accomplished on the Baltimore and Ohio, which initially had a board of engineers consisting of two to three officers on loan from the U.S. Army. Their charge was to lay out the route while a civilian superintendent of construction supervised the building activities. This system lacked harmony and finally led to a dispute between the engineering board and the construction superintendent. In May 1830, after the initial thirteen miles of track opened, Captain McNeill of the board of engineers charged superintendent of construction Wever with insubordination and with falsifying contract amounts. Ultimately, the company's board of directors sided with Wever and dissolved the board of engineers. By June 1830, the army engineers had been reassigned, but they already had completed the survey of the entire route to the Ohio River. Yet other problems, including the mountains of western Maryland and Virginia, delayed

completion of the line until the end of 1852.⁹ By then, Jervis had completed two railroads and had made major contributions to two more. Of
course, on the Mohawk and Hudson and the Saratoga and Schenectady,
Jervis's two earliest roads, he did not have the problems that faced the
Baltimore and Ohio engineers.

In keeping with his habit of moving rapidly ahead on a project,
Jervis selected the two resident engineers for the railroad in less than a
week after his own acceptance. On March 15, he offered John Clark,
recently resigned from the Delaware and Hudson Canal, one of the
positions and designated his brother, Timothy Jervis, for the other.¹⁰ In
his letter to Clark, Jervis revealed that some of the directors of the
Mohawk and Hudson suggested requesting assistance from the U.S.
Army Corps of Engineers "to obtain the benefit of their scientific aid."
Jervis believed the majority of the board to be against the plan. He may
have been hopefully speculating, since his feelings on the subject were
"decidedly against committing the execution of such work to such
men."¹¹ Jervis did not explain why he disliked the West Pointers.¹² He
may have resented their formal engineering education or felt their training did not prepare them to build railroads. Upon receiving affirmative
replies from Clark and Timothy Jervis, Jervis informed James Renwick
of their appointment, assuring Renwick that the hiring of his brother did
not represent a conflict of interest. He also took the opportunity to state
the need for assistant engineers, rod men, and axemen.¹³

As soon as the organization of his force was complete, the principal
engineer commenced his preliminary survey for the railroad route, which
was to be built between Albany and Schenectady, New York. Jervis could
propose a suitable route, but its final approval was up to a committee
consisting of John Jacob Astor; Lynde Catlin, company treasurer; and
James Renwick.¹⁴ According to a contemporary account of the building
of the road, the Jervis route "was generally three fourths of a mile north
of Mr. Fleming's line except at the two terminations. It is believed that
no part of Mr. Fleming's plan has been adopted."¹⁵ In other words, the
line ran a straight sixteen miles between the two cities, terminating at the
Hudson River at Gansevoort Street in Albany and at Mill Street near the
original Erie Canal in Schenectady.¹⁶

By mid-July 1830, Jervis had progressed in his work to the point
that he finished a twenty-two page report to the company. The document
described the materials to be used in track construction and the manner
in which the track would be laid. The report also provided a detailed
breakdown of cost estimates, which was a preliminary step in all Jervis
projects.¹⁷ Meticulousness in making calculations was a Jervis trait in his
professional life as well as in his personal business affairs.

In planning construction of the line, Jervis decided that the rail timbers were to be of white pine, six inches square, and from twenty-one to twenty-four feet in length. White pine was preferred because of its strength and resistance to warping. Jervis considered the use of Southern yellow pine, but found it too expensive and "dealers in it given to deceiving their customers."[18] Stone blocks measuring fifteen inches square by sixteen inches high and placed four feet apart on center would support the rail timbers. The blocks, embedded in gravel, would elevate the timbers two or three inches above the surface of the ground. The wooden rails would be between four feet nine inches and five feet apart, with an estimated life of about twelve years.[19] The iron part of the rail, that upon which the train wheel rested, consisted of "a plate 2½ inches wide on the bottom with the upper edges so curved as to reduce the top width to 1⅞ inches and to be 9/16 of an inch in thickness . . . " with a weight of approximately 19½ tons per mile.[20]

The principal engineer also suggested the construction of a McAdamized horse path so that horses could be used as a source of power as well as locomotives.[21] This foresight was substantiated by the fact that, although the railroad had originally intended to use locomotives only, the opening of the road to traffic found both horses and locomotive steam power in use. The horse path continued to be "used more or less until the locomotives were fully prepared."[22]

Ground was broken for the Mohawk and Hudson in Schenectady on August 12, 1830. Within one year of the beginning of the work, twelve miles of single track had been completed.[23] Apparently the construction of the Mohawk and Hudson moved ahead rapidly and routinely. The land between Albany and Schenectady was a sandy plain described by Jervis as "a table land of fair character for a good line and easy grades." The chief obstructions to the rapid completion of the entire line were the steep approach grades to the level area between the two cities. These were inclines of "near[ly] two hundred feet from the Hudson and over one hundred feet from the Mohawk."[24]

The elevation from the rivers through the use of inclined planes were, to Jervis, simply in keeping with prevailing theories about locomotive tractive power. Construction of a railroad on steep inclines, such as those at Albany and Schenectady, "at that day was regarded as impracticable without the planes with stationary power."[25] An alternate route that might have resulted in the elimination of the need for the planes met strong opposition from some of the citizens of Albany who objected to a railroad in the heart of the city.[26]

While work was progressing on the roadbed and track, Jervis made a suggestion to the company directors that was illustrative of his farsightedness. Influenced by his unsuccessful Delaware and Hudson experience, Jervis posed the possibility of the future adoption of an all-iron rail. To prepare for this, he recommended that the blocks supporting the wooden stringers be spaced three feet apart instead of four, which would provide better support for the heavier rail.

Jervis favored the change even though it would add approximately $1,100 per mile to the cost of construction.[27] He informed the railroad directors of his opinion about using the iron rail the day before he received a letter from Renwick on the same subject. According to Renwick, the use of an all-iron rail was foremost in the minds of the directors—so much so that they delayed taking action on the "proper form" for a rail until a meeting with Jervis could be arranged. The meeting, in John Jacob Astor's office, produced no immediate change in the original plan for the rails, but it did result in closer spacing of the support blocks.[28]

For the track gauge, the chief engineer wanted 4 feet 9 inches (4 feet 8½ inches is now considered standard gauge), which would carry an engine weighing between 3 and 3¼ tons. The gross weight of each carriage should be one ton; the sixteen passengers per carriage and their luggage were estimated to weigh 1½ tons. At five carriages per train, the resistance to the working power of the engine was determined to be 327.90 pounds, allowing for an average speed of twelve miles per hour.[29] In comparison with English locomotives, the one recommended by Jervis was rather small. It was clear that the experience he gained from the problems with the Delaware and Hudson's Stourbridge Lion on iron-capped wooden rails was not forgotten. The lighter American-made locomotive cost more than English engines, but Jervis, nevertheless, wrote of his engine plan, "the importance however of a light Engine I view to be too great to allow such difference in expense [cost of new molds and patterns] to have an essential influence."[30]

Since the Mohawk and Hudson Company already had ordered English machines, Jervis's campaign for the adoption of an all-iron rail continued into the autumn of 1831. Obviously he hoped to at least convince the directors that the planned second track be built of iron, since by that time the first track was nearly completed.

The arrival of the railroad's second locomotive, an English import, in late summer 1831 and its subsequent trial runs evoked the following communication from Jervis to Churchill C. Cambreling, a company director. "The English engine is doubtless too heavy for the road and this is clearly shown from the little work she has done. It is decidedly my opinion she should not be used on this road as nothing but an iron road is sufficient for such a weight. . . . "[31]

Jervis elaborated on the subject of an iron rail in a second letter to Cambreling written a little more than a week later. The nine-page document began with a response to a request by Cambreling for some cost comparisons between timber and iron rails. Reference was made to other railroads, including the Liverpool and Manchester. Again the question of the weight of the English engine arose, but Jervis placed a new emphasis on it. He referred to the "character of a passenger business" as one that "demands the least practical interruption. The expectations of the public have been so much excited in reference to rapid travelling (and that must be by locomotive steam power) that they will not be satisfied with moderate speed say 10 or 12 miles per hour. They must have 15 as a regular business." Jervis typically pointed to economy in informing Cambreling that "larger engines may be used on an iron road with very little increase of their daily expense, and will therefore be more economical for the work they do than those which must be used on a timber rail."[32] Jervis admitted that the wooden rails did not break under the weight of the English engine, but the locomotive caused the wood to compress. "Without iron rails I have no doubt that we will abandon the use of the English engine."[33]

Cambreling was not totally convinced of the need for the more expensive rails, since he wrote back to Jervis, "I have examined wooden rails [on the Baltimore and Ohio Railroad] . . . to see whether iron has been driven into wood but I cannot perceive that the slightest impression has been made. I saw cars and loads of 8–10 tons each on 4 wheels." Cambreling did admit, however, that even though heavy freight cars were used "constantly," locomotives were "only occasionally used."[34]

The Jervis-Cambreling correspondence on the rail material was written after the initial runs of not only the English locomotive but also of the railroad's first engine, the American-made DeWitt Clinton. The DeWitt Clinton was built to Jervis's specifications for a lightweight machine that would be less injurious to the rail. The completed engine weighed 6,758½ pounds and was capable of producing ten horsepower. DeWitt Bloodgood, a contemporary writer, described it as "being much less in proportion than that of the best English engines. As it stands on the rails, it can be very easily moved by a single hand!"[35] The railroad's English engine, the Robert Fulton, arrived on August 27, 1831.[36] A product of the Robert Stephenson works, it weighed nearly twice as much as the American engine, and the load was not evenly distributed over the four wheels, since 8,745 pounds rested on one pair of wheels.[37] This gave Jervis cause for concern because the weight on a single wheel was two and one half times greater than the load on a wheel of the Clinton.[38]

While the English locomotive was still in transit, the initial public run of the DeWitt Clinton was made on the ninth day of August 1831.[39] Except for the legendary hazards encountered from the billowing smoke, the flying sparks, and the lack of air brakes, the trip was a success because most defects, which had been revealed earlier on the test runs, had been remedied. Jervis's locomotive was designed, or perhaps more accurately intended, for the use of anthracite coal. His intention to use anthracite was not particularly novel or innovative. When the Stourbridge Lion was first fired during the tests at the West Point Foundry in June 1829, hard coal from the Lackawaxen region of Pennsylvania was used. Both the Tom Thumb and the York, two Baltimore and Ohio engines used prior to the DeWitt Clinton, burned anthracite coal. Thomas Earle in his *Treatise on Rail-Roads* recommended its use and included descriptions on the geography of the Pennsylvania anthracite regions.[40] However, the hard coal was found to pack in the Clinton's furnace to such an extent that the air blast required to burn it tended to melt the grates and the nozzle of the pipe from the wind reservoir. As a result, the fuel was changed to wood. Additional problems that were corrected resulted from the surging of water into the cylinders, the low termination of the eduction pipes in the chimney causing a poor draft, and the large size of the chimney itself.[41]

The Mohawk and Hudson continued in operation until December 31, 1831, when traffic was halted until the following spring. In his history, Frank W. Stevens simply states that operations were suspended. A communication from James Renwick to Jervis on December 28 revealed that the closing was due to "lack of materials." There was no indication of what was meant by this message, which ended with a statement that the road would "remain closed until further notice."[42]

Lack of evidence makes it hard to determine the extent to which the Clinton or the English engine were used on the railroad before operations ceased at the end of 1831. Bloodgood, in November 1831, said that passengers were being carried in coaches drawn by horses as well as by locomotives "whose powers are not yet conclusively tested."[43]

"Something didn't work right," according to Stevens in his account of the beginning of the Clinton's second season.[44] He based this statement on the fact that on April 14, seven hundred dollars was paid to the West Point Foundry for two pairs of wheels and eccentrics.[45] Apparently the defects of the Clinton required more than wheels and eccentrics, since the engine was still inoperative in late April.

Jervis wrote to Adam Hall, builder of the locomotive, to notify him that the water tubes in the machine were leaking. After calling Hall's attention to the manner in which the tubes were secured in the Robert

Fulton, Jervis stated "I am apprehensive we shall not make her worth much after all.[46] To this, the disgusted Jervis added that the engine had cost as much or more than horse power. He admonished Hall on the poor quality of workmanship evidenced in the locomotive's performance and rather sarcastically noted, " . . . if the engine goes well, with a good load, there is no doubt about the beauty of the thing."[47]

Hall's defensive reply came quickly. He insisted the boiler tubes had been adequately tested and believed the problem resulted from a combination of an improper water level in the boiler and lack of an experienced locomotive engineer. Hall continued with a second warning about the water level and cautioned Jervis against a possible explosion.[48]

Jervis's reaction, if any, is not known. It is known that the DeWitt Clinton continued to malfunction, making it necessary to install a new boiler before the end of 1832. Finally, the company sold the engine in April 1835.[49]

Compared with subsequent locomotives, Jervis says little of the Clinton in his writings. His "Historical Sketch of the Mohawk and Hudson Railroad," written thirty-five years later, simply describes the locomotive as being "quite light, but . . . able to haul a train of 80 to 100 passengers."[50] His autobiography omits mention of the engine in the section on early locomotives and reference to the Clinton appears only once in the chapter on the Mohawk and Hudson Railroad.[51] The omission could have been due to Jervis's unwillingness to recognize faulty workmanship.

Jervis was dissatisfied with the West Point Foundry as early as December 1831. Correspondence between the chief engineer and William Kemble, foundry superintendent, indicates Jervis's concern over the rolling stock contract being altered to the advantage of the foundry. Kemble evidently changed an order for wheels and axles to include seats for passenger wagons. Jervis challenged the change by questioning " . . . what right or where can there be the least propriety of your assuming to change — for seats that you now furnish. . . . " Jervis was not satisfied with the seats manufactured by the company; therefore, he had not ordered them. Additional items, such as tools, also were sent, but had not been ordered. Jervis, mindful as usual of detail and economy, itemized these and other materials for which he felt the charge had been exorbitant and deducted their cost from the total bill.[52]

Apparently, the wheels, as ordered, were also less than satisfactory because Jervis set out to improve upon them. By July 1833, he had accomplished this and announced his achievement in an illustrated letter to the editors of the *American Railroad Journal*. The chief improvements in his new wheel over the wheels made for the DeWitt Clinton

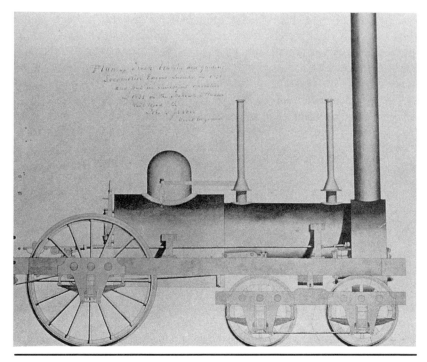

Fig. 3.1. Jervis's locomotive experiment, 1833. Drawing courtesy of Jervis Public Library.

were the inclusion of a "feather" edge on the flange, which tended to allow for better stability on the rail, and an increase in weight. Twenty pounds were added to each wheel for a total weight of 275 pounds. This increased the strength of the wheels over the older ones, which had experienced a twenty-five percent breakage rate when run at an average speed of fourteen miles per hour.[53]

The objections Jervis had to the workmanship at the West Point Foundry and the lack of trust he had in its management did not prevent him from ordering a second locomotive from the company. Perhaps it was in deference to the fact that both James Renwick and Governeur Kemble, Mohawk and Hudson directors, were also on the board of the foundry.

The locomotive's design followed a plan originated by Jervis that employed a forward movable truck. Instead of a locomotive resting on four fixed wheels, Jervis's plan called for substituting a four-wheeled truck in place of the two front wheels. The purpose of the truck was to guide the rear driving wheels into curves on the railroad. The movable or bogie truck was Jervis's most important contribution to railroads. In August 1832, David Matthew, superintendent of construction of the Mohawk and Hudson, described the Jervis-designed engine as having:

> nine and a half inch cylinders, sixteen inch stroke and had two pairs of driving wheels five feet in diameter, and set aft the furnace; had four wheels, thirty-three inches diameter in the truck. This truck was placed under the front end of the boiler for support, attached by a strong pin, and worked upon friction-rollers so as easily to follow the curves of the road, as the fore-wheels of a carriage upon common roads.
>
> The boiler furnace was five feet long, by thirty-four inches wide, with three inch tubes, and made to burn anthracite coal.[54]

In addition to his description, Matthew stated, "with this engine I have crossed the Mohawk and Hudson Railroad from plane to plane, fourteen miles, in thirteen minutes, making one stop for water. I have tried her speed upon a level, straight line, and have made one mile in forty-five seconds [eighty miles per hour] by the watch. She was the fastest and steadiest engine I have ever run or seen, and she worked with the greatest ease." He later wrote that "this was the first bogie engine or truck . . . ever built in this country or any other."[55] Jervis named the locomotive Experiment.

The Experiment was the first locomotive whose design was distinct from those used on English roads. But the truck principle itself was known prior to the Jervis-designed machine. William Chapman, an English inventor, patented a "bogie" truck in 1812. It was meant for use on a rail wagon. As described, "the wheels of [Chapman's] swivel truck moved around the rail or circumference of the curve as the vehicle above it took the chord of the arc."[56]

Jervis's personal library contains several volumes relating to English railroads.[57] Of these, the work of Thomas Tredgold is of particular interest in that pages are marked that contain references to carriages supported by movable four-wheel trucks. The description of the eight-wheeled carriage includes the statement, "If one frame with its four wheels be removed, and an axle with two wheels applied in its place, the carriage would have six wheels, and it would be easy to adjust the load so that the pressure on each pair of wheels would be equal."[58]

Jervis's contribution was to apply the principle to the locomotive and to adopt it for regular use on a railroad. It was upon this adaptation only that Jervis based his claim of "the sole responsibility of introducing this improvement in railway machinery." He also pointed out that he "took no patent for the invention." As a result, he was not publicly recognized as its inventor, but "as an American engineer, it was a satisfying compensation to be able to present to the railway interest a valuable improvement. . . ."[59] Additional consolation was the fact that "an American engineer, in the face of English practice, should have devised a plan, which at the time was considered very radical, of introducing a truck . . . which, after thirty-seven years of experience, is now adopted on every engine of nearly fifty thousand miles of railroad in America."[60]

But lack of sufficient recognition had reached the point of bitterness by the 1870s. Jervis's autobiography includes a passage in which he credits the Corning administration of the New York Central with acknowledging him as the inventor of the truck and complimenting him with a free pass on the railway. "But," Jervis added in one of his infrequent vitriolic statements, "Mr. Vanderbilt . . . refuses me such compliment, which I think my devotion to railway affairs entitles me to. The railway fare that I pay is of no great importance, but I think I am entitled to the compliment. . . . " Jervis pointed out that his inventions were in daily use on Vanderbilt's railroads, and it was for that reason that Jervis felt he had not been "justly dealt with."[61] Not wanting to miss an opportunity to extol the virtue of hard work, Jervis concluded his remarks with the reminder that he and his wife both have a life pass on the Hudson River portion of the Vanderbilt line (he had directed its construction), allowing them to "ride there in the enjoyment of a privilege I have earned by hard labor."[62]

While it is true that Jervis did not patent his movable truck engine, he frequently and emphatically defended his claim to being solely responsible for its introduction. Much of this was prompted by the contention that others had developed a truck locomotive earlier than the Jervis engine.

Most notable of the contenders was Horatio Allen with his locomotive, the South Carolina. Allen's contract with the Charleston and Hamburg line allowed him to be absent during the summer to avoid the unhealthy season in the South. During the summers of 1830 and 1831, Allen journeyed to the Albany area to spend his leave time with Jervis and to observe the work on the Mohawk and Hudson.

Both Jervis and Allen worked on a solution to the problem of developing an engine that could negotiate curves with ease and yet run at high speed, since the emphasis at the time was on the passenger trade. Because merchants and other potential railroad investors were aware of the low cost per ton mile to ship goods by water, they continued to assume that trade in heavy freight could not be taken from water transport.

Fig. 3.2. Horatio Allen's South Carolina locomotive for the Charleston and Hamburg Railroad. Drawing from William H. Brown, *The History of the First Locomotives in America,* New York: D. Appleton and Co., 1871, 170.

Both men had a "lively impression of the failure of the 'Stourbridge Lion' and were specially intent on devining [*sic*] a relief for the rails [distributing the weight] by some method of increasing the number of wheels. . . ."[63]

Jervis noted that the English method of solving the problem was to place the weight on more wheels, but keep all the wheels on the same frame. Both he and Allen regarded this as impractical for use on curved track. In arriving at his solution, Jervis's main concern was not whether the plan would work, but whether it would work safely on curves at high speed. He discussed the plan with Allen, who apparently liked it. The two men had an "extremely cordial" relationship and "interchanged the various views [they] entertained in a most frank and unreserved manner."[64]

Yet, eventually the discussions between Jervis and Allen led to a divergence of views about the truck engine. Allen became committed to a plan for a double truck engine on eight wheels, which was simply to connect two frames to a single boiler and firebox. He felt it necessary to take this approach to maintain an adequate number of drivers.[65] However, Jervis disliked its complexity and saw problems arising from the "working of machinery on two frames that must be constantly varying their parallelism."[66]

Allen's South Carolina was built in 1831 and put into service the following year.[67] Jervis wrote in his autobiography that had the South Carolina been successful, he would have rejoiced at Allen's achievement.[68] But, as Jervis pointed out in a letter to the editor of the *Railroad Gazette,* his plan was a success and Allen's a failure. In the forty years since the introduction of the two plans, "I do not know that Mr. Allen's locomotive is seen on any railway. Mine may be seen on 50,000 miles of railway."[69]

In reflecting on his innovation, Jervis admitted that he lacked complete confidence in the reliability of the truck. It was Allen who, impressed with the idea, assured him that it would work safely. In fact Allen was the "only engineer of any considerable experience who favored [Jervis's] views."[70]

In any case, as Jervis had admitted, credit for the invention of the truck principle could go to neither Jervis nor Allen. "All we are entitled to," according to Jervis, "is our respective plans for adopting this principle . . . to passenger speed."[71] This point was reiterated by Jervis at the conclusion of the section on the Mohawk and Hudson in his autobiography. "The truck itself was not a new idea with me," he emphasized, since "it had in principle been used, but was generally supposed to be impracticable for high speed."[72]

The Jervis claim to the introduction of the forward movable truck engine has been accepted by several historians who have concentrated on the development of American railroad technology. William H. Brown credited Jervis with originating the truck plan for locomotives.[73] Robert Thurston, in a history of steam engines published seven years after Brown's book, also recognized Jervis as responsible for the new type engine. Thurston wrote that in 1832 " . . . the first locomotive was built of what is now distinctively known as the American type—an engine with a truck or bogie under the forward end of the boiler." It was built at the West Point Foundry "from plans furnished by John B. Jervis."[74]

More recently Brian Hollingsworth, an English railroad expert, described Jervis as "one of the great benefactors of mankind . . . who in 1832 introduced the pivoted leading truck or bogie" in locomotives.[75] Contemporary verification of Jervis's pioneer effort can also be found in John White's history of American locomotives. According to White, " . . . the six-wheel engine or 'Jervis type' enjoyed a brief but intense popularity in the United States. It performed well in mixed service and was our first national type, a distinctive American locomotive." White noted that the "great years for the 4-2-0 [wheel arrangement] were between 1835 and 1842 when it was built almost to the exclusion of any other wheel arrangement."[76] White explained that the boiler and valve gears were a direct copy of the standard Stephenson design but the running gear was a radical departure from the type used on British engines.[77]

This new "distinctive American locomotive" design resulted from Jervis's observation that the rigid frame of English locomotives was not satisfactory for American tracks.[78] Locomotive builders were quick to adopt the Jervis-designed 4-2-0. One of the most notable, Matthias Baldwin, visited the Mohawk and Hudson Railroad, was favorably impressed with the Jervis truck engines, and built his next locomotive, the E. L. Miller, on the Jervis plan.[79] White pointed out that in accord with common practice concerning locomotive reforms, Jervis failed to patent his design and it was "freely given over to the industry."[80]

The performance of the Experiment was so favorable that similar locomotives were ordered for the Mohawk and Hudson and for a new line being built by Jervis between Saratoga and Schenectady. The Saratoga and Schenectady Railroad had been chartered in February 1831 with Churchill C. Cambreling as its first president.[81] Under the circumstances, it was not surprising that Jervis was asked to make a reconnaissance of the terrain through which the new railroad would pass.

On March 21, 1831, he informed the Saratoga and Schenectady directors that he had completed preliminary surveys of two possible routes and both appeared satisfactory.[82] Jervis's cost estimate of either route was just over $10,000 per mile; the total for twenty-two miles was estimated at $221,267.62. However, Jervis advised the directors "that if it should be thought important to travel at a greater velocity than 10 miles per hour it may be effected by adopting a carriage proportionably lighter or by constructing a stronger road." Jervis favored the stronger road, although it meant an additional cost of more than $1,000 per mile over the original estimate. Jervis also recommended a track gauge of four feet nine inches, since it would be advantageous to have the carriages the same as those of the Mohawk and Hudson.[83]

Another aspect of Jervis's "stronger road" that was innovative to railroad building in the United States at that time was suggested by his resident engineer. Jervis appointed William C. Young as his subordinate on the Saratoga and Schenectady. Young "proposed and practically introduced . . . the use of cross-ties in lieu of stone blocks and foundations, which formerly sustained the sleeper to which the strap-rail was spiked."[84] The wooden ties provided a rail base more elastic than stone and one upon which the rails were less apt to become uneven as a result of the heaving or sinking of the stones.

In a May 1833 article in the *American Railroad Journal,* Jervis briefly described the first engine ordered especially for the Saratoga and Schenectady. After stating that he had prepared its plans in December 1832, Jervis added only that it be mounted on six wheels and constructed in England at the Stephenson works. Delivery was anticipated sometime

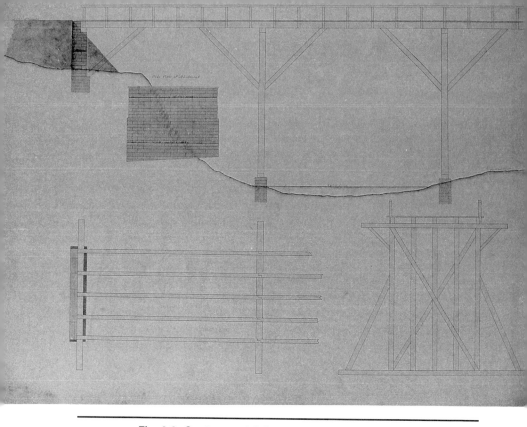

Fig. 3.3. Saratoga and Schenectady Railroad bridge, c. 1832. Drawing courtesy Jervis Public Library.

during June 1833.[85] The completed locomotive, the Davy Crockett, was nearly identical in appearance to the Experiment.

Prior to his order for the Davy Crockett, Jervis had directed that the first Stephenson engine delivered to the Mohawk and Hudson be converted to a 4-2-0. This was the Robert Fulton, a Stephenson Sampson–class engine mounted on four wheels. The conversion, done under the supervision of Asa Whitney at the Mohawk and Hudson shops, was completed in early 1833.[86] According to John White, Jr., the rebuilding of the engine was particularly difficult. The locomotive had inside cylinders, making it necessary to use bell cranks to connect the cylinders to the new rear driving wheels.[87] The machine was used on the Mohawk and Hudson and may have been used on the Saratoga and Schenectady prior to the arrival of the Davy Crockett. Jervis noted that " . . . the ease and smoothness of her motion, over that she had when on four wheels, is very striking."[88]

In the same letter to the *American Railroad Journal* in which he described the running of the Robert Fulton, Jervis gave his initial impression of the Davy Crockett. Its movement was "almost as smooth and steady a motion as a stationary engine."[89] His enchantment with the Stephenson locomotive was expressed again four decades after his original observations. He described his first ride on it as a "great delight. The smooth action of its parts and the steadiness of its motion gave me a great satisfaction."[90] Actually, Jervis took his first ride on the Stephenson six-wheel engine approximately two months after he resigned his position as chief engineer of both the Saratoga and Schenectady and the Mohawk and Hudson in April 1833.[91]

Although Jervis returned to the construction of waterways after his resignation from the railroad, the change was by no means permanent. As a pioneer in railroad engineering, Jervis had introduced to American railroads the steam locomotive. Although the first attempt was unsuccessful, he kept his faith in steam power and recommended its use on the Mohawk and Hudson. The favorable experience with engines on the Mohawk and Hudson caused Jervis to experiment with an alteration in the basic design of locomotives and develop the movable forward truck. This innovation certainly was one of the most significant in the history of railroading. With these accomplishments as a background, it was inevitable that Jervis would return to railway building.

While Jervis was employed on the Chenango Canal and briefly on the Erie enlargement, the shift from water to rail transportation had already commenced. By the mid-1840s, Jervis returned to railroads and spent the following two decades, the final years of his active practice of engineering, building and managing rail lines. All this occurred, however, only after Jervis supervised the digging of at least one more canal.

4

Canaling Again

ALTHOUGH RAILROADS had made their appearance in New York, the state was still in the euphoria of the canal boom. By the early 1830s, a number of canals were being constructed throughout New York to connect with the successful Erie. The "Grand Canal" itself was being considered for enlargement by a legislature that was seeking to expand upon its earlier good fortune.

The Chenango Canal was one of the lateral canals that owed its existence to the Erie. That is, like the other New York canals that were built along the route of the Erie, the Chenango's purpose was to open canal transportation to a portion of the state not adjacent to the Erie main line. After several years of agitation, the people of the Chenango River valley were successful in getting a waterway built through their area.

Their success was due largely to the candidacy of John Tracy, a valley man on the Democratic ticket for lieutenant governor in 1832. A Democratic victory that year prompted Governor William Marcy to recommend the construction of the canal in his annual message to the Legislature in January 1833. The following month, the New York Legislature passed an act authorizing the construction of a canal "from Binghamton, in the county of Broome, up the valley of the Chenango River, to its headwaters, and thence by the most advantageous route, to the Erie Canal."[1]

On April 12, 1833, the Canal Commissioners appointed John B. Jervis as chief engineer.[2] The naming of Jervis may have stemmed from the 1833 report by the Assembly Committee on Canals. The report made special mention of coal as potential canal freight and singled out the Delaware and Hudson Canal as an example of a successful enterprise that derived most of its revenues from coal.[3] Jervis, a builder of the

Delaware and Hudson, was a logical choice. Perhaps a more important reason for his selection was his acquaintance with at least three members of the Canal Commission, most notably William Bouck, a prominent Democrat and future New York governor.

Statistics compiled by the Canal Commissioners in 1830 showed the Chenango "had not much promise of commercial success."[4] But, true to his devotion to the profession, Jervis commenced his duties on the Chenango with the same degree of careful attention that he would have given to a more important assignment.[5] His initial instructions to his engineering staff required their first object to be "to ascertain the most favorable route, within the district allotted to the completed line having regard to economy in construction, general utility and good taste in the symmetry and beauty of the line and works connected therewith."[6]

Finding "the most favorable route" was one of the two major problems confronting Jervis and his engineers in the construction of the Chenango Canal. When it authorized the canal, the State Legislature itself had determined the route from Binghamton to the headwaters of the Chenango River. The problem was that from the upper Chenango to the Erie, a distance of between twenty and thirty miles, the choice of the canal line was left up to the engineers. The only stipulation was that the canal between the Chenango River and the Erie Canal could not use the water of either the Oriskany or Sauquoit creeks.[7] With this in mind, Jervis laid out several possible routes for the Chenango to connect with the Erie. Included were proposals to enter the main line canal at Utica, at Rome, and at various points in between the two communities. Jervis even considered places as far west as Durhamville and the Oneida Creek, both of which were approximately ten miles west of Rome.[8]

Even before he commenced the surveys for the northern route, Jervis came under pressure from various individuals who attempted to persuade him to use his influence with the Canal Commission to locate the canal through their areas. A letter from Simon Newton Dexter extolled the virtue of the Oriskany Creek route and made it quite clear that the canal would help his many mills throughout the creek valley. Dexter was well acquainted with Jervis and closed his letter with, "I wish no favors and I know you too well to expect any—If you think this route, all things considered is best—I do not doubt you will give it your support."[9] A week after Dexter's correspondence came a request from a resident of western Oneida County who wished to know whether or not the Chenango Canal would be located in the valley of the Skenandoah or Oneida Creek. The letter not only emphasized the value of the Skenandoah Creek valley as a canal route, but the author also attempted to influence Jervis's opinion of the Utica route. According to the letter, the

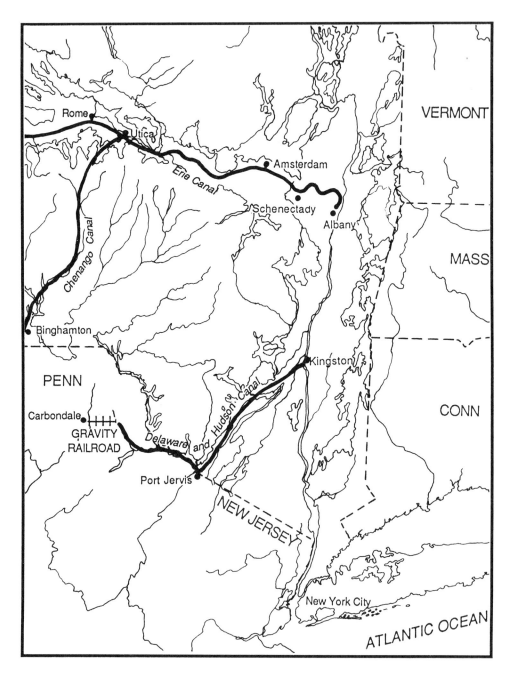

Fig. 4.1. New York canal routes, 1830s.

people of Utica were not particularly interested in the Chenango Canal.[10]

Ultimately Jervis made no particular recommendation, but simply submitted statistics on all the potential routes. After personally examining each route, the Commissioners decided to terminate the northern end of the canal at Whitesboro since the expense of building along this route was less than all other routes except one.[11] By the spring of 1834, however, the Legislature passed an act changing the location of the northern terminus of the canal and putting the junction with the Erie at Huntington's Basin in the city of Utica. This was done as a result of petitions from Utica citizens and with the understanding that the people of Utica would pay the more than $42,000 of additional cost for the Utica route.[12]

The second major problem confronting Jervis in the construction of the Chenango Canal was, from an engineering standpoint, much more difficult to resolve than the choice of a route. The Chenango Canal was an interbasin canal—that is, a canal that connects two separate river or creek watersheds. The difficulty this presented was the finding of an adequate water source for the summit level, as Jervis noted in a report to the canal commissioners. His solution to the problem was reservoirs, but he cautioned that "a reliance on artificial reservoirs to so large an extent as is contemplated in the projected work, is quite novel in the history of American Canals." He pointed out that reservoirs had been successfully used to some extent in other countries, but "limited experience in this should lead to great caution in all the plans and calculations connected with their construction, and the supply of water they are expected to furnish."[13]

Because there had already been failure in the use of reservoir supply systems in the United States, skeptics predicted that the Jervis plan would not work. European experience showed that reservoirs would retain only one-third of the total rainfall.[14] Jervis silenced the opposition by proving the Europeans to be in error. He constructed a rain gauge that showed that forty percent of the rainfall would remain in reserve in the artificial lakes.[15] By that time, Jervis's confidence in the reliability of reservoirs as a source of supply was such that he concluded a report to the Canal Commissioners by stating that he had no doubts the system would be adequate for the wants of the canal.[16]

Jervis's measurement of rainfall and runoff has been called "a hallmark in the history of American hydrology."[17] Ultimately seven reservoirs were built on the canal's summit level[18] under the direction of Jervis's able assistant William Jarvis McAlpine.[19]

The reservoirs proved to be more than adequate since they not only furnished abundant water for the Chenango Canal but, by 1841, helped supply the Rome level of the Erie Canal. Although the cost of their construction was great, "the reservoirs proved of immense value to the State."[20] The canal itself was completed by autumn of 1836, but the opening was delayed until spring of the following year.[21] Jervis's report to the Canal Commissioners in 1836 informed them that the canal was nearly completed. He pointed out that the total cost of construction would be $1,976,821.76. This exceeded his estimate made three years earlier by only $116,972.63.[22]

Except for the reservoir water supply system, [23] the Chenango Canal was not particularly challenging to Jervis. This, plus the small chance for success accorded the canal, caused his lack of enthusiasm about the project. While employed on the Chenango, Jervis began a search for a more interesting position. He had no lack of job offers and, although most were for relatively minor projects,[24] at least one concerned a major railroad undertaking.[25] Jervis accepted none of the offers.[26] Apparently the only one in which he expressed interest in early 1835 had been filled prior to his inquiry.[27] Ultimately Jervis took a position that, in a sense, he had been flirting with during his tenure as chief engineer of the Chenango works. The new appointment brought him once again to the Erie Canal.

The prospect of returning to the Erie Canal as a division chief was attractive to Jervis. The Erie had already demonstrated its worth and, unlike the almost insignificant Chenango, it was a project that could enhance his reputation. When talk of an Erie enlargement began to circulate, Jervis had thoughts of returning to the main line. Even so, personal feelings prevented him from actively soliciting an appointment. Perhaps the memory of his having refused Commissioner Seymour's offer of a good position on the Erie a decade earlier stopped Jervis from asking his old friend to intercede on his behalf. Instead, Jervis chose a more indirect approach, which eventually brought about his appointment to a position on the Erie.

As early as 1833, Jervis received a request from Jonas Earll, Jr., a member of the Canal Commission, to come to Rochester and inspect the Genesee Aqueduct. Earll wrote that "Mr. Bouck and myself thought it important that you should examine that work."[28] The rebuilding of the aqueduct at Rochester was among several canal projects recommended to the Legislature in 1834. These projects represented the first step toward an enlarged canal.[29] The next solicitation came from William Bouck himself in early 1834. The canal commissioner asked Jervis to submit a plan for a second set of locks ten feet longer than the ones used on the canal at an estimated cost of approximately $10,000 per lock.[30]

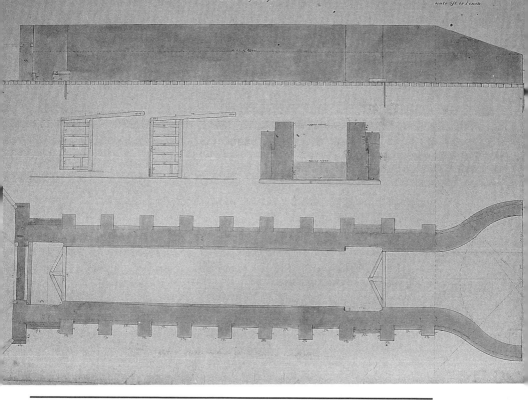

Fig. 4.2. A lock for the original Erie Canal (1823) or for the Chenango Canal (1834). Drawing courtesy Jervis Public Library.

Jervis became more involved in Erie business as each year passed. This was due in no small way to the influence and design of William Bouck. During the winter of 1834–1835, Bouck asked Jervis to make estimates comparing the economy and capability of the existing Erie Canal with the proposed enlarged waterway.[31] Shortly after Jervis submitted the requested calculations to Bouck, he was asked by the Canal Commission to examine the works at Little Falls. The commissioners were concerned about the effect a proposed dam across the Mohawk River would have on the canal. In a detailed report on the subject, Jervis carefully reviewed every influence the dam might have on the Erie.[32] This was the final unofficial connection Jervis had with the anticipated Erie enlargement project.

On May 11, 1835, a law was passed authorizing the canal commissioners to enlarge the Erie Canal and to construct double sets of lift-locks as soon as the commissioners felt this to be in the public interest.[33] By July 8, the canal board adopted a resolution declaring that the work on the enlargement should start as soon as possible,[34] and two weeks later, at a meeting in Utica, it named the engineers who would be in charge of making the survey. They were John B. Jervis, Albany to Fultonville; Nathan J. Roberts, Fultonville to Frankfort; Frederick C. Mills, Frankfort to Lyons; and Holmes Hutchinson, Lyons to Buffalo.[35]

Although Jervis did not actually solicit the appointment, he must have felt comfortable with the assignment. He had been an engineer on the eastern section of the Erie Canal prior to his work on the Delaware and Hudson Canal, and Nathan Roberts, who was named to head the section west of his, had been Jervis's first party chief when work commenced on "Clinton's Ditch" in 1817. Since the survey was to begin immediately and since Jervis was still chief engineer of the yet unfinished Chenango project, he again called upon William McAlpine to do the initial field work for the Erie enlargement. But, according to Jervis, "though I was in charge as chief engineer of the [Chenango] canal, I gave a large share of personal attention to the question of [the] enlargement."[36]

The reports of the engineers were submitted to the canal board in October 1835. The Jervis-McAlpine survey caused Jervis to recommend two major changes in the route of the Erie Canal. One involved approximately one mile of the ditch and was deemed necessary for the construction of an aqueduct across the Schoharie Creek. In the construction of the original Erie Canal, provision had been made for crossing the Schoharie by damming the creek downstream from the line of the canal. The dam raised the level of the creek to canal level and created a stretch of slack-water through which a canal boat could pass. However, damming the Schoharie proved to be extremely difficult because of the violence of the creek during the freshet season. Dams of various kinds were tried but none were entirely satisfactory, so Jervis recommended an aqueduct as a solution to the problem. The increase in traffic on an enlarged Erie Canal would demand a reliable stream crossing.[37]

The other route change Jervis recommended to the canal board was longer and much more complicated in all aspects. The route of the old canal crossed the Mohawk at Cohoes, paralleled the north bank of the river for thirteen miles, then crossed back to the south bank at Schenectady. Two aqueducts, one 748 feet long and the other 1,188 feet, were required for this route. Jervis recommended the construction of the enlarged canal along the south bank of the Mohawk, thus eliminating the need for the aqueducts.[38] The October report also contained estimates on tonnage of boats and costs of construction for a canal six feet deep and sixty feet wide, for one seven feet by seventy feet, and for one eight feet by eighty feet.[39]

Jervis was particularly intent on convincing the Canal Commission that the line of the canal from Cohoes to Schenectady should be changed. It followed that a man who, throughout his life, was dedicated to economy and the elimination of waste wherever possible, should press for the new route. McAlpine, sent back to take a second look at the canal between Cohoes and Schenectady, reported his findings to Jervis on November 23.

The following day Jervis notified the Canal Commission of McAlpine's concurrence about the change and advised the commissioners that the expense for the new route would be approximately $100,000 greater than enlarging the present canal. But, Jervis added, "the extra expense of this line will stand against the hazard and expense of maintaining two expensive aqueducts. Aqueducts with wooden trunks are to be avoided in all cases where the line can be maintained without too great additional expense, or the sacrifice of the convenient accommodation of trade and navigation."[40] Jervis concluded the letter by urging the adoption of a resolution to change the line to the south side of the Mohawk.[41]

The canal board approved Jervis's plan for the Schoharie aqueduct, but board members remained divided on the matter of the Cohoes-to-Schenectady line. The location of the canal between the two communities had been a difficult decision when the original Erie was built.[42]

By early 1836, Jervis left the Chenango Canal to work full-time as chief engineer of the Erie's eastern division, taking William McAlpine, his principal assistant, with him. Jervis commenced his assignment by reiterating his argument in favor of eliminating the two Mohawk aqueducts. He informed the commissioners that he knew there would be problems.

> To change the line of a public work after investments have been made should only be done when the considerations of public utility clearly overbalance its injurious influence on private interests. The proximity of the Country afforded by this case to the Eastern termination of the Canal is such that only a limited amount of property . . . is shipped to or from it on the Canal, the Shops and Taverns that supply the boatmen navigating the Canal embraces the most prominent interest, and through them the contiguous country participate in furnishing the agricultural articles that are wanted in this traffic. To change the route to the opposite side would not wholly destroy this interest but . . . would create a closer competition from the people on the new route.[43]

Jervis added to his argument that the new route would have five fewer locks than the present one.[44] This was important in decreasing the time for passage from Albany to Schenectady and in saving on future lock maintenance as well as in reducing the cost of lock construction.

The final decision of the Canal Commission was to maintain the original line. The idea of abandoning such a long stretch of existing canal for which the state had already purchased a right-of-way prevailed against the arguments of supporters of a new route.[45] The fact that the commissioners and Jervis were not in accord on this and certain other matters concerning the canal[46] was not, in terms of Jervis's career, of great importance.

Jervis's work on the Erie enlargement ended a few months after his appointment as head of the eastern division when he was approached in September 1836 by a committee of the Croton Aqueduct Commission and offered the position of chief engineer of that work. Even though he enjoyed his work on the Erie, the prospect of building one of the first urban water systems proved to be so attractive to Jervis that he accepted the offer the following month.[47] In doing so, he embarked on a difficult, controversial, and perhaps the most important assignment of his engineering career.

Jervis's role in the canal building of the 1830s, although not as important as some of his other assignments, did contribute to his experience and training in preparation for his major project, the Croton Aqueduct. Added to this was his development of a new method of measuring rainfall and his improvement on the existing methods for stream gauging. These developments were widely recognized, and they represented Jervis's most important contributions to canal construction while he was employed on New York's canals.

5

A Different Kind of Waterway

THE SELECTION of Jervis as the man to direct construction of the Croton Aqueduct project was due, to a large extent, to his experience with artificial waterways. Most of his two decades as an engineer had been spent constructing canals. It is true that Jervis lacked experience in building aqueducts, but, for that matter, so did most American engineers. For centuries, aqueducts had been used to supply water to European cities; however, there were few in use in early nineteenth-century America. Hence, the Croton project provided Jervis with a variety of new engineering experiences. Not only was there the aqueduct itself, which was both above and below ground, but there were its several diverse structures. The dam on the Croton River, the High Bridge over the Harlem River, and the receiving and distributing reservoirs were among the additional structures Jervis designed and built as part of the Croton project.

By the fourth decade of the nineteenth century, New York, a city with some 250,000 inhabitants, was still without an adequate method of furnishing a constant supply of good water to a majority of its people. During the preceding half century, a number of attempts had been made to provide water to New Yorkers, ranging from the cisterns and wooden pipes of the Manhattan Company to the attempts of Levi Disbrow and the promoter John Sullivan to bore wells into the island's rock. None of the methods used to supply water were satisfactory, and New York was forced to continue relying on an inadequate and impure supply.

Lack of pure water and an almost nonexistent sewage system caused the city to remain at the mercy of fires and cholera epidemics. In fact, it was the merciless cholera epidemic of 1832 that brought New York closer to an adequate water system. The loss of 3,500 lives, compared, for example, to Philadelphia's loss of 900, moved the city government to look into an aqueduct supply. It was believed that Philadelphia's ability to flush the streets regularly had kept down the death toll. In the fall of 1832, a committee of New York aldermen visited the successful Fairmount Works in Philadelphia and, impressed by the operation, they returned to New York and recommended that surveys be made to locate a sufficient source of water.[1]

Efforts to find a plentiful supply of stream water for New York City were not limited to the 1830s. Two earlier inspections had been made, and in both cases the examiners reported in favor of the Bronx River as an adequate water source.[2] Beginning in the fall of 1832, several new surveys were made; although there remained some support for the Bronx, it began to appear as though a better source was the Croton River in northern Westchester County.[3]

The water commissioners, who were appointed by the New York Common Council to study the water supply program, reported on February 16, 1835, in favor of the Croton River as a water source. Their report was an amalgam of the recommendations of two engineers hired by the commissioners, John Martineau and David Bates Douglass. To provide a water supply, the commissioners proposed to erect a dam near the mouth of the Croton, and they recommended an enclosed stone aqueduct from the dam to the distributing reservoir in Manhattan — except for the Harlem River crossing, which would use inverted siphons of wrought iron pipes eight feet in diameter.[4] An average of the cost estimates of the two engineers produced a sum of approximately $4,150,000, to which was added $1,262,000 for the distribution pipes in the city, for a total of about $5,412,000.[5]

The report of the water commissioners was seconded on March 4 by the Common Council's Committee on Fire and Water. Common Council approval of the plan was followed by a public referendum held April 14 through 16, 1835. The plebiscite resulted in approval of the Croton plan by a vote of three to one. The way was now clear for the water commissioners to proceed with the construction of the aqueduct.[6]

The building of the Croton Aqueduct was divided into three major segments or projects: the aqueduct and its receiving and distributing reservoirs in New York City; the dam on the Croton River, built to create the Croton reservoir; and the Harlem River Bridge or High Bridge, the largest bridge of the aqueduct system. According to historian Nelson Blake, "the most authoritative description of the Croton works is John B. Jervis, *Description of the Croton Aqueduct*."[7] It seems logical, then, to rely on Jervis for an account of the works.

The route of the Croton Aqueduct paralleled the Hudson River for nearly forty miles from the Croton River to the Murray Hill distributing reservoir on Manhattan Island.[8] The aqueduct top was arched, the bottom an inverted arch, and the side walls vertical with a slight inward bevel, making the brick-lined interior space wider at the top than at the bottom. The greatest interior width was 7 feet 5 inches, and the greatest height 8 feet 5½ inches.[9] Thirty-three ventilators were constructed at one-mile intervals to provide air circulation through the aqueduct. Many also doubled as entrances to the water tunnel. Six waste weirs were built to allow excess water to escape from the aqueduct. They also doubled as ventilators. No less than 114 stone culverts carried the aqueduct across the many small streams along the route.[10]

Water from the aqueduct flowed into two reservoirs, a receiving reservoir in north-central Manhattan and a distributing reservoir in the south-central part of the island. The receiving reservoir covered more than thirty-five acres and had a capacity of 150,000,000 imperial gallons. Its walls consisted of earthen banks protected on the outside by a stone facade.[11] In listing the advantages of a receiving reservoir, Jervis noted that although the Croton waters were pure enough to eliminate the need for filtration, in times of turbid water, the reservoir's large capacity would allow any dirt particles in the water time to settle.[12] The 20,000,000-gallon distributing reservoir, two miles south of the first, was on 5th Avenue, between 40th and 42nd streets (the present location of the New York Public Library). Its walls were of hydraulic stone masonry and averaged 45 feet above street level. The exterior was coped with an Egyptian cornice, which gave the work a pleasant appearance.[13]

The main reservoir was the lake formed by the construction of a dam across the Croton River, seven miles upstream from its junction with the Hudson River near Ossining.[14] The Croton Dam, the first big masonry dam in the United States,[15] was forty feet above low water in the river.[16] The resulting lake was some five miles long and covered an area of about 400 acres.[17]

According to Jervis, the dam "was one of a kind: a completely unique combination of two ancient types, earth-fill and masonry. The result was an earth embankment about one hundred and thirty feet long and a composite spillway section about two hundred and seventy feet long."[18] The spillway was in the form of an ogee curve; that is, the lower face commenced on a curve with a radius of fifty-five feet and continued to within ten feet of the top. At that point, a reversed curve, on a radius of ten feet, carried the face over to meet the back wall. The back of the dam was vertical with occasional offsets.[19] A second dam, nine feet high, was constructed 300 feet below the main dam. Its purpose was to "set the water back over the apron of the main dam, and, form a pool to check the water as it [fell] on it."[20]

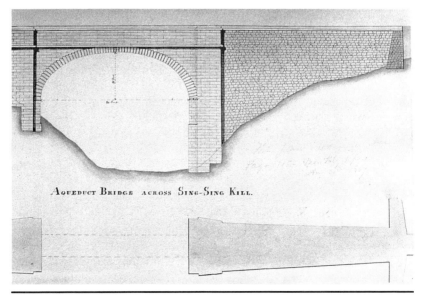

Fig. 5.1. An aqueduct bridge for the Croton project, 1837. Drawing courtesy Jervis Public Library.

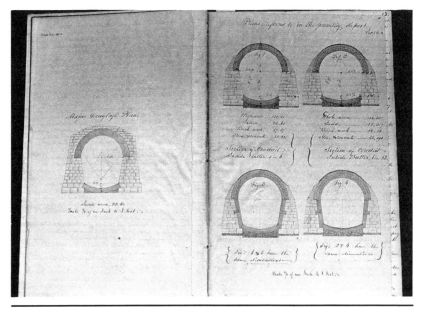

Fig. 5.2. The Croton Aqueduct, detail from Jervis's notebook, probably 1837. Notebook courtesy Jervis Public Library.

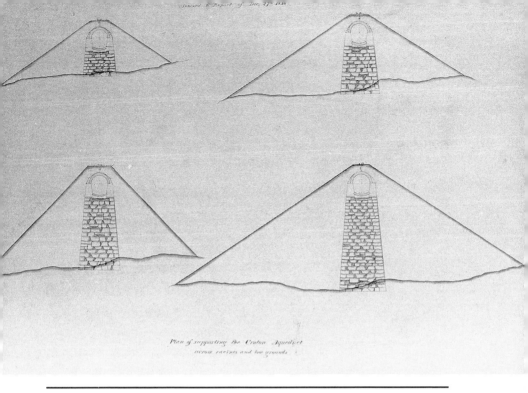

Plan of supporting the Croton Aqueduct
across ravines and low grounds

Fig. 5.3. The Croton Aqueduct, detail of plan. Drawing courtesy Jervis Public Library.

The Croton Dam put Jervis in the vanguard of modern hydraulic engineering. The use of the stilling basin and the ogival spillway became accepted practice in dam building.[21]

However, the most notable structure of the Croton Aqueduct was the High Bridge. Officially called Aqueduct Bridge, it was constructed over the Harlem River, one of the four important crossings specifically mentioned in Jervis's description of the aqueduct.[22] In terms of total size, there were few structures of any kind that could approach the bridge at the time of its construction.[23] The length of High Bridge was 1,450 feet, and its height from high water line to the top of the parapets was 114 feet.[24] The bridge consisted of fifteen masonry arches, eight spans of eighty feet and seven spans of fifty feet.[25] The arches were unusual in that "unlike most stone arches, the loads from above the arch ring (actually, an arch slab) were carried to the ring by a series of masonry walls instead of the usual earth fill."[26] This reduced the "dead load" between the sidewalls or spandrels and "permitted a more economical design."[27] Even with this economy, the bridge cost more than $800,000 to build.[28] The High Bridge, with its size and novelty of construction, greatly enhanced Jervis's reputation. It also played an impor-

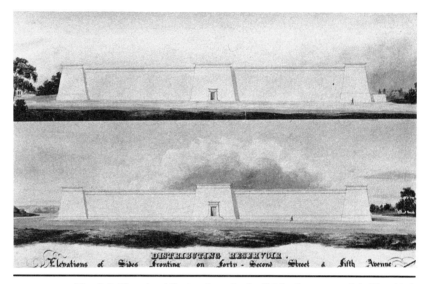

Fig. 5.4. Facade of Croton Aqueduct's distributing reservoir in New York City. The reservoir was located at the present site of the New York Public Library main branch on Fifth Avenue, between Fortieth and Forty-second streets. Drawing courtesy Jervis Public Library.

tant part in the major dispute of the Croton project, the Douglass-Jervis controversy.

John B. Jervis was not the first chief engineer of the Croton. His predecessor, David Douglass, was appointed soon after the project was authorized and remained in the position until he was replaced by Jervis on October 11, 1836. Although Douglass was fired, due largely to bad relations with the water commissioners, he was not without supporters. A contemporary work on the Croton credited Douglass, at the time of his dismissal, with having brought the Croton plan to "the present maturity." Jervis was mentioned only as the successor to Douglass.[29] However, recent historians of the Croton Aqueduct have recognized the value of Jervis's appointment. Blake felt that the "Commissioners made an excellent choice" in naming Jervis to succeed Douglass. Others tend to agree with Blake.[30]

Once appointed, Jervis wasted little time in assuming the responsibility of his position. Since the terms of his contract allowed him to complete plans already in progress on the Erie enlargement, Jervis had to rely on his assistants to take charge temporarily of the Croton operations.[31] Edmund French, a young West Point graduate who had resigned from the Army, was chosen to head the engineer's office.

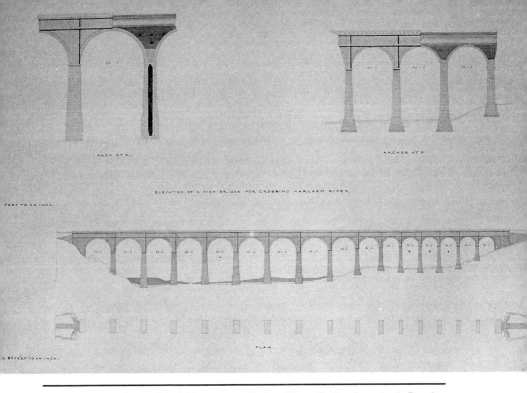

ARCH AT A.

ARCHES AT B.

ELEVATION OF A HIGH BRIDGE FOR CROSSING HARLAEM RIVER.

FEET TO AN INCH.

PLAN.

80 FEET TO AN INCH.

Fig. 5.5. High Bridge, across Harlem River (Croton Aqueduct). Drawing courtesy Jervis Public Library.

The chief engineer's directions to French and others provide some insight into Jervis's devotion to business. After telling French to keep the office in order, Jervis issued a directive calling for the removal of all "articles that do not belong to it [the office] and which only promote confusion. Allow no one to derrange [sic] the order of the office or to remove papers of any kind without direction. Allow no smoking and no play of any kind in the office. In all respects let it be strictly a place of business and for no other purpose."[32] Henry T. Anthony, a resident engineer, was not excluded from the scrutiny of the chief. Anthony was scolded for not beginning work on the line earlier in the morning than he had been to take advantage of every daylight hour.[33] These letters to French and Anthony are of interest in that they do more than simply set the mood for Jervis's tenure as chief engineer. They are also an excellent record of his character. Jervis's lifestyle was marked by a complete and constant devotion to business and the profession. He quite naturally expected his subordinates to live and work in the same stoical manner.

By the end of 1836, Jervis was in New York City preparing plans and specifications for the general aqueduct work.[34] In the interest of economy, he reduced Douglass's staff of nineteen engineers to five for the winter season.[35] Jervis missed no detail in his efforts to save money.

He expected the engineers to furnish their own surveying instruments as this arrangement was "most compatible with the proper dignity and character of the profession, and is best in a business point of view."[36] He even issued orders on as relatively insignificant an item as colors for the engineers' drawings. "I have never allowed Engineers for water-colors," he informed French, "as I have always considered a box of colors should belong to every Engineer."[37]

Once the work on the line commenced in the spring of 1837, Jervis reminded each resident engineer to see to his work in the "best interest of business." To check on this, Jervis would frequently visit the line.[38] Jervis also requested that the residents keep a monthly time sheet on employees "in order that absences can be deducted from their pay."[39] This too was in keeping with the "best interest of business."

By the end of 1836, Jervis submitted his first report to the water commissioners. The document, complete with illustrations, indicated that Jervis was satisfied with Douglass's plan for the interior of the aqueduct. The proposal called for a tube having an arched top and bottom and vertical, parallel sides. Jervis likewise concurred with Douglass's plan to use brick and mortar as construction materials, except for the stipulation of hydraulic cement as a precaution against the possible erosion of the mortar by ground water.

The cost of materials and labor for the aqueduct was estimated at "between $93,899.52 and $94,348.32" per mile.[40] Always mindful of thrift, Jervis later revised his initial calculations to include variations in the masonry side walls of the aqueduct. This change permitted the use of less brick and concrete per line foot of aqueduct, which would make a difference of about $500,000 on thirty-five miles of aqueduct.[41]

With the arrival of the 1837 construction season, Jervis made additional appointments to the engineering department, of which the most important was the selection of Horatio Allen as his principal assistant.[42] Jervis also named his younger brother William to a resident's position in charge of a division of the line.[43] The appointment of James Renwick, Jr., to a minor engineer's position was of some interest in view of his later prominence as an architect. The son of Jervis's old friend James Renwick, Sr., the younger Renwick was given the job of second assistant to resident engineer Peter Hastie.[44] Renwick remained with the Croton project for 5½ years before resigning over a dispute with Hastie. Separation from the Croton project proved to be fortuitous in view of Renwick's subsequent change to a career in architecture.[45]

The increase in the engineering staff[46] hastened the completion of the surveys, and by April 26 bids were let for eight miles of aqueduct from the Croton Dam to Sing Sing. At the end of the summer of 1837, a second portion of aqueduct was placed under contract. By then, work was in progress on approximately half the length of the waterway.[47]

Since the construction of the aqueduct was moving ahead in good order, Jervis decided to visit other urban waterworks to expand his knowledge of aqueducts. In May he travelled to Philadelphia to inspect its water system, and in September he went to Washington, D.C., to view the Potomac Aqueduct.[48] The Potomac Aqueduct was of particular interest to Jervis because of similarities between it and the Croton in terms of the basic problems and proposed solutions. Jervis subsequently corresponded with the chief engineer of the Potomac Aqueduct, Col. J. J. Abert, on the subject of the Harlem River bridge.[49] The bridge and the Croton Dam were the only two structures of the project that were troublesome to Jervis: the bridge because of the controversy over its dimensions and design and the dam because of the forces of nature and a miscalculation on the part of the chief engineer.

By February 1837, Jervis presented a plan that called for constructing a dam fifty feet high of "substantial masonry" across the Croton River.[50] The length between the abutments was to be one hundred feet and the thickness of the dam sixty-nine feet at the bottom and seven feet at the top. The forty-foot average thickness was "not required, but is adopted to carry an easier slope to carry off flood waters."[51] The well-illustrated document was detailed both in construction specifications and in the manner of regulating the water level after the dam was completed.[52] As originally designed, an immense earthen embankment 250 feet long, 250 feet wide at the base, and 55 feet wide at the top was constructed to complete the damming of the Croton. It was fifteen feet higher than the waste weir of the masonry dam and was used to block the old channel of the river.[53] This type of dam could be built more economically than an all masonry structure.

The water commissioners reported in January 1841 that the Croton Dam was "now all but completed."[54] All that remained was to finish the embankment to its full width. This would never occur, since "in the early morning hours of January 8, 1841, the Croton project received its most serious setback."[55] A combination of two days of heavy rain and melting snow caused an unprecedented amount of water to enter the new reservoir. The waste weir or overfall of the masonry section of the dam had been built to handle a possible water flow four to six feet deep.[56] However, on January 8, the water rose fifteen feet above the waste weir, bringing it to the top level of the earthen embankment.[57]

The chief engineer's report maintained that "the embankment stood well, and gave no indications of failure, until the water rose to near the surface, and passed through between the frozen and unfrozen earth about 20 inches below the top."[58] However, "after the breach was made in the embankment, large masses of heavy ice came down from the reservoir, which soon broke down the unfinished protection wall, and carried off nearly the whole embankment."[59] The masonry portion rested on solid rock and therefore was not damaged by the water.[60]

Jervis was at the scene of the break within hours of its occurrence. He later wrote that the "view was indeed sad and the aspect was severe in the extreme. No one without such experience could imagine the severity with which this scene, with its attending circumstances, affected me."[61]

Upon determining the extent of the damage, Jervis made a report to the water commissioners in which he "had nothing to say but to state the facts."[62] After relating the amount of damage sustained by the works, he defensively stated that the flow of water over the weir presented a "rush of water that I could not have believed would ever have been so suddenly collected in the Croton."[63] The high water mark that came at 4:30 AM on January 8th was not anticipated in view of the water level the previous day. In fact, the water continued to rise "at the rate of 14 inches per hour on a reservoir [of] over 400 acres in addition to the discharge of the immense volume over the weir of the dam. The result has been disastrous. . . . "[64] Jervis estimated that $75,000 would be needed to repair the break.

Jervis closed the report with a curt statement about the greatest loss of the flood. "It appears that 3 lives were lost one at the dam and 2 at Baily's wire factory."[65] If it seemed that Jervis was rather terse about the deaths connected with the flood, it was because he would have been unlikely to include anything but the basic facts in a report to the commissioners.

Jervis was not blamed for the collapse of the embankment. The water commissioners felt that although the flood was disastrous in some aspects, particularly in the loss of life, it presented less of a problem than if it had happened after the works were complete.[66] The commissioners expressed satisfaction that "all the aqueduct work, on the line, has stood remarkably well, and the culverts have been found ample to discharge the water from the valleys and streams, and the embankments have been but little washed or damaged by this unprecedented storm."[67]

Jervis was directed to take steps to prevent a reoccurrence of the failure of the dam by replacing the destroyed earthen section with one of stone laid in cement. The new part of the dam was to be 180 feet in length, which, when combined with the masonry portion that withstood the high water, would make a stone dam with an overfall of 260 feet.[68]

This presented a problem that Jervis had hoped to avoid. The original weir section rested on solid rock that could resist the damaging

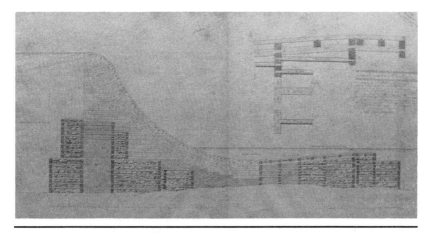

Fig. 5.6. Cutaway view of the Croton Dam, showing masonry and log cribbing. The Croton Dam pioneered the use of the ogival (or reverse) spillway. Drawing courtesy Jervis Public Library.

effects of falling water. The new or north section would rest on gravel, making it necessary for Jervis to improvise a structure that would reduce the velocity of the falling water. To achieve this, he conceived the idea of building the lower face of the dam in the shape of a reversed curve, to gradually turn the water from a vertical to a horizontal position.[69] Further reduction of the destructive action of the water on the gravel bottom was accomplished by constructing a composite apron of timber cribbing, concrete masonry, loose stones, and elm and hemlock planking. Also, a stilling basin was formed by building a dam nine feet high about 300 feet below the apron that would break the force of the water after it left the apron.[70]

Work on the new dam commenced in the spring of 1841. By January 1843, two years after the tragic flood, the commissioners announced the completion of the Croton Dam.[71] The second dam, of sound design and construction, was used until superseded by a larger structure in 1906.[72] Its sixty-four years of service might be said to have exonerated Jervis from his error in calculating high water when he planned for the first dam.

Although the bridge across the Harlem River met with no disaster such as befell the Croton Dam, the bridge was the center of Jervis's problems while he served as chief engineer of the aqueduct. Jervis advised the water commissioners in December 1837 that he was studying the question of the Harlem crossing. His report referred to the earlier proposals of Canvass White, Martineau, and Douglass for carrying water over the river. White had recommended the use of iron pipes resting on a low bridge; Martineau had agreed with White and called for an "inverted syphon" of wrought iron pipes supported by a low bridge. Major Douglass differed with the two and suggested a high bridge of stone masonry to maintain the regular grade of the aqueduct. Jervis told the commissioners that he would consider the problem and the various plans to determine the kind of structure that would "most economically secure the desired object."[73]

The chief engineer submitted plans for both a high bridge and a low bridge. The high grade level would be 163 feet above river bottom and an average of 138 feet above tide. The arch spans over the river would be eighty feet wide and those over land fifty feet. A length of 1,450 feet would be needed to maintain the grade.[74] The plan using the inverted syphon required a much lower bridge. A single eighty-foot-long arch, fifty feet above high tide, would be all that was necessary to allow for navigation of the river. The remainder of the river would be crossed by a stone embankment on the north side of the arch and an arcade of three smaller arches on the south side. Two parapet walls would be built on either side of the structure's top to hold the four 36-inch cast iron pipes necessary to allow the passage of nearly 50,000,000 gallons of water per day. The pipe chamber would be covered with four feet of earth to protect the pipes from frost.[75] Jervis estimated the cost of the siphon and low bridge at $426,027. The cost of the high bridge was calculated at $935,745, more than $500,000 more than the lower structure. Hence, Jervis recommended the inverted siphon pipes and low bridge for the Harlem crossing.[76]

The water commissioners concurred with Jervis's choice and listed seven reasons for their support of the plan. As might have been expected, the first two referred to the excessive cost of the high bridge. However, the next four reasons expressed concern over the construction of such a large work. They discussed the limited experience of engineers in sinking piers in "so great a depth of water and mud,"[77] and they also considered the injurious effects of frost and leakage. The length of time needed to build the high bridge was mentioned as a factor that would delay the waters of the Croton from reaching New York City. Finally, the commissioners stated that the fifty-foot clearance of the large arch of the low bridge would be sufficient for the passage of vessels that might be used if the Harlem River were made navigable.[78]

Obviously, the water commissioners felt that the low bridge was best for the purpose of the aqueduct, but, in their report to the Common Council, they admitted that "as far as architectural display is involved, the high bridge has the preference."[79] The commissioners advised the

Fig. 5.7. Cross-section of the stone arch for the Croton Aqueduct. Drawing courtesy Jervis Public Library.

aldermen that if they, the assistant alderman, and the mayor preferred the high bridge, it would be built.[80]

This option left an opening for controversy; Jervis, as chief engineer, ended up being the man in the middle.

Opinions about the two plans began to polarize, and the newspapers were quick to join in the fray with articles arguing the pros and cons of the two bridge plans. The *New York American* attacked the sagacity of the commissioners and the chief engineer and claimed that unlike Major Douglass, Jervis's predecessor, they did not "enjoy such a reputation for and acquaintance with either the principles of science applicable to the business on which they were engaged or . . . a practical knowledge of what had been elsewhere accomplished. . . . " The article questioned Jervis's cost estimate for the high bridge as being "too extravagant" and also suggested that the siphons would not suffice for "large masses of water."[81]

An answer to the *American,* anonymously authored by Jervis, appeared a few days later in the *Journal of Commerce.* Aside from a defense of the use of the siphon, it provides insight into Jervis's feelings about criticism of public officials. "The correspondent of the *American* thinks the Commissioners are above criticism," wrote Jervis. "In a free country the acts of all public men are supposed to be subjects of criticism; none are so high as to claim exemption; and the commissioners will not probably object to any fair and honorable examination of their proceedings."[82] But, continued the engineer, "it is not proper . . . to admit the allegations brought forward without facts, or arguments to support them. . . . "[83] Jervis felt that the motivation for the *American* to print the damaging article did not come solely "from patriotism and devotion to the public good."[84]

On March 15, three days after the appearance of Jervis's unsigned letter in the *Journal of Commerce,* a statement supporting Jervis appeared in the *American.* It referred to the allegation that Jervis was opposed to the high bridge because it was originally the plan of Douglass and dismissed the charge as being absurd, as anyone who knew Jervis would not make such a statement.[85] Jervis felt the letter had been written by Horatio Allen. Additional letters and articles in support of Jervis and his plan for a low bridge appeared in other newspapers. The *Evening Post,* in recommending the low bridge and siphons, cited correspondence of approval from Frederick Graff, superintendent of the Philadelphia Water Works.[86] If anything about the controversy remained clear by the end of March 1838, it was that either the low bridge or the more expensive high bridge would be satisfactory for the Harlem crossing.

On March 31, Jervis was called before a joint committee of the Common Council and was asked whether he considered the high bridge impracticable. Jervis replied that "the high bridge was necessarily a work more difficult to construct and more liable to failure than the low bridge and iron pipes" and added "if it was decided to build a high bridge . . . I should recommend the use of pipes . . . even on the high bridge."[87] When the committee hinted that Jervis might be afraid to undertake the high bridge, he replied that he "considered it a duty to present the two plans inasmuch as there was a great difference in expense. . . . "[88]

The Common Council did not approve of Jervis's plan to substitute inverted siphons for a high bridge because they felt a low bridge would "do great damage by destroying navigation" on the Harlem River.[89] On July 9, 1838, the Council's views were reflected by the Board of Assistant Aldermen, which adopted a resolution in favor of the high bridge. The measure also contained a provision for submitting the question to the electorate of the City and County of New York.[90]

Apparently, the water commissioners were not impressed by the action of the aldermen, since they began to let contracts for the siphon bridge. However, the proponents of a high bridge remained undaunted in their drive to prevent the interruption of river navigation. In the end, they successfully appealed to the State Legislature; on May 3, 1839, that body passed a law "prescribing the manner in which the Croton Aqueduct shall pass the Harlem River." The act provided for the building of either an aqueduct bridge with arches of "not less than one hundred feet from the usual high water mark of the river" and having a span of "at least eighty feet" or a "tunnel under the channel of the river."[91]

The law of May 3 came as no surprise to Jervis. Several months earlier he had written to Colonel Abert informing him of the controversy over the Harlem crossing. Jervis told Abert that it most likely would be necessary to construct a high bridge "essentially to maintain our grade over the valley. I cannot say . . . that I regret this as you know Engineers are prone to gratify a taste for the magnificent when there is a good reason for the execution of prominent works."[92] If Jervis had been afraid to tackle the high bridge, as the joint committee of the Common Council had implied nine months earlier, then by the end of 1838 he had not only overcome his fears, but had turned them into enthusiasm.

In accordance with the wishes of the Legislature, the water commissioners directed their chief engineer to prepare plans for both a high bridge and a tunnel. The May 3 act of the Legislature called for a bridge at least 100 feet above high water. By June 1, Jervis submitted a design for one that was lower than the grade level bridge planned by Douglass and still met the legal requirements. A bridge of less height would be less expensive. As on the low bridge, inverted siphons could be used to move the aqueduct water across the bridge and then return it to grade level. The total cost of the bridge, including the addition of ten percent "for contingencies," was estimated at $836,613.[93] Jervis also considered the possibility of a wooden aqueduct bridge instead of a masonry one. A wooden bridge would be less expensive to build, but would be susceptible to damage from fire, rot, wind, and salt water; hence, Jervis rejected the idea.[94]

Jervis's proposal for the tunnel under the river called for the dredging of mud from the river bottom to allow a frame for a coffer dam to be sunk on the sand. After the coffer dam was in place, two fifty-horsepower steam engines would be installed in order to pump the water from the pit. Then the tunnel masonry and iron pipes for carrying the water could be put in place.

Jervis found it hard to prepare an estimate for the tunnel because he lacked experience in placing a coffer dam of the size required. The dimensions of the dam, 400 feet long and 40 feet wide, would have made it very difficult to put in place. He referred to the problems involved in the building of the Thames Tunnel in London, and he believed that, when completed, the Thames undertaking would cost four times as much as the original estimate. Therefore, the estimate for the Harlem Tunnel included a fifty percent addition for contingencies and totalled $636,738. In explaining the unusually large contingency budget, Jervis advised the commissioners of the "uncertainty in estimating for work done under a heavy pressure of water."[95]

In making his recommendation as to which structure he favored for crossing the river, Jervis first pointed out that either would take longer to complete than the aqueduct itself. The bridge could be built in five years and the tunnel, if the coffer dam could be placed, would require four years to construct. In the interim between the completion of the aqueduct and the finishing of the Harlem crossing, "a temporary twenty-two inch main could be put down for about $30,000 and then taken up for about $20,000 and used to supply the city mains."[96]

The chief engineer then indicated his preference for the high bridge, even though he estimated that it would take a year longer to build and would cost nearly $200,000 more than the tunnel. Jervis admitted that the "high bridge I have heretofore endeavored to avoid, is a work of great expense, and attended with much difficulty in its execution," but "it is better to adopt it than the plan of carrying the aqueduct by a tunnel under the river. Could I have the same confidence in the estimate for the tunnel that I have in the Bridge," he explained, "I should have less confidence in coming to this conclusion. . . . "[97]

Jervis ended his report by saying that he would dutifully build the kind of structure that the water commissioners desired. He had no doubt, though, that the masonry bridge with iron pipes would be the most suitable and when completed, "will be viewed as the most satisfactory work."[98]

The commissioners agreed with him and on June 15, 1839, they advertised for bids for the high bridge. The contract was awarded on August 13.

The start of construction produced an unforeseen problem for Jervis and the engineering staff. It had been supposed that a rock foundation could be found for the bridge piers. But a thorough examination revealed that although there was rock on both sides of the river, there were places beneath the river where rock could not be located at eighty feet below high water. As a result, several of the piers would require a pile foundation.[99] This brought up the question of whether or not the piles would support the weight that would be placed upon them. As there were no known methods or experiments to test the strength of the piles, Jervis "proposed an experiment to determine the question."[100]

Horatio Allen was placed in charge of the test. He began by setting up a hydraulic press to bring pressure on the pile to be tested. The remainder of the trial, in Jervis's words, was as follows:

> This pile was round oak, fifteen feet long, and had been driven about twelve feet. It was fifteen inches in diameter at the upper end and probably eleven inches at the lower end. A piling machine was placed over it before the trial, and three blows struck with a hammer weighing fourteen hundred pounds, falling through a load of thirty feet. The pile sunk under the hammer an average of one inch at each blow. A lever was fitted to determine the motion of the pile under the pressure of the hydraulic ram of one to fourteen. The pile withstood a pressure of sixty tons without any perceptible movement. It yielded a trifle under sixty-five tons but resumed its original position after the pressure was removed. This yielding was doubtless due to elasticity in the pile and in the medium in which it was driven.[101]

The experiment, which "may well have been the first full-scale test of pile foundations in the United States,"[102] proved satisfactory as a method for determining the load strength of bearing piles.[103] The piles supporting the piers of the High Bridge have borne their load satisfactorily for 141 years.

Although the aqueduct and its structures were sufficiently complete by June 1842 to allow the initial passage of water into New York City, the high bridge required an additional seven years to finish.[104] It was very near completion when George Templeton Strong called it a "very great piece of work."[105] Strong's statement exemplified the popular attitude towards the entire Croton project, its disputes and immense cost notwithstanding. Henry Tanner, in his *Description . . . of Internal Improvements Throughout the Several States* (1840), devoted nearly eleven pages to the Croton Aqueduct and a mere two pages to the Erie Canal.[106] He commented on both the greatness and the cost of the project, taking notice of the considerable difference between the original estimate and the final cost. He predicted that the aqueduct "will not fall short of $10,000,000."[107] One month after Croton water entered the city, Jervis estimated a total expenditure for the Croton of one million dollars less than Tanner's figure.[108] Both predictions were within $500,000 of the final figure for the project.[109]

Apparently, New Yorkers were willing to readily bear the expense of this major investment in consideration of the long-awaited returns. The official celebration that took place on October 14, 1842, was immense. Philip Hone captured the mood of the city two days before the carnival when he wrote, "nothing is talked of or thought of in New York but Croton water. . . . It is astonishing how popular the introduction of water is among all classes of our citizens, and how cheerfully they acquiesce in the enormous expense which will burden them and their posterity with taxes to the latest generation."[110] The Croton River at last flowed through the streets of New York, and Jervis's most notable waterway was finally a reality.

Tanner reflected the thoughts of those who beheld the great works of the Croton when he wrote of the "true character and magnitude of this important work" and how it would "stand the test of time, and answer all the purposes for which it was designed."[111] The statement also was a tribute to the project's chief engineer. Jervis, faced with the difficult task of designing the Croton Aqueduct with its many diverse structures, produced a system that furnished a rapidly growing New York City with water for more than half a century without serious problems or breakdown.

The Croton system itself was responsible for the city's phenomenal growth, for without it "there could not have been a doubling of the narrow island's population between 1845 and 1855. Nor could the city's economy have developed as rapidly" because hotels and the "growing number of steam engines and steamships" all depended on Croton water.[112]

Jervis had some plans and drawings he inherited from Major

Fig. 5.8. Profile of the Manhattan portion of the Croton Aqueduct. Drawing courtesy Jervis Public Library.

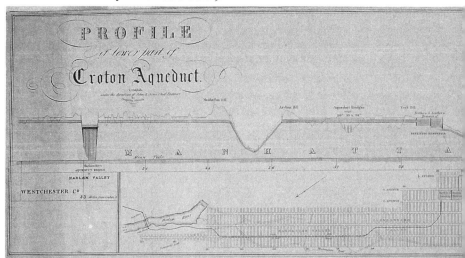

Douglass, but most of the structural design was his own. He altered Douglass's ideas for the aqueduct tunnel and for the Harlem River bridge. It was the massive bridge with its hollow wall construction and inverted siphons that was Jervis's most spectacular achievement of the Croton project. A close second, though, was the main reservoir dam. The novel reverse curve design of the dam with its stilling basin was a major addition to Jervis's long list of engineering innovations.

Of course, the two Manhattan reservoirs should not be excluded from Jervis's accomplishments. The distributing reservoir, in particular, exhibited a form that was both functional and pleasing to the eye. The plain Egyptian facade differed from the more elaborate European Gothic architectural styles that were becoming popular in the United States, but it satisfied Jervis's tendency to relate design to function. There is little doubt that, in total, the Croton Aqueduct represented the complete maturation of Jervis the engineer.

Since there was still much work to complete, the introduction of Croton water into New York City did not mark the end of Jervis's tenure as chief engineer. He continued in that position throughout the 1840s. Although Jervis was less active after 1842, in relation to the actual construction, than he had been during the six years preceding the opening of the aqueduct, the years were not without problems.

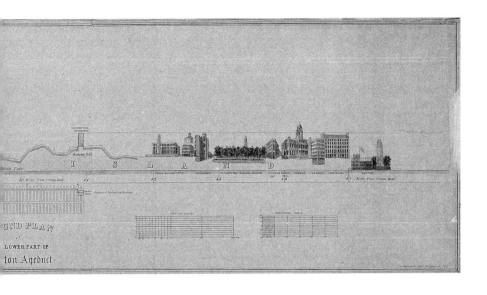

In addition to the growing controversy with Major Douglass and his friends, the chief engineer's pride was injured by the action of the Common Council on September 12, 1842. Following a controversy between the Common Council and the water commissioners over control of the aqueduct works within New York City, the Legislature determined that the water commissioners' power should end at the Murray Hill distributing reservoir. On September 12, the Common Council voted to organize its own Water Board and appointed Horatio Allen as the board's chief engineer. Allen was to have charge of laying the water mains.

Jervis, who received fourteen votes in the balloting for the position, noted the event in his Croton letter books and saved a clipping of a letter to the editor of the *Evening Post,* written by Allen on September 13. In an explanation of his acceptance of the post, Allen stated that he would not have sought the appointment if Jervis had been a candidate. It was Allen's opinion that Jervis would not have accepted the job even if he had been elected to it. Next to the clipping, Jervis wrote the following comment: "This letter does not quite answer — I did not seek the office and Mr. A. knew I was dissatisfied that a Chief Eng. should be made — I wanted a different title given to it — The letter seems more to look to a justification of Mr. A. than to do justice to myself."[113]

There is sufficient evidence to support Jervis's contention that he did not desire to be engineer to the Water Board. Apparently neither did he look forward to the possibility of sharing the glory of the Croton with another chief engineer. In any case, the matter was insignificant when compared to what might have happened to Jervis's strengthened engineering reputation as builder of the Croton. The revelations of the Douglass supporters could have severely damaged Jervis's status if the Douglass people had been successful in making good their claims.

6

The Douglass Affair

WHILE JERVIS was at the pinnacle of his engineering career as the chief engineer of the Croton Aqueduct, he became embroiled in a controversy that would hound him for more than half a century. Jervis's opponent in the fight was his predecessor on the Croton works, Major David B. Douglass.

The Douglass affair gave Jervis cause for concern because it could have damaged his professional standing. Not only was he worried about his reputation as an engineer, but the altercation between the two engineers also brought out accusations that Jervis was little more than a tool of the Albany Regency, New York's Democratic machine.

Although the attacks on Jervis did not damage his renown as an engineer, they did serve to emphasize the possibility that Jervis owed his appointment to politics. The charges of spoilsman engineer greatly incensed Jervis. He vigorously denied them, but found it difficult if not impossible to provide positive proof that he was not a political appointee as the Douglass people charged.

The dispute between Major Douglass and his friends and Jervis and his supporters had its origins on October 11, 1836, with the firing of Douglass and the hiring of Jervis. However, the act of the Legislature in May 1839 that called for constructing a high bridge over the Harlem River and the appointment of a new Board of Water Commissioners on March 17, 1840, brought on open warfare between the opposing sides. Since the new water commissioners were Whigs and since the Douglass people had cried political foul in 1836, there was every reason to believe that Jervis, who had been chief engineer for about 3½ years by that time, would be replaced, perhaps by Douglass.

David Bates Douglass had served as chief engineer of the Croton project from June 2, 1835, until October 11, 1836.[1] Controversy had prevailed throughout his employ on the New York water project. As early as June 1833, Douglass led a party of surveyors into Westchester County to collect data for the presentation of yet another opinion on the proper source of New York's water supply. The Douglass survey supported the findings of Colonel DeWitt Clinton that the Croton River was the best water source.[2] Although Douglass's report was not well received by those who opposed the Croton River as a water source, the report placed him in good favor with Myndert Van Schaick, one of the leaders of the Croton faction. Alderman Van Schaick was not a member of the Common Council's Fire and Water Committee, but he made his opinions known to the committee.

In October 1832, the committee began its own survey headed by the renowned Benjamin Wright, then New York City street commissioner. Wright's reports, submitted early in 1834, supported the earlier William Weston and Canvass White recommendations in favor of the Bronx River as a source.[3] In spite of Wright's reputation, Van Schaick felt from the beginning that Wright was in error in confining his survey to the Bronx watershed. To support Van Schaick's contention, Clinton was retained to conduct a survey.

Van Schaick was so strongly convinced that the Croton was the best choice that he drafted a proposal asking the Legislature to pass a law that would direct the governor to appoint five water commissioners. The commissioners in turn would conduct their own survey and report the findings on or before November 1, 1833. In January 1833, both the aldermen and assistant aldermen agreed to the Van Schaick plan.[4]

The Van Schaick proposal received additional support when it reached the Legislature, since its sponsor had recently been elected to the State Senate. On February 26, Governor William Marcy signed the water commission bill into law. Van Schaick then selected five men to serve on the commission and prevailed upon Governor Marcy to appoint them.[5] All those named to the commission were Democrats "who enjoyed a high reputation for honesty and practical business experience."[6] Stephen Allen, former New York mayor and proponent of the Croton as the water source, was elected chairman.[7] The water commission then named Major Douglass as its surveyor. Undoubtedly, the choice of Douglass was based on his favoring the Croton as a water source.

In reporting in favor of the Croton, Major Douglass submitted a plan that was almost assured of acceptance by the commission. However, his recommendations, which included the dam across the Croton River, the closed masonry aqueduct, and the high aqueduct bridge across the Harlem River, carried a price tag of nearly $5,000,000. Douglass's figure was double that of Clinton's, and this resulted in considerable criticism of his report.[8] The water commission not only asked Douglass to reexamine his calculations, but it also hired John Martineau to make still another survey.

Martineau managed to trim one million dollars from Douglass's figure by moving the dam closer to the mouth of the Croton, thus shortening the total length of the aqueduct, and by eliminating the expensive high aqueduct bridge. As an alternative to the high bridge, Martineau suggested the use of an inverted siphon of iron pipes to cross the Harlem River.[9] The acceptance of the amalgamated plan of Douglass and Martineau by the appropriate commissions, committees, and councils meant that construction on the aqueduct could begin. It was at this point that Douglass was selected as chief engineer.

Douglass's first task as the new head of the Croton project was to lead a surveying party into Westchester County in the summer of 1835. He regarded his first two surveys as merely preliminary and wished to obtain a more detailed view of the line. The delay did little to promote good relations between Douglass and water commission chairman Stephen Allen, since Allen was anxious to show progress on the aqueduct. He also was interested in economy, and to this end he limited the size of Douglass's engineering party.

It took a full year from the time of Douglass's appointment for him to furnish maps of the route to the water commission. Further delay occurred when Douglass undertook a fourth survey of the line "in order to improve its location."[10] Again Douglass asked for a large force, and again Allen limited the size of the engineer's staff. By the fall of 1836 the surveys were complete, but additional delays resulted from lack of bid specifications. Douglass provided excuses and continued to request a larger staff. Allen and the other commissioners could no longer tolerate the delay. They began to have doubts about Douglass's engineering ability. Douglass was given an opportunity to resign; he refused to do so and was then removed.[11]

At this point the water commissioners turned to John B. Jervis. With his acceptance of the offer, Jervis automatically was drawn into the controversy between Douglass and the water commissioners. The feud lasted nearly fifty years. Douglass, his family, and his friends defended the major's engineering skill and explained his dismissal in simple terms of party politics. Douglass was a Whig and all but one of the commissioners were Democrats.[12] Hence, he was fired so a good Regency Democrat could take credit for building the great Croton Aqueduct. That Jervis was a Democrat and had powerful friends in the Albany Regency cannot be denied. Also, the fact remains that the Democrats had controlled New York at the time Jervis was named to head the Croton

Fig. 6.1. John B. Jervis, c. 1835. Photo courtesy Jervis Public Library.

project. However, the argument that attributed all to politics was an inaccurate oversimplification.

Beginning in the early 1820s, Democratic-Republicans in New York State led by Martin Van Buren welded together a political machine that, aided by New York City's Tammany Hall, dominated state government and politics for nearly two decades. Van Buren's increasing national interests led him to create the "Albany Regency" to dominate state politics and ensure the continuing support of his powerful home state bastion. Initially, the Regency was a select group, influential among which was William Marcy, a three-term New York governor in the 1830s.

The adoption of a new state constitution in 1821 made it easier for the Regency to control New York. This constitution significantly increased the appointive power of the governor. The reservoir of patronage that was centered in that office added to the effectiveness of Regency control. In addition, the anti-Regency element was divided and, with the exception of the charismatic DeWitt Clinton, lacked strong leadership. Even when Clinton triumphantly returned to the strengthened governor's office in 1824 after a two-year absence, Van Buren and the Regency were able to come to terms with Clinton over patronage. Clinton was an independent whose chief interest was the governorship. However, he lacked a party organization. In 1826, the Regency Democrats went so far as to surreptitiously back him for reelection in return for patronage. Clinton's death early in 1828 removed this last impediment to complete Regency control.

Until 1834, the chief opposition to the Democrat-Republicans, or simply Democrats after 1828, came from the National Republicans. But the National Republicans declined in strength after 1828 when their president, John Quincy Adams, was defeated by Democrat Andrew Jackson. During Jackson's two terms, federal patronage funneled into New York to Regency Democrats through Jackson's active supporter, Martin Van Buren. By 1833, Van Buren was Jackson's vice-president.

Another hinderance to strong anti-Regency opposition in New York was the emergence of several new parties. Aided by the extension of the franchise after 1821 to virtually all adult males, parties sprang up that reflected a variety of views and issues. The most prominent of the newcomers was the Anti-Masonic Party. Although originally an outgrowth of rural opposition to the Masonic Order, it quickly metamorphosed into an antimonopolistic organization.

By 1828, the party had come under the leadership of Thurlow Weed, an Albany newspaperman. Weed, long opposed to Van Buren and the Regency, had been searching for a vehicle to challenge them at the polls. At first, however, all the Anti-Masons did was to more completely fragment the opposition to the Democrats, assuring the Regency of even greater political control. Weed's dream party was a union between the National Republicans and the Anti-Masons, but ideological differences prevented this until 1834.

Of the many descriptions of politics in the Empire State during the antebellum years, perhaps the most succinct and accurate was that of a contemporary observer who likened New York's political machinery to "a labyrinth of wheels, within wheels."[13] Not only did patronage enter into the political scenario, but politics were played against a background of bank charters, the new industrial philosophy versus the traditional agrarian theme, various reform movements from workers' rights to women's rights, the state debt, national expansion, and the issue of slavery. Of all, the most destructive to party cohesion was the slave question. Out of this divisive controversy was born the Republican Party in 1854 with its free-soil platform.

Even Jervis, a faithful Democrat for at least three decades prior to the election of the state's first Republican governor in 1856, gave up the party of Jackson and followed his free-soil sympathies into the ranks of the new party. However, when the Republican Party's most important predecessor in New York emerged in 1834, Jervis was unwilling to leave his Democrats to join the new Whig organization. This raises the question of the extent of Jervis's political involvement prior to the 1850s.

In 1834 New York City was given approval from the state legislature to elect its own mayor. It was the first time that the anti-Jackson coalition brought forth its Whig Party ticket. Thurlow Weed finally realized his goal. Mutual hatred of the Democrats brought National Republicans and Anti-Masons together to form the Whig Party, even though earlier they lacked harmony in their views on banks, monopolies, and the extent of government.

During the next twenty years, Whigs battled the Democrats in New York and throughout the nation. The modernist Whigs advocated an activist role for the central government, particularly in supporting improvements that would stimulate and aid the economy. The traditionalist Democrats wanted to confine the role of government to that of protecting the rights and property of citizens. In New York State, the debate between the two parties often centered on the future of the state's canal system. To put it simply, the Whigs favored enlarging and expanding the system regardless of the state debt and the Democrats were against spending more on canals. This was the basic dichotomy in the late 1830s. However, with the increase of free-soil and antislave agitation during the mid-forties, the party lines in New York State became less distinct.

Jervis was a strong advocate of internal improvements. As a builder of canals and railroads, it makes sense that he would have been. Yet Jervis remained a Democrat. One historian of pre–Civil War New York's politics presented a description of a New York Whig as a genteel Presbyterian or Baptist upstater of high moral character who "regarded with grave suspicion the raffish character of the Democratic party, especially its strong appeal to the newly arrived Irish and German immigrants."[14] Jervis could well have posed for this verbal picture, right down to his feelings about the Irish. However, Jervis continued to be a Democrat.

Finally, when a Whig governor appointed a Whig Board of Water Commissioners in 1840, it certainly seemed likely that the new board might have removed a known recipient of Democratic patronage or at least brought pressure on Jervis to become a Whig. Jervis certainly fit the Whig pattern, and — politically — changing parties might have been a wise move. However, Jervis remained a Democrat, although a relatively quiet Democrat.

The point is that for all of his Regency friends and his involvement in public projects, Jervis remained apart from the game of party politics. There is no evidence to support the Douglass faction's allegations that Jervis actively campaigned for the Croton job or that he sought out the support of his political contacts. The fact that Jervis was a Democrat certainly did not hurt him, but his best recommendation for the position was his known skill as an engineer.

Undoubtedly Jervis's friendship with Benjamin Wright was also an asset. Wright was a powerful ally for Jervis because he had done the 1834 study of water sources for New York City, he had been appointed as street commissioner of New York City in 1831, he was friends with Governor Marcy, and he had an outstanding reputation as an engineer. The extent to which Wright intervened, if at all, for his former assistant is unknown. However, Wright's faith in Jervis, particularly on the Delaware and Hudson project, was known among people of influence in New York City. If this can be considered "political influence," then Jervis unquestionably was the beneficiary of it.

In fact, if Jervis's steadfast adherence to the Democratic Party in New York State during the 1830s and 1840s was economically motivated, it was his banking interests, not his engineering jobs, that accounted for the primary motivation. The state legislature controlled the issue of bank charters. During much of the time between 1820 and 1850, the Democrats controlled the Legislature. Given Jervis's interest in banks and the lack of a compelling reason to leave the Democratic Party, Jervis remained a Democrat.

The nearly fifteen-year domination of state politics by the Regency began to weaken when the Whigs took control of the Assembly after the election of 1837. Earlier that year, Martin Van Buren had reached his long-sought goal when he was sworn into the presidency. Unfortunately, part of the legacy Van Buren inherited from the Jackson administration was an economic policy that contributed to the nation's first deep depression. The Depression of 1837 occurred only a few months after Van Buren took office, but it plagued his entire term. It was a contributing factor to Whig success in the Assembly elections in 1837, and the depression continued to help Whig candidates during the next three years. However, since Democrat William Marcy remained in the governor's mansion for a while and the Democrats retained control of the Senate, Jervis's position was not in jeopardy.

But in 1838, Whig William Seward defeated Marcy for the governorship; in 1839, the Whigs completed their move for control of state government by capturing a majority of the Senate. Early in 1840, Governor Seward, with the consent of the State Senate, removed all the water commissioners except Whig William W. Fox and appointed a new board.[15]

To the friends of Major Douglass, this seemed an ideal time to campaign for the reinstatement of their man. As far as they were concerned, politics had been responsible for Douglass's removal. Now politics could be used to return Douglass as chief engineer.

As it turned out, this would be more difficult than the Douglass supporters imagined. Jervis had established a fine reputation for his able and efficient management of the engineering department. Also, Jervis had remained as aloof from politics as was possible for a chief engineer appointed by a politically selected commission. Jervis's approach was in accord with his ideas on professionalism and the engineer.

When the Democratic commissioners submitted their final report to the Board of Aldermen in March 1840, it contained an expression of confidence in Jervis and the recommendation that he be retained in his position. "We cannot forebear expressing the hope, therefore, that our successors will avail themselves of the talents and acquired knowledge of Mr. Jervis, for the further prosecution of a work of so much importance to this city. The advantages in retaining his services, and also of his present assistants must be obvious. . . . " The commissioners had in mind not only the abilities of the engineers, but also the "practical knowledge which is only acquired by years of attention and familiarity with the subject."[16]

Meanwhile, the opposition was preparing its attack. Appropriately, the battle was opened by the *New York American,* the journal that had stood against the commissioners in the bridge controversy. Applauding Douglass and condemning the Democratic board, the *American* claimed that the water commissioners used Major Douglass's talents to draw up the aqueduct plan and then fired him because they "considered an eleve [*sic*] of the Albany Regency a more suitable instrument to subserve their political object than a Whig." The newspaper called on the new Whig commissioners to correct the injustice and not let an "old soldier . . . lie under any unmerited obloquy."[17]

Actually, the July 18 article was typical of the many newspaper stories during the campaign. That is, the pro-Douglass forces tended to focus on the Democratic water commissioners as the source of evil, rather than on the chief engineer. Even so, Jervis could not avoid the conflict. Such charges as were made against him usually were allegations of his role in pressing for Douglass's removal in order to make room for his own appointment. Also, the charges were an attempt to impugn Jervis's reputation as an engineer by insinuating that his political connections were his chief qualification.

Revitalized and encouraged by the editorials, Douglass himself took up the pen. In October, the hero of the defense of Fort Erie[18] directed a blast against the water commissioners. He reiterated the charge of political patronage and stated that Jervis's appointment was assured as early as 1835. Douglass charged that Stephen Allen's "private talks with [William] Bouck at the Democratic Convention in Baltimore" were aimed at securing a replacement for him as chief engineer.[19] Douglass was supported in his foray by the Whig *American,* which cried patronage and claimed that "all the contracts, with unimportant exceptions were given to Loco-Focos and that the Loco-Foco Chief Engineer still remains in office."[20]

These allegations considerably upset Jervis, who thought them a slur on his professionalism. He felt his conduct was above reproach and stated so soon after the appearance of the Douglass article. Jervis wrote that "in all their [*sic*] communications with me, the Board placed the subject of my engagement on professional grounds only."[21] He insisted that at no time during his tenure on the Croton or any other project did he attempt to use political influence. If politics had entered into his appointment as chief engineer, he had no knowledge of it. Consistent with his philosophy, Jervis assured his readers: "A political Engineer . . . has a very low standing in my estimation."[22]

In his autobiography, Jervis reiterated his ignorance of the political leanings of the engineers and contractors on the Croton. He noted that a canvass by a member of the Whig board showed a roughly equal division in terms of the political affiliation of engineers and contractors. Jervis insisted that it would have been difficult for the water commissioners to favor certain contractors without his knowledge. No inquiry was made about party membership when candidates were presented for appointments to the engineering department.[23]

Stephen Allen defended the chief engineer against the charges of using political influence. According to Allen, Jervis neither sought favors from his political allies nor did he impose upon his influential friends. On the Croton project, Jervis asked for nothing but a position in the engineering department for his younger brother. What seemed curious to Allen was that Douglass had waited four years to state publicly his "charges" against Jervis.[24]

Additional support for the argument that Jervis did not give an advantage to Democrat Party members can be found in a letter from John Bloomfield to his nephew. Bloomfield reminded Jervis that, in relation to his possible dismissal by the Whig commissioners, they "can not charge you with directly using your influence . . . " to favor Democrats. However, " . . . they may say that your known opposition to the Whigs [as a known Democrat] can well have an evil influence" and may think it necessary to remove you.[25] Jervis was as close to his Uncle Bloomfield as he was to anyone. He had few secrets from his uncle and freely asked Bloomfield's advice on many matters. The December 11 letter was one of counsel and was a good analysis of the Douglass controversy. It served to remind Jervis that Douglass sought to do the same thing that Jervis was seeking: to "defend his professional reputation."[26]

While he was in the chief engineer's position, it is highly unlikely that Jervis "played politics." The weight of evidence is against it, and it would have been too contrary to Jervis's character for him to have done so. However, the role, if any, that Jervis's political friends played in his appointment and the extent to which Jervis had advance notice of Douglass's removal remains open to question.

Perhaps a possible answer can be found in a series of articles on the Croton written by Myndert Van Schaick in 1845. Van Schaick, in his attempt to establish his claim as the first to suggest the Croton water source, said it was he who recommended Jervis to Stephen Allen, as early as the latter part of 1835. Reluctantly, Van Schaick did admit that Allen's quick approval of the Jervis appointment suggested to Van Schaick that Allen had been approached earlier on Jervis's behalf.[27] Following Allen's consent, a meeting took place between Van Schaick and Jervis in Albany during the winter of 1836, at which time Van Schaick "presented to the mind of Mr. Jervis . . . those considerations of ample pay and exalted fame which finally, after much negotiation, induced him to relinquish his employment on the Erie Canal."[28]

Again it was Stephen Allen who intervened on Jervis's behalf. Reinstated to his post as chairman of the water commissioners because of a change of politics in Albany, Allen denied that Van Schaick had been instrumental in obtaining Jervis's appointment as chief engineer.[29] His statement, rather tardy in its publication, might have been in the interest of the reputation of his chief engineer or it might have been a case of self-interest. Allen was another of a growing crowd of individuals who claimed to have given birth to the idea of the Croton Aqueduct.

Within a week of Allen's statement, Jervis, prompted by a letter from Van Schaick asking him if he recalled their conversation of the winter of 1836, responded to Van Schaick's earlier claims. Jervis's reply was noncommittal about his understanding of the legitimacy of Van Schaick's offer. Jervis did not deny the meeting with Van Schaick, but said that he regarded the conversation "as expressing the wishes of an old friend rather than as an authorized negotiation. If you [Van Schaick] treated the subject as an authorized agent it has escaped my memory."[30] Jervis ended his statement with the comment that since he was employed at the time on the Erie enlargement, there was no reason that he should have been interested in a new engagement. Apparently, though, within a few months Jervis's interest had shifted.

The letter to Van Schaick was not enough to close the issue of Jervis as the Regency appointee. Certain questions about his appointment continued to keep alive the possibility that Jervis was a "political" engineer. Perhaps when the Jervis-Douglass dispute was reopened in the 1870s, the Douglass supporters had these questions in mind in their attempt to vindicate Major Douglass.

First, there was the matter of the Jervis–Van Schaick meeting. A letter from Stephen Allen, published a few days after the Jervis letter of May 19, pointed out that Jervis did not admit that Van Schaick made him an offer of a position.[31] Of course, Jervis had claimed a lapse of memory and did not deny it either. Understandably his powers of recall did not improve after thirty years when, as the question came up again, he flatly denied having been approached by anyone prior to the visit of a committee from the water commissioners. The committee, consisting of Stephen Allen and Saul Alley, called on Jervis in September 1836, several months after his meeting with Van Schaick.[32]

Next, there were the many letters that Jervis received late in 1842 requesting him to use his influence with Governor Bouck to obtain appointments.[33] Requests for jobs were nothing new; Jervis received plenty of them while in charge of various projects. The novelty was that the requests were for jobs that had nothing to do with engineering, such as the New York City posts of Resident Physician and of Inspector of Pot and Pearl Ashes. Numerous petitions were from Myndert Van Schaick.[34] This may have been coincidental, or it may have been Van Schaick's way of collecting for a favor.

Finally, there was Jervis's insatiable ambition and his continual quest for the challenge. Several instances have already been cited as proof of this. The Erie enlargement offered only a slight enhancement of Jervis's professional reputation. The Croton was a much more attractive prospect. Van Schaick's offer would have provided Jervis with an opening made to order for his advancement, and he could have had the Croton job without first going to his Regency friend Bouck. As keen as Jervis may have been on upgrading his professional standing, it was not within his character to solicit a position. And, of course, Bouck preferred that he remain an engineer on the Erie. If Jervis and Bouck did discuss the possibility of Jervis's appointment to the Croton, a record of their conversations is not to be found among their papers.

The Whig water commissioners may have concurred with Douglass's supporters in the belief that Jervis was a Regency man. If they did, it did not sway their decision to keep him in the chief engineer's position. Undoubtedly, the fact that the aqueduct was progressing in good order prevented Jervis from being removed.

Another factor may have been the Whigs' plans to economize on aqueduct costs. The water commissioners felt it was imperative to reduce costs since the amount the Legislature had authorized them to raise was now exhausted. The commissioners appealed to the New York Common Council and finally to the state Legislature for assistance. On July 26, 1841, new legislation allowing the commissioners to raise an additional $3,500,000 was passed. The act also granted them the option, with the assent of the Common Council, to discontinue construction of the High Bridge and substitute instead inverted siphons and iron pipes.[35] Ironically, it was the Whig Douglass who had recommended a high bridge. Jervis had suggested the more economical system of siphons and pipes supported by a low bridge. With this in mind, the commissioners could have regarded it as wise to retain Jervis.

Public pressure prevented a change to the Jervis plan of pipes and inverted siphons. Construction on the High Bridge continued and yet Jervis remained in the chief engineer's job. He developed a certain rapport with some of the Whig commissioners and became a friend of at least one, John D. Ward.[36]

However, Board Chairman Samuel Stevens's apparent acceptance of Jervis did not prevent him from insulting the chief engineer at the time of the great Croton celebration in October 1842. In arranging for the procession, Stevens placed himself in a coach near the head of the parade, leaving Jervis to walk with the rest of the engineering corps. Only a chance discovery of the fact by Governor Seward prevented the humiliation from occurring. Seward invited Jervis to ride in his carriage.[37]

The parade incident marked the end of a difficult period for Jervis as chief engineer. The three years of Whig administration and the attacks by Douglass and his supporters kept Jervis in fear of losing a position that was important to him. Early in 1843, the former Democratic water commissioners were reinstated by Governor Seward's successor, William Bouck. Stephen Allen was back in the chairmanship, and Jervis no longer had to fear being discharged on account of his political affiliation.

With the threat of removal gone, Jervis's final six years as head of the Croton engineering department were relatively uneventful. In fact, during part of that period, he was actively involved in other projects. On June 30, 1849, Jervis resigned as chief engineer of the Croton Aqueduct.[38] Before the end of the year, Major David Bates Douglass died. These events should have meant an end to the controversy involving the two engineers. Instead, it marked only the end of the first phase of the dispute. After an interim of a quarter of a century, the controversy was rejoined.

The second round of the Douglass affair was sparked by a biographical sketch of Jervis that appeared in the September 15, 1874, issue of the *New York Evening Post*. The article, much of which was devoted to the Croton, heaped acclaim upon Jervis and hailed him as the man who "has done more for the city of New York than any other engineer."[39] Within a month, a letter was sent to the *Evening Post* reminding the people of New York of Major Douglass's role in the Croton works. The correspondence, signed "M.D." emphasized the part that Douglass had played in the design of the aqueduct, with the author claiming that Douglass's chief fault was that he was not a politician.[40]

By the end of November, the newspaper received a reply to "M.D.'s" letter from Rome, New York. It was Jervis's final response to the charges made against him by the Douglass faction. The 3,500-word statement was a history of the proposals of Major Douglass versus the plans of Jervis. Jervis commented on the aqueduct and its important structures in terms of the extent to which they represented Douglass's proposals. As to the structure of most controversy, the High Bridge, Jervis noted that Douglass recommended a similar bridge, but the one that had been built was planned and executed by Jervis. The former chief engineer recalled that Major Douglass—although appointed engineer under favorable circumstances—had, within seventeen months, apparently so lost the confidence of the water commissioners that they had removed him.[41] Finally, Jervis asserted that when he was selected he

took the appointment with no acquaintance with the board and through their [sic] administration and three successive changes by political action, with a strong influence for the reinstatement of Major Douglass, yet I was retained until the work was completed, and I retired on my own unsolicited resignation.

The fact that the aqueduct has served its functions more than thirty years shows that my critics were in error, and the several boards justified in trusting my engineering ability.

After adversely criticizing my works, it is unreasonable that the late Major Douglass should have the credit of my labors after success has been realized.[42]

In his conclusion, Jervis alluded to the unsupported allegations that he had conspired politically to obtain the chief engineer's post. This was a reiteration of what he had written in the first part of the letter about the claim that he sought favors from his political friends.

Apparently these statements did not put the matter to rest. Major-General George W. Cullum, in a book on the U.S. Army Engineers published five years later, claimed that the removal of Douglass was, in part, political. As a successor to Douglass, the commissioners appointed a "gentleman with whom it appears they had been in correspondence for some time."[43] This latest defense of Douglass stated that the dismissal was also due to a disagreement between Douglass and the commissioners over the system of granting contracts. Douglass's views "were not their [the commissioners] views. He was for them an impracticable man."[44] Jervis did not reply to these suggestions of political complicity. He either did not know of the book, which, given his interest in reading, seems unlikely, or he felt he had said enough on the subject.

Major Douglass, without a doubt, was responsible for some of the initial work on the Croton. Jervis readily admitted this fact. However, contrary to the claim of Douglass and his supporters, his was a limited role. Credit for the final plans and the completion of the notable work rightly belongs to Jervis. Jervis neither stole Douglass's plans nor worked for the major's removal.[45] No evidence indicates "that Jervis in any way conspired with Allen for Douglass's removal in order to further his own career." Jervis "was a better engineer than Douglass," which undoubtedly worked more in favor of his superceding Douglass than any other factor.[46]

However, the questions raised about Jervis's relationship to the Regency are not as easily answered. Lack of conclusive evidence in either direction prevents a positive statement that might finally settle the matter.

The Douglass affair obviously had a deep and lasting impact on Jervis. One-third of his "Facts and Circumstances" was devoted to the Croton Aqueduct project, of which half was concerned with the Douglass controversy. It is unfortunate that the affair came in conjunction with what was perhaps Jervis's greatest triumph. In reality, the stigma of political engineer worried Jervis a great deal more than was necessary. Whether or not he was a Regency appointee had little effect on the quality of his work or on his conduct as chief engineer.

7

Not Only an Engineer

THE ROUTINE WORK on the Croton Aqueduct after 1842 and the decision to relieve Jervis of the responsibility for planning the water distribution system for New York City meant that the chief engineer was able to turn his attention to other matters. During the remainder of the 1840s, in addition to presiding over the completion of the Croton, Jervis helped plan a water supply for the city of Boston. He also laid out a railroad between New York City and Albany and served two years as chief engineer of the road.

Jervis's activities during the forties were not confined to his profession. He continued to be involved in farming, banking, investment property, and the general merchandise business. His political interest increased as did his concern about the possible spread of slavery into the new territories beyond the Mississippi. As always, he remained a strict adherent to his religion. Jervis also read a great deal. His library reflected his primary interests and included volumes on subjects other than those in which he was actively involved.

Some indication of Jervis's character and his involvements other than civil engineering can be gained by examining his personal library. The collection, which continues to remain much as it was when he used it, contains more than 1,100 volumes.[1] Its diversity reflects the multifaceted individual responsible for its assemblage. Naturally, many of Jervis's books pertain to civil engineering and related subjects, such as topographical surveys and mechanics. A number of scientific journals line the shelves as do works on American and English architecture. However, most of the volumes in the collection are on subjects not directly related to civil engineering or the building arts. They can be divided into five general categories: humanities, social sciences, natural sciences, agriculture, and religion.[2] Books pertaining to religion are the most numerous and account for more than one-fourth of the total collection. If notations in the margin and underlining are any indication of the use Jervis made of his books, then it is safe to say that he used his library. The wonder is how—considering the time spent at his profession and his reading—Jervis was able to find time for anything else.

However, he did find time for other interests, many of which considerably added to his financial standing. Salary increases resulting from career advancement, as well as his frugal lifestyle, enabled Jervis to divert funds into investments.[3] The investments, for the most part, were managed by others in whom Jervis placed his trust. This approach was in keeping with his philosophy about the propriety of engineers becoming involved in matters other than their profession.

Jervis felt that the "man who, by a proper economy, is able annually to lay something by as an investment from his earnings is only exercising the prudence necessary to provide for age or infirmity." Jervis advised that "all men should do this," since it puts them at ease about the future.[4] However, Jervis made a distinction between investing for the future and speculating from a "thirst to be rich." He felt that an engineer should secure a proper salary and then give his undivided attention to his professional duties. Jervis warned that the engineer whose mind is preoccupied with speculation will not become eminent in his field. As evidence of this, Jervis noted that several engineers known to him "were always on the alert for speculation," but none of them gained a good reputation as an engineer.[5] Hence the reasoning behind Jervis's almost casual approach to the management of his finances.

Undeniably, Jervis was aware of how his funds were invested, and he occasionally made observations on such matters as the state of banking. But Jervis's preoccupation with his engineering work necessitated a reliance on others to make his investments. He chose his agents well and, for the most part, he profited from his investments.

Most of Jervis's surplus funds went into bank securities. By the time Jervis was appointed chief engineer on the Croton Aqueduct, he held stock in at least seven banks.[6] His relationship with the banks in which he invested was largely limited to occasional letters from bank officers informing him of stock dividends. The importance of this kind of correspondence should not be overlooked, though, since it meant that Jervis was making acquaintances with influential persons throughout New York State. One such individual was Washington Hunt, president of the Lockport Bank and Trust Company. Hunt, a Whig, was elected governor of the state in 1850 and was a known friend of internal improvements, especially the Erie enlargement.

Jervis's activities in banking widened his circle of contacts and might have been partially responsible, along with his Regency friends, for keeping him in the Democratic Party. During the decade in which Jervis began investing in banks, the Democrats held continual control of the Legislature and, therefore, of bank chartering. After 1804 New York law required the chartering of banks. In 1827, the Legislature increased its political influence over banks by increasing the degree of state control over banking. Given Jervis's growing investment in banks, it was logically to his advantage to remain a Democrat. However, his allegiance to that party never faltered in the bleak years following the Depression of 1837, when most banks suspended the redemption of paper bank notes for specie and many banks closed their doors.

In 1839 the Whigs completed their takeover of the Legislature, but Jervis remained in the Democratic ranks. Even when, in 1840, his esteemed Uncle Bloomfield drank "hard cider" and went to the "Log Cabin" because of the Whig's stand on internal improvements, Jervis remained loyal to the party of Jackson and Van Buren.[7] Perhaps his position on the Croton would have been less vexatious had he switched to the Whig Party.

Actually, it was during his early years on the Croton project that Jervis became the most actively interested in banking matters. These years coincided with the financial crisis following 1837, and Jervis's involvement, in addition to investment, was that of giving advice on proper management. In reply to a request from the cashier of the Bank of Rome for information on the "state of the money market," Jervis provided the latest financial news from New York City. He also used the opportunity to warn the cashier against unwise practices such as issuing too large a quantity of paper notes.

As a stockholder, Jervis preferred to manage conservatively rather than "depend on hazardous profits." It was his belief that the current emergency would not end until the old manner of "getting a living by industry and economy takes the place of wild speculation and extravagance."[8] The following year, Jervis reiterated his feelings on speculation, one of the roots of the hard times, to Azariah C. Flagg, a member of the Regency's inner circle and the state comptroller.[9] Jervis's reaction to the Depression of 1837 was obviously an attempt on his part to protect his interest in banking. He freely offered advice to bankers throughout the crisis, which represented the extent of his comments on banking until after the Civil War.[10]

During the late 1820s and throughout the 1830s, Jervis was also engaged in another banking activity: the making of loans. The choice of individuals to whom the loans were made and, to an extent, the amount of the loans was usually left to his Uncle Bloomfield. As early as 1827,

Bloomfield notified Jervis of a request from two Rome businessmen for $1,750. Jervis agreed to the loan.[11] By 1830, Bloomfield informed Jervis that he was "almost constantly applied to for money." He requested that Jervis send him a draft in case "something worthwhile arises."[12] By this time, Jervis had made loans to half a dozen residents of the Rome area.[13]

An indication of Jervis's character as a businessman can be found in his transactions with the prominent Oneida County entrepreneur, Simon Newton Dexter. Dexter had known Jervis for about ten years before he attempted to borrow money in June 1838. Jervis's reply to Dexter's request for a loan of $1,800 portrays the engineer as something akin to the stereotyped villain of a late nineteenth-century melodrama. Jervis's answer, communicated to Dexter through John Bloomfield, was that Jervis was unwilling to accept Dexter's note without at least two co-signers who were to be men designated by Jervis. Dexter's reply to the terms was:

> I was not a little surprised at the communication — now I supposed that you knew that my note was as good as either of the gentlemen you require as endorser — it is so many years that you have known me and my standing as to property. . . . I should hardly suppose you would ask me an endorser for $1,800 — 6, 9 and 12 months — I surely should not have asked it on your note — An endorser and a good one — I expected to give — but I did not expect that these men would be selected by you that *you knew never* endorsed even for each other . . . of course, therefore, no arrangement can be made with you.[14]

Dexter wanted the loan to purchase some judgments that Jervis himself held against the Scriba estate, a late eighteenth-century patent that encompassed most of Oswego County and a portion of western Oneida County. The last paragraph of Dexter's letter made reference to the Scriba lands in a final compassionate plea for Jervis to change his mind. Dexter informed Jervis that a Mr. Dundas, "who appears to be an excellent man, was anxious to save something for old Mr. Scriba's sister — and could the arrangements have been made with you the homestead could have been saved."[15] Jervis was unmoved by the sad tale and did not change the terms for the acceptance of Dexter's note.

The reason that Jervis imposed the seemingly harsh conditions may have been that he already held a mortgage for more than $3,000 against some land belonging to Dexter. The mortgage was paid, but not before Dexter had to request a three-month extension on the loan.[16] Although it was Bloomfield who acted as the intermediary in these transactions, it was clearly Jervis who dictated the terms.

In addition to taking mortgages on land, Jervis also became involved in a popular business of the early nineteenth century: land specu-lation. While employed on the Delaware and Hudson Canal, Jervis pur-chased lots in Honesdale, the Pennsylvania terminus of the canal. Mindful of his advice against engineers becoming involved in anything that would distract their attention from their profession, Jervis left management of the Honesdale property in the hands of his agent, Rus-sell F. Lord, his successor as chief engineer of the Delaware and Hudson.

All of Jervis's property was near the canal, with some of it adjacent to the canal basin. Within less than a decade of purchase, all of Jervis's parcels in Honesdale were sold, with Jervis taking back mortgages on many of the lots. Indications are that his Honesdale property maintained its value even during the hard times of the late thirties and early forties.[17]

During the early 1830s, Jervis made several rural land purchases in Oneida County, although at least one parcel was property that adjoined the village of Rome. A hiatus in his land speculation activities occurred in 1837, when Jervis became cautious because of the adverse financial situation.[18] The interruption was brief, however, and by the following year Jervis was buying land once again. During the next three years, he acquired his father's 115-acre farm in the town of Rome and also pur-chased some excellent commercial property in Rome village, including three brick stores on the main street. Jervis bought other business prop-erty in Palmyra, New York.[19] During the 1830s, his land purchases to-taled nearly $25,000.[20]

Once again it was John Bloomfield who served as Jervis's agent and advisor for land purchases in the Rome area. His correspondence with Jervis indicated that he was always alert for land at bargain prices. Bloomfield's letters also revealed that he was not reluctant to ask Jervis for advance knowledge of public improvements that would cause appre-ciation of land values. In one such instance, Bloomfield had an opportu-nity to buy land in Rome that had the potential of bordering on the enlarged Erie Canal. The exact route of the enlargement had not yet been made known by the canal commissioners. Hence Bloomfield was hesitant, since he was unsure whether the land value would appreciate sufficiently for him to pay the high asking price and still make a profit. Bloomfield suggested that Jervis, because of his "intimacy with the Canal Commissioners," might "be able to judge what they will do" about choosing a canal route through Rome.[21] Unfortunately, Jervis's reply to the request remains undiscovered, but given his relationship with his uncle, there is reason to believe that Jervis would have aided Bloomfield whenever possible. One thing is certain: the Jervis investments managed by Bloomfield were good ones that added to Jervis's growing wealth. The same could not be said of all Jervis's financial ventures.

Not all Jervis's investments in the Rome area were managed by Bloomfield. During the time he was employed on the Croton project, Jervis was involved in three partnerships that included other members of his family. His youngest brother, Benjamin, was with Jervis in all three partnerships. A brother-in-law, William Brayton, was a partner in the second, and brother William Jervis was a member of the third partnership.[22] The business combinations included the operation of mercantile stores in Rome; in Cazenovia, a village thirty miles southwest of Rome; and in Taberg, a small village ten miles northwest of Rome. A gristmill and sawmill in Taberg were also included in the operation.[23] Benjamin Jervis, approximately twenty years old when the first partnership was formed, managed the business of the first two partnerships and Jervis supplied most of the capital.

The partnerships involving Jervis and his family were largely failures. The first, between Jervis and Benjamin, involved stores in Cazenovia and Taberg. The business agreement was expanded early in 1838 to include William Brayton. Shortly thereafter, a mercantile establishment in Rome was added to those already in operation.[24] To facilitate the business expansion, Benjamin felt that $10,000 would be needed to finance the new "B. F. J. and Company." Jervis contributed the total amount in return for which he would receive one-third of the profits of the firm.[25]

Jervis's willingness to finance the firm stemmed from his desire to have Benjamin live in Rome where he could be near their "aged and infirm family." Since the other Jervis brothers chose "professions of a rambling character," Benjamin seemed the logical one to remain and pursue the mercantile business.[26] Unlike many of his other investments, the partnership with Benjamin was "by no means a matter of speculation," but was in consideration of responsibility to Jervis's family.[27]

This feeling of obligation was strong enough to cause Jervis to contribute the capital even against the advice of another of his wife's brothers, Henry Brayton, an officer in the Bank of Rome. Brayton advised Jervis that he was not getting a large enough return for his investment. Brayton felt that Jervis "ought not to furnish more than $6,000 or $8,000 to share 1/3 profits. . . . "[28] As it turned out, Jervis would have been wiser to contribute nothing to the "company." After a year and a half of mixed reports on the business and requests from Benjamin for an additional $1,500,[29] the partnership was dissolved.[30] "B. F. J. and Company" was a failure.

There seems to have been one dominant factor that resulted in the financial failure of the company: the unsound practices of Jervis's two partners. A letter from banker Henry Brayton to Jervis in New York City pointed out to the engineer where his partners had been in error. Brayton, replying to a letter from Jervis in which Jervis related his fears of a large loss, felt that the losses might not be as bad as were at first indicated. Brayton confided that he was "still of the opinion that could you [Jervis] have had the supervision of the establishment or could Benjamin and William made up their minds to follow your advice," the business could have prospered. Jervis's partners preferred to do "a *large* business more for the name than the profit." If they had instead "first commenced moderately and safely for profit rather than name they might have eventually worked themselves into a snug profitable business."[31]

Brayton then characterized his brother William as an individual who often "carried all steam and no ballast" and therefore not one who was willing to heed advice. Benjamin Jervis's weakness was his willingness to "let customers have his capital to do business upon while he himself pinches along on credit." Brayton hoped Benjamin had profited by his error.[32]

Apparently Jervis felt his brother Benjamin had profited from his experience since, incredible as it may seem, he entered into another partnership with him. The new business arrangement may have been an attempt by Jervis to recoup his losses or it may have been the result of Benjamin's plea for another chance. A few weeks after the breakup of the first partnership, Jervis received an apology from his brother. Benjamin feared that he had lost Jervis's confidence, and he assured his older brother that, given another opportunity, he would once again "engage in business vigorously."[33] Since Jervis still owned the commercial property, it was simply a matter of reorganization and recapitalization. Again, much of the money was furnished by Jervis. This time William Jervis was brought into the partnership to aid his younger brother Benjamin in the management.

This final commercial venture of the Jervis brothers was no more successful then the previous one had been. By early 1842, Jervis received word from William that business was so poor at the Taberg store that the income there could not cover expenses. He felt the store should be closed and the stock moved to the Rome store. William bemoaned his loss of a year's labor at the store, but admitted it was little compared with the capital investment lost by Jervis. William sought Jervis's advice as to future action and informed his older brother that Benjamin would "go along with any plan since he has nothing to lose and has already been the cause of considerable loss to you [J. B. Jervis]."[34] Within a month of William's letter, the partnership was dissolved, and William had agreed to purchase the mill property in Taberg from Jervis.[35]

Whereas failure of the previous partnership could be attributed to poor management, the last partnership seemed to have failed due to lack of business. The decline of commercial activity precipitated by the national crisis of 1837 reached a low in 1842. The mercantile business of the Jervis family was not immune to the bad economic conditions. Perhaps the news of the passage of the internal improvements "stop and tax" bill by the state Legislature hastened the decision to abandon the partnership. Since the Rome area benefited from construction on the Erie enlargement and Black River Canal, a halt to canal building was certain to be detrimental to local businesses.

The causes for the failure of Jervis's mercantile venture were, to the major investor, unimportant compared to the loss of his invested capital. However, Jervis accepted the loss with little complaint. Jervis tolerated failure from his brothers, especially young Benjamin, that he would never have accepted from those under his supervision. On his part, Benjamin looked up to his older brother with unceasing admiration.[36] The relationship between Jervis and his brothers as business partners is one of the few instances that provides insight, albeit limited, into Jervis's relations with his family.

Another side of Jervis's character is shown in his attitude towards other members of his family, especially his two wives. As the oldest of seven children, Jervis did not lack companionship during his childhood. Yet the man that became acclaimed for his many engineering accomplishments was a distant, reserved individual.

This was especially true in his relationships with women, even though he grew up literally surrounded by females. Three sisters followed within nine years of his birth, and Jervis was thirteen before his first brother was born. This meant that during his years on the farm at Rome, Jervis bore all the responsibility that, had there been other brothers, would have been divided among the male children. Next to his father, Jervis was the "man of the house." Under those circumstances, he might have grown up feeling at ease around women. Lacking evidence to the contrary, we can only assume that his relationships with the opposite sex were as stilted during the first third of his life as they were throughout the remainder of it.

Undoubtedly, Jervis's deep Calvinistic convictions had an effect on his behavior towards women. Perhaps more influential in this sense was the outcome of what possibly was Jervis's first important romance. While he was a resident engineer on the Erie Canal, Jervis developed what apparently was more than a casual friendship with a young lady in Amsterdam. The liaison lasted about a year, during which time Jervis's work on the canal kept him in the eastern Mohawk Valley area. However, when work was halted at the end of the 1821 season, Jervis returned to Rome and remained there from November 1821 until April 1822. He did not visit Amsterdam during that time. In the spring of 1822, Jervis discovered to his surprise that in his absence his "friend" had married.[37] His ignorance of the change of heart of his "friend" is clearly demonstrated in a letter to her in March in which he indirectly suggested a closer relationship between them.[38] Although Jervis later indicated that he bore her no malice,[39] the impact her rapid courtship and marriage had on him was marked.

During the next three years, Jervis's letters to his sisters Ann and Betsy and to his Aunt Bloomfield reveal his disappointment and his determination to accept "God's will." Typical of these letters was the one addressed to Ann Jervis less than two months after his discovery of the marriage. After telling his sister that he resigned himself to the loss, Jervis reminded her that one should accept the "injunctions of our heavenly Father." Although "it is instinctly our duty to do all in our power to promote our own happiness," human emotions should be subordinate "to the will of his holy providence—with the consideration that all earthly objects are secondary and our highest hopes of happiness beyond the confines of this cloudy and tempestuous atmosphere."[40] Jervis sought solace in his religion to help explain and compensate for what had occurred.

Finally, in 1825, Jervis declared to his sister Ann that passion could, at times, prevent good judgment. In the margin of the letter, he added: "If we are governed by prudence, we shall not be governed by passion which is more or less productive of evil."[41] With this as a maxim, he approached his marriages of the following decade.

Jervis, the man who seemingly found it so difficult to communicate his inner thoughts and feelings to people, especially women, was married twice. His first marriage, to Cynthia Brayton in June 1834, occurred while he was employed on the Chenango Canal. During the five years of their marriage, Jervis went from one project to another without a break. Cynthia's fragile health often prevented her from accompanying him; consequently, she spent much of the time with her family in Westernville, near Rome.

During absences from her husband, Cynthia corresponded with him frequently. Her letters to Jervis contain insight into his choosing to marry at age thirty-eight. According to his wife, Jervis was a lonely man who needed the companionship that a wife could provide him. Cynthia felt that it had been loneliness that had caused Jervis to become more involved in his work in order to fill the empty hours.[42]

Jervis's need for his wife's companionship continued unabated, even during the hectic early years of the Croton project. He corresponded with Cynthia at least twice weekly, his letters revealing how lonesome he was for her, while hers showed love for Jervis and how she anxiously awaited their reunions.[43] It must have been with great anticipation that Jervis and his wife looked forward to the birth of their first child in the spring of 1839. On May 9, a daughter was born, who lived only a few hours. The rigors of childbirth were too much for Cynthia, who died five days after her daughter. Virtually nothing is known of Jervis's reaction to the death of his wife and child. He was alone again and sought solace in his work on the Croton and in the comfort of his religion.

Jervis, now in his mid-forties, apparently felt the need to marry again. The loneliness that Cynthia had so often written about was noticed by others. Uncle Bloomfield was among those who advised Jervis to look for another wife and, within less than a year of Cynthia's death, Jervis had done so. Bloomfield was delighted,[44] as were the members of Cynthia's family, who expressed their best wishes for his future happiness.[45] On June 16, 1840, Jervis and Eliza R. Coates were married.[46] Except for the fact that her health was better than Cynthia's, Eliza was similar to her predecessor. She was an obedient, devoted wife who much regretted the absence of her husband.[47] Eliza outlived her husband in a marriage that lasted nearly forty-five years, but was without issue.

Although Jervis's second marriage was a lasting one in which he found happiness, sorrow continued to stalk his life, especially during the years of the New York projects. His sister Maria died from complications of childbirth in 1828.[48] His sister Betsy suffered a mental breakdown and spent six months in a retreat for the insane in Hartford, Connecticut.[49] A few months before the death of his own wife and daughter, Jervis's brother Timothy lost an infant daughter.[50] Then in the 1840s, Jervis's father died, as did his beloved Uncle Bloomfield.

The letters from his family that informed Jervis of these several deaths almost always contained references to religion and the will of God. For example, Jervis's brother lamented that the death of his infant daughter had "blasted our fond hopes." However, Timothy was quick to add, " . . . may God in his infinite mercy sanctify this severe lesson to the advancement of our spiritual interests and his glory."[51] Jervis's father had written that Maria Jervis had "died in the triumph of faith. . . . perfectly resigned to God's will."[52] Obviously, religion was as much a part of their lives as it was a part of Jervis's own.

The introduction to FitzSimons's *Reminiscences* points out that religion was one of the two major subjects that dominated Jervis's life. The editor also notes Jervis's concern about the "apparent contradictions between science and religion."[53] It was only natural that a man with an inquiring mind searching for exact answers should question that which could not be proved by a formula or experiment. However, the forces exerted upon Jervis were too great for him to reject religion or relegate it to a Sunday-only position.

Jervis was, as has been stated, part of a family of religious people. Three of his relatives were ministers. However, it was more than simply the attitudes and occupations of his family that kept Jervis a believer. Religion was an important part of Jervis's life because it provided him with answers. The "will of God" was a solution for those events that seemed to defy rational explanation. Jervis sought and found solace in religion for the many sad events of his life. A writer sketching Jervis's appearance during the second half of his life could not have been more accurate when he described the engineer as "quiet and unassuming" and one who "might have been taken for some studious clergyman."[54]

The Last Eastern Engineering Projects

THE APOGEE of American nationalism that followed the War of 1812 and coincided with the building of the Erie Canal in the late teens and early twenties had turned in the opposite direction by the mid-1840s. A series of events in the previous decade laid a firm foundation for the sectional strife and the inter-party and intra-party warfare that shook the forties. These events also opened a chasm between North and South that finally produced in 1861 the ultimate sectional conflict, the Civil War.

Politically, New York suffered as much or more than the other northern states as a result of the events of the 1840s. Although he never wrote about it, possibly because of preoccupation with his beloved engineering, it may have been during the forties that Jervis's adherence to the Democratic Party began to falter.

New York's Democrats had struggled through the early forties. They were plagued by a Conservative versus Radical conflict as well as by the governorship of the popular Whig William Seward. In 1842, Conservative and Radical Democrats managed to embrace barely long enough to elect Conservative William Bouck to the governorship. Bouck was Jervis's friend from the Erie and Chenango canal days. But Bouck was limited to a single two-year term because the brief Conservative-Radical love affair quickly turned sour and the running sore of Anti-Rentism refused to heal.

The Anti-Rent conflict, an uprising of tenant farmers in eastern New York against their landlords, broke out during the administration of Bouck's predecessor, William Seward. This conflict bothered Bouck throughout his term and helped to destroy the administration of Bouck's successor, Democrat Silas Wright. However, Wright had his administration filled with other problems as well.

Silas Wright became governor of New York in the same 1844 election that put Democrat James K. Polk in the White House. Once in Washington, Polk named former New York governor and Regency man William Marcy to head the War Department. Unfortunately, Polk, apparently naive to the full extent of turmoil within New York's Democrat Party, tended to funnel the valuable patronage into the Empire State through Marcy instead of Governor Wright. Marcy and Wright were of different factions within the party. If this was not enough to widen the gap between New York's Democrats, other events were in the offing that would almost hopelessly divide the Democrats in New York for nearly twenty years.

Early in 1845, Congress passed the bill to add Texas to the United States. The annexation of Texas caused relations with the Republic of Mexico to become strained nearly to the breaking point. Although Texas had won its independence from Mexico in 1836 and had existed as a republic in the interim, Mexico never recognized Texan separation. Polk was a known expansionist, and throughout 1846 Congress discussed the possibility of war with Mexico.

One of the debates was over a bill to add to the strength of the United States Army. A Pennsylvania Democrat named David Wilmot attempted to add a provision to the bill that would have banned slavery from any territory taken by the force of the about-to-be-strengthened army. Although Southerners beat back the Wilmot Proviso, a segment of New York's Democrats thought it a good idea. When the expected war with Mexico broke out the following year, the American victory that resulted added about a third of Mexico to the United States. Debate raged over whether or not the new territory should be open to slavery, and in New York the Proviso Democrats gained strength and became known as Barnburners.

These Barnburners were willing to take a strong stand against the extension of slavery into the territory won by war. In doing so, they spoke out against the Democratic administration. As a result, they were called Barnburners by their Democratic opponents, who compared these free-soil Democrats to farmers who were willing to burn down their barns (destroy the Polk administration) to get rid of the rats (the extension of slavery). The Barnburners called their opponents in the Democrat Party Hunkers. In other words, they were Democrats who sacrificed principles to maintain their power and patronage. During the remainder of the forties, New York's Barnburner and Hunker Democrats continued to squabble, one result of which was domination of the governorship by the Whigs from 1846 to 1852.

Jervis remained reticent throughout the breakup of his party, at least in his correspondence. The same could be said of those who wrote to him. As usual, project talk was the order of the day. Even in 1848, when many New York Barnburners closed ranks with the new northern-based Free Soil Party, which was dedicated to preventing the spread of slavery, and even when that party nominated New York Barnburner Democrat Martin Van Buren, Jervis remained quiet. No record exists of whether his vote went to Van Buren or to the nominee of the regular Democrats, Lewis Cass. In any case, both Van Buren and Cass lost to Whig Zachary Taylor.

His party's bloodbath in the 1840s and the growing popularity of the movement to stop the spread of slavery must have been on Jervis's mind as he gazed on the waters of the North Atlantic during his voyage to England in 1850. The decade of the forties had ended. Soon Jervis would end his unswerving allegiance to the Democrat Party.

Jervis spent much of the 1840s in New York City, but occasionally he found time to return to his farm in Rome. If it could be said that he had a hobby, it was agriculture, although as much as he enjoyed his farm, he did not neglect his profession. In addition to completing the Croton, Jervis was involved, to varying degrees, in several other projects during the 1840s. These were either waterworks or railroads and tended to be anticlimactic compared to his earlier works.

In 1845, Jervis received at least four requests for his professional services. The first came from Halifax, Nova Scotia. The municipal authorities asked Jervis to recommend an engineer from the Croton project that they could invite to Halifax to study the feasibility of an urban water supply. Jervis replied that he would like an "excursion" to Halifax and therefore would come himself. He asked $250 plus expenses for his service, explaining that the fee was "not a larger charge than would probably be made by an engineer of much less experience," but it would be satisfactory since he desired to make "a tour of that kind" anyway.[1] Jervis left for Halifax on August 16, and he was back in Rome by the end of September. His activities in Halifax did not extend beyond advice on the possibilities for a water supply.

Soon after his return to Rome, Jervis received an invitation from the directors of the Erie Railroad to join a three-man commission whose task was to choose the best route for the Erie between the Shawangunk Mountains (Port Jervis) and Binghamton. Jervis must have felt in good company on the commission when he found that his friend Horatio Allen was also a member.[2] The Erie Railroad commission, like the Halifax job, was of short duration and did not interfere with either of the two more important appointments Jervis received in 1845.

The first, in Boston, was his first major project wholly outside New York State. Impressed and encouraged by the examples set by Philadelphia and New York, the city of Boston began moving rapidly in the direction of an urban water system. By 1845, the discussion on the water system had settled down to a debate between the merits of Spot Pond, north of Boston, and Long Pond (Lake Cochituate), west of Boston, as the best source for the city's water. The struggle between the opposing factions was kept alive by the results of a public referendum on May 19, 1845 in which Bostonians rejected a proposal that would have given a distinct advantage to Long Pond. At this point the Common Council's water commission decided to seek advice from the "highest authority" and appointed a study commission consisting of one person from New York and one from Philadelphia. Jervis was selected along with Professor Walter Johnson, a Philadelphia chemist.[3]

At first, Jervis was reluctant to serve on the commission. He had made a general examination and concluded that the project was essentially one of engineering. "Not having any previous acquaintance with my associate but the fact that he was not professionally an engineer," Jervis decided "not to enter upon the service unless the engineering was placed entirely in [his] hands."[4]

That Jervis should make such a decision was perfectly consistent with his character and regard for the engineering profession. Johnson was not an engineer, and Jervis felt strongly about the need for professional engineers to conduct the survey. To Jervis, any other method of approaching the task simply would not make sense. Also, his concern with his own reputation was such that nothing less than a reputable engineer would be suitable to Jervis as a co-author of the report.

Jervis was actually suggesting that he be the only member of the commission, but the Boston water committee "wanted the moral force of two commissioners."[5] A compromise acceptable to Jervis was reached when it was suggested that both Jervis and Johnson sign the report, but that Johnson's duties on the survey consist only of those that did not "conflict with the general engineering."[6]

When the survey got underway, it was not Jervis but Henry Tracy who did most of the field work. Tracy, one of the principal assistants on the Croton project, conducted studies of all possible sources under consideration for Boston's water supply.[7] Because there was much support for both Spot Pond and Long Pond, the chief water sources under consideration, Jervis was pestered by many—including the water committee—for some hint of his conclusions. However, not even Tracy was informed of Jervis's opinions. This was not because of lack of trust on Jervis's part, but it was so Tracy could honestly deny any knowledge of Jervis's plan.[8]

Apparently the committee grew impatient for an opinion. Having had no luck with Jervis or Tracy, they went to Johnson. In Jervis's words, " . . . my associate had been rather leaky but he was unable to quote me, and the committee appeared to think I should at least give them an intimation."[9] Much to the dissatisfaction of the water committee, Jervis refrained from giving them "an intimation" until the work was completed.[10]

On November 18, Jervis and Johnson submitted their anxiously awaited report to the water committee. Their findings showed that Spot Pond was insufficient for Boston's water needs, but that Long Pond would furnish the needed 10,000,000 gallons daily at an estimated cost of $2,651,643.[11]

All previous controversy over Jervis's obstinacy notwithstanding, Jervis's final comment on the report was simply that it "was generally satisfactory, and the work was authorized to be constructed."[12] The water committee was obviously more enthusiastic about the report. Its members were impressed enough to forget past differences and invite Jervis to become consulting engineer of the waterworks.

Jervis agreed to the offer and promised to visit Boston as often as necessary in return for a $3,000 annual salary.[13] Jervis remained in his post as consulting engineer until the end of 1848 when the works were completed and Cochituate water entered Boston. The Cochituate furnished "practically [Boston's] entire supply" until a conduit to the Sudbury River was completed in 1878.[14]

The Cochituate Aqueduct, although a prestigious assignment, was not as demanding of his time as Jervis's final New York project. In addition to completing the Croton Aqueduct, his most important work in the late 1840s involved supervising the construction of the Hudson River Railroad. The proposed rail line between New York City and Albany began to be a reality in 1845 when James Boorman, a wealthy New York businessman, succeeded in raising about half of the $6,000,000 needed to build the road. The remaining $3,000,000 was to be raised by a public stock issue. Jervis's association with the railroad came as a result of his position with the Croton Aqueduct. Among the original directors of the company were, in addition to Jervis, Saul Alley and Stephen Allen, the Democratic water commissioners who had been in charge of the building of the Croton.[15]

While associated with the Hudson River Railroad, Jervis's task was one not only of building but also of selling. The promoters of the railroad envisioned a route that would connect New York City and East Greenbush, a village on the east bank of the Hudson opposite Albany. Many potential investors felt that the proposed railroad could not succeed, since they feared that competition from the steamboat traffic on

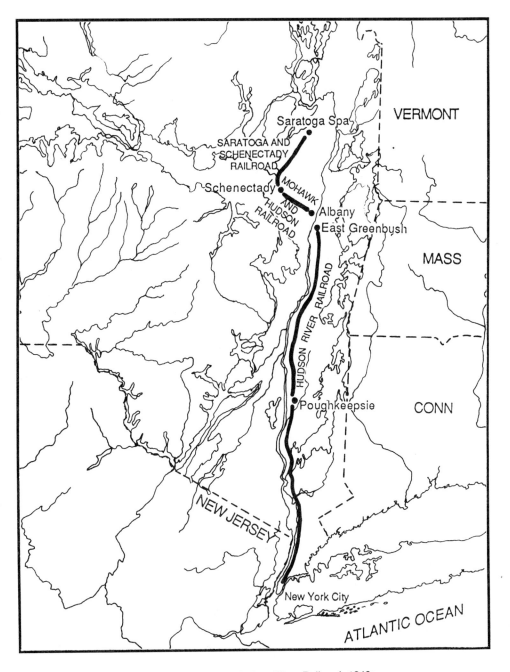

Fig. 8.1. Route of the Hudson River Railroad, 1840s.

the Hudson would render the railroad unprofitable. Also, the line would be generally parallel to the route of the New York and Harlem, a railroad already under construction several miles east of the proposed Hudson River Railroad.[16] When Boorman approached Jervis in the summer of 1845 with the proposal that he conduct a preliminary survey, the latter "had a favorable opinion of the enterprise, but well understood the difficulty in convincing capitalists that it would be a commercial success."[17]

Jervis began the feasibility study in the autumn following Boorman's visit. Again the reliable Henry Tracy was picked to do much of the field work. The report was prepared for presentation to a meeting that was held on January 23, 1846, at New York University and was presided over by New York City Mayor William F. Havemeyer.

Naturally, part of the document was devoted to technical data about the engineering aspects of the railroad. Jervis recommended double track from New York to Poughkeepsie, but a single-track from Poughkeepsie to East Greenbush.[18] The cost per mile of single track railroad was estimated at $11,200.[19] The $6,000,000 needed to build the railroad could be recovered in a relatively few years from the projected $485,000 annual net revenue.[20] Jervis supported his estimates with statistical quotations from the *Westminster Review, Hunt's Merchants Magazine,* and an army engineer's report on Hudson River travel.[21] The report concluded with a reaffirmation of the belief that a railroad could successfully compete with steamboats and would be a sound business venture.[22]

The summary of the Jervis report was, in a sense, a reaffirmation of what he had stated three weeks earlier in a newspaper article. In early January, Jervis had begun his campaign to convince New Yorkers that a Hudson River rail route could be a success. New Yorkers had little interest in railroads because they did not recognize their superiority to steamboats in passenger transportation. "However," Jervis advised, "the railroad will soon dispel the belief that the steamboat is alone in rapid transportation."[23] Jervis explained to his readers that trains travelled upwards of thirty miles per hour and that in England they regularly travelled forty to fifty miles per hour. While steamboats could make the passage to Albany in ten to eleven hours, trains could do the same in less than half the time. To Jervis it was a simple fact: "New Yorkers [had] not made a good railroad from their city to Albany because they [were] suffering under the delusion of steamboats."[24]

Although Jervis and the chief promoters of the railroad were convinced of the soundness of the venture, many potential investors remained skeptical. Their doubts were encouraged by those who openly opposed the project for business reasons. As early as 1842, a group of Poughkeepsie businessmen had attempted to get a charter for a railroad that would generally follow the Hudson shore. They were blocked in the Legislature by the steamboat interests. In 1846, it was not the steamboat supporters, but the backers of the New York and Harlem Railroad who led the fight against the proposed road. They were joined by many landowners along the river, who, in a burst of early environmentalism, argued that the railroad would destroy the natural beauty of the river bank.[25]

The New York and Harlem protested that it would be unfair for the Legislature to charter a second competing railroad since the lawmakers had recently chartered the Harlem Company. The promoters of the Hudson River line denied that they were attempting to destroy the Harlem road. They pointed out that each railroad had its own district and that the lines would be twenty to twenty-five miles apart from each other.[26]

One enthusiastic supporter of the Hudson road did consider the possibility of the Legislature allowing only one railroad between Albany and New York City. "If but one road is to be considered," he wrote, "it should be the river route."[27] This writer argued this on the basis of the convenience and ease of travel of the Hudson River Railroad route as compared with the line of the New York and Harlem. He also pointed to the character of the men involved in the Hudson River project. Before listing them, the writer asked, "Are there any black sheep amongst them? Are they not commercial men of standing, merchants of wealth and high respectability, and citizens and manufacturers whose interests you are bound to look to?"[28] The name J. B. Jervis headed one of the columns on the list.[29]

The supporters of the Hudson River Railroad were successful. They won their charter in May 1846. A capital stock of $3,000,000 was authorized. Within a month, an eighteen-page prospectus was published, half of which was the original Jervis report.[30] The document claimed the road would do a larger business than any on the continent with a return of not less than seven percent.[31] The advantages of the line listed in the prospectus notwithstanding, when the subscription books were opened in September, only a few persons other than the future directors purchased company stock.

Although the public response was disappointing, the railroad supporters remained undaunted. Several newspaper articles and pamphlets were added to those already published in support of the project. Jervis again lent his voice to the attempts to change the attitude of New Yorkers towards the railroad. The arguments he used in an article published in November were reminiscent of those used the previous January. Jervis continued to criticize New Yorkers for their lack of interest in railroads, and he appealed to their self-interest by asking, " . . . can New York afford to remain indifferent to the subject of railways" in the struggle among cities to reach the western trade?[32] Jervis accurately predicted that railroads would eventually be built from Cleveland into Indiana, Michigan, and Illinois. As the extension of the western roads occurred, " . . . it must be evident to all who watch the movements of the times, that without the aid of railroads, New York must lose in her relative superiority as the great centre of American commerce."[33]

Apparently, this kind of propaganda, as written and repeated by Jervis and other supporters of the Hudson River Railroad, was effective. On March 1, 1847, the subscription of the necessary $3,000,000 was completed. Four days later, the Hudson River Railroad Company was officially organized. Jervis, a member of the first board of directors, was appointed the chief engineer of the railroad.[34] The amended act of incorporation gave him until March 20, 1851, to complete construction of the line.[35] What seemed like ample time to build a 140-mile railroad turned out not to be, when apparently unforeseen problems, other than engineering problems, began to appear.

Prior to the start of construction, it was not only necessary to survey the line, but to acquire a right-of-way. Although many of the landowners were willing to sell, some were reluctant and slow to recognize the advantages. Jervis demonstrated his impatience with the property owners in a monthly report to the directors. He seemed at a loss to comprehend the reason for their unwillingness to sell when the potential for increase in property value should have been adequate inducement for a sale.[36]

To those landowners concerned about the scenic beauty of the river, Jervis explained that the "natural scenery would be improved; the shores washed by the river would be protected by walls of the railway; and the trees, no longer undermined and thrown down by the river would grow more beautiful; and that the railway thus combining works of art with those of nature would improve the scenery."[37]

The objections of the property owners notwithstanding, Jervis appears to have been correct in his assessment of the railroad's effect on the beauty of the river. A more recent comment on the success of Jervis's objectives suggested that with the possible exception of canals, railroads are "the least intrusive and most harmonious"[38] relative to nature of the various forms of transportation. Jervis's proposal was "nature methodized by means of the railroad." In other words, the railroad would "transform the wild natural growth" into a "more parklike setting."[39]

For proof of Jervis's accomplishment, a modern comparison can be made between "the discreet contour-hugging lines of the former Hudson River [Railroad] . . . with the squat Tappan Zee bridge of the New York Thruway." The bridge is "intrinsically offensive," appears to be "sinking into the water," and it "obstructs one of the great river vistas of the world."[40] Yet, at the time, the recalcitrance of the property owners so disturbed Jervis that he advised the directors that should the railroad not acquire the right-of-way, it might be necessary to abandon the enterprise.[41] Within a few weeks, however, enough easements had been purchased so that by the beginning of July, land maps were nearly complete for the first fifty-five miles of the line, although there continued to be difficulties with some landowners.[42]

As soon as most of the land for the line was secured, the directors let the first contracts. As far as the actual railroad was concerned, Jervis specified that the crossties be seasoned chestnut, 7 inches wide by 7 inches deep by 7½ feet long.[43] For the rails, Jervis wanted an inverted "T" that weighed seventy pounds to the yard. Although he was aware of the new "I"-shaped rail that had recently been developed in England, he rejected it because he felt the "I" rail less able to bear lateral strain.[44]

Actually, the road itself was the least of the problem. The roadbed was the major obstacle. Jervis later noted that the character of the roadbed route did not permit construction on the railroad to be started as promptly as on inland roads. Embankments had to be built across bays and along the shore of the river, and it was necessary to protect the earthworks from river erosion by a wall of stone fill. Until the protection wall was built to the high tide level, the work had to be regularly interrupted to wait for the ebb tide.[45] Further problems arose in this operation because it was necessary to transport the stone fill by boats, a method of transportation unfamiliar to most contractors and one resulting in "indecision and delay."[46]

While construction continued on the lower section of the line, the survey of the Fishkill to Albany segment was started. The work on the contracted section was largely under the direction of principal assistant Edmund French, a former assistant on the Croton Aqueduct.[47] The survey of the line north of Fishkill Landing was placed under the direction of John T. Clark, who was assisted by William Jervis. Clark had been with the engineering department on the Delaware and Hudson Canal, and William Jervis had previously worked on the Croton.

Clark surveyed both a route along the margin of the Hudson River and one that ran inland from the river.[48] Upon reviewing Clark's report on the two lines, Jervis indicated his preference for the water-level route since it would permit the entire railroad to be built without a noticeable grade, hence, making greater speed and economy in engine size possible.[49]

Jervis's decision, made public on January 12, 1848, caused "great local excitement . . . [and] was attacked with much severity by those who entertained different views as to the policy recommended."[50] Letters were sent to railroad directors by several area residents and stockholders in an attempt to cause the board to reject Jervis's route. Their reasons for favoring the inland route ranged from the old reliable river competition to community self-interest.[51] Jervis felt that the true explanation for the opposition to the water route was that some stockholders had land along the inland route.[52] In any case, the Board of Directors eventually accepted Jervis's recommendation and adopted the river route.[53]

The controversy over the route north of Fishkill was only one of the problems Jervis had to cope with during the winter of 1847–1848. In December 1847, the Board of Directors pushed up the date for completing the railroad to Fishkill from 1849 to fall 1848. The chief engineer warned that considerable extra expense would result from the need to employ more laborers to meet the new deadline. Jervis estimated 5,000 workers would be required,[54] or about 2,000 more than normally employed.[55]

While Jervis and the engineering department were struggling with the demands of the new completion schedule, the directors changed their decision and gave Jervis until spring 1849 to complete the section. However, as the time limit was extended, so was the northern objective. Poughkeepsie, twenty miles beyond Fishkill, was the new target. It was this New York City to Poughkeepsie section of the railroad, completed during Jervis's tenure as chief engineer, that was the most difficult to build.

Both the river and the land seemed to conspire against the easy completion of the line. The rock cutting in the Highlands was the most difficult Jervis had encountered on any project. Not more than one or two feet could be drilled per day. Of particular difficulty was the cutting of a tunnel 842 feet long at a place ironically known as Breakneck Hill. Several contractors were forced to relinquish the job before Jervis was able to find one who could complete the tunnel.

In keeping with his policy of damaging the countryside as little as possible, Jervis saw to it that the excavated material was used as fill. The movement of the earth and rock from the excavations to the artificial embankments "greatly increased the labor" but resulted in "very little borrowing of materials."[56] This produced the double benefit of "avoiding the necessity of mutilating the country . . . and the expense of double cutting."[57]

Added to the difficulty of excavation and earth-moving was the problem of keeping the workers on the project. Numerous strikes plagued the line during the 1848 work season. Jervis blamed them on the constant feuding among the Irish workers. Jervis had strong feelings towards Irish responsibility for the strikes. Although these workers did not start every strike, there is reason to believe that in this instance Jervis was largely correct.[58]

A final obstacle — an outbreak of cholera among the laborers — prevented the completion of the railroad to Poughkeepsie until December 1849. However, the first forty-two miles to Peekskill were in operation by the first of October.

In July, Jervis anticipated the event by cautioning the directors and the public that the road should not be judged immediately after its opening. If given a chance, the railroad "will exhibit its capacity to maintain a successful competition with steamboats in the transit of passengers."[59] Still the promoter, Jervis added that when the railroad was completed, " . . . the valley of the Hudson will then present the facilities its natural location and the state of science demand to meet the social and commercial wants of the extensive and rapidly increasing trade."[60]

Jervis seemed compelled to defend the railroad as a sound business venture. Perhaps his feeling was due in part to the necessity of raising the cost estimate for the completed work. In August, Jervis estimated that the amount needed to build to Albany would be $1,865,330 greater than his original estimate of $6,000,000.[61] The chief engineer defended the increase by claiming that it was "not more than might be expected in a work of this magnitude" and that it fell "far short of what had been experienced in similar works."[62] Perhaps Jervis, while trying to account for the excess cost, recalled the warnings of those who had campaigned against the water route as being too expensive. As it was, his calculation of 1849 was less than the final total expended by more than $2,000,000.[63]

On August 17, 1849, Jervis tendered his resignation as chief engineer. It was not the difficulty of the work nor the cost overrun but failing health that caused him to resign. The Board of Directors, " . . . having seen that the pressure of his arduous duties was undermining his health, were convinced that they could do not otherwise than meet his wishes."[64]

William C. Young, former chief engineer of the Utica and Schenectady Railroad, was named to succeed Jervis. The Hudson River Railroad Directors honored Jervis for his service by appointing him consulting engineer, a position he held until the following spring.[65] But perhaps a greater accolade was contained in Young's acceptance statement. He responded to the Directors:

> I have the more readily accepted the office, to which you have appointed me, under the arrangement you have made to continue the services of Mr. Jervis as Consulting Engineer. To him I owe a debt of gratitude for early professional patronage which years of personal and professional respect for him have not yet paid.
> I am, in a great measure, of his school of Engineers, and shall carry forward his great plans of this project, with a view to sustain his well earned reputation. . . . [66]

The Hudson River Railroad was completed under Young's direction on October 1, 1851. Six days later, Young succeeded James Boorman as president of this important line, which helped revitalize the nation's chief metropolis.[67]

Railroad historian William Stanton Root wrote just after the beginning of the twentieth century that the building of the Hudson River Railroad had an effect "upon the commercial and industrial prosperity of New York City" that "cannot be estimated." Root explained that the railroad contributed to the city's growth by opening up the residential areas of northern Manhattan and above to the main business district in the southern part of the island.[68] More recently, urban historian Edward K. Spann noted that the Hudson River Railroad's "all-weather route" to the Albany area enabled "New York to tap into a line of upstate railroads which ran west to Buffalo."

Within two years the railroads between Albany and Buffalo became the New York Central system. By pushing through a link to this system, New York City countered "the western designs of Boston" and made "itself the chief Atlantic terminus of the expanding national railroad network."[69] This expansion was particularly notable between Buffalo and the Mississippi River in the 1850s. This was all the more reason why the arrival of Jervis's Hudson River line at East Greenbush across from Albany in 1851 was a very timely one. It served to help strengthen the economic recovery New York City had been enjoying since the mid-1840s.

Upon his retirement from the Hudson River line, Jervis left for Europe and a much needed rest. However, he was too deeply involved in his profession to take a complete vacation from it. When an invitation from the renowned English engineer Robert Stephenson arrived, requesting Jervis's presence to observe the completion of the bridge across the Menai Straits between Anglesey Island and the Welsh mainland, the

American engineer readily accepted.[70] Jervis spent the remainder of the four-month tour inspecting engineering works in England and on the Continent.

Jervis's health was much improved by the trip. When he returned home, he was ready to plunge into work. Almost immediately Jervis began his next railroad project, which would take him into the Midwest during the pre–Civil War decade of rapid railroad expansion.

9

To the Mississippi and Beyond

JERVIS RETURNED from his European trip with his health much improved. The internationally famous fifty-five-year-old engineer was at the pinnacle of his career. The country he returned to in 1850 was embroiled in controversy stemming to no small extent from the recent acquisition of territory that fulfilled the push to the Pacific.

The settlement of the Oregon question in 1846 and the end of the war with Mexico in 1848 had resulted in the addition of land to the American republic, the vastness of which was only superficially understood. At practically the same moment that the peace commissioners were securing for the United States Mexico's sparsely populated northwestern province of California, gold was discovered. Suddenly, Americans east of the Mississippi River were seeking the fastest way to get to the Pacific coast. In little more than a year, California had sufficient population to ask for statehood.

Late in 1849, California asked to join the Union as a free state. The request triggered a new round of sectional controversy because the slave states wanted the southern portion of California open to slavery. This and other matters related to slavery continued to fuel debates in Congress. The legislative agreement that was reached, known as the Compromise of 1850, temporarily ensured a relative calm between the dissident sections of the United States. New economic energy resulted from the short-lived political tranquility.

One manifestation of this economic energy was vigorous railroad building, particularly west of the Appalachians. The 1850s, especially those years prior to 1857, witnessed the building of the most miles of track of the three decades of railroad construction prior to the Civil War. During the 1850s railroads reached the Mississippi, spanned the mighty river, then frantically attempted to bridge the distance to California by challenging the almost trackless Great American Desert. The outbreak of the Civil War in 1861 temporarily halted the banding of East to West with iron.

However, the war was more than a decade away in 1850 when Jervis headed into the Midwest to build railroads or, more accurately, to build and manage them. During the fifteen years that followed, Jervis made the career transition from builder, to builder-manager, to manager. It was a logical development for a man who had advocated multiple roles for engineers.

While working on the Hudson River Railroad, Jervis had suggested, partly because of failing health, that his duties be changed from those of civil engineer to those of general superintendent. The directors of that line chose not to accept the change. Jervis had to wait until he went west to try his hand at management.

Following the lead of their eastern predecessors, the states of the Ohio Valley and Great Lakes region launched ambitious transportation building programs in the 1830s. However, they lacked the population and capital of the eastern states, and many of their largely state-financed canals and railroads suffered considerably during the depression years of the late 1830s and early 1840s.

One such road was started by the state of Michigan at the Lake Erie port of Monroe. This road was supposed to run across the southern part of the state, perhaps to Lake Michigan. Construction began in 1837, but the road was only built as far as Hillsdale, a distance of some seventy miles. Beset by financial problems, the state finally sold the ailing line in 1846 to an investment group headed by Elisha Litchfield, a Detroit attorney. The price was $500,000, of which $450,000 was to be paid over nine years.[1]

The price of the rickety railroad was a questionable bargain since the road's strap iron and timber rails were falling apart and its small amount of rolling stock was in poor repair. Yet the stockholders were prepared for the challenge, as many of them were Litchfield's wealthy family and friends from New York State. A Litchfield in-law, Teunis Van Brunt, from Cazenovia in central New York, became the first president of the new Michigan Southern Railroad.

The directors had tough work ahead of them, beginning with repairing existing track. Under the terms of the charter, they also had to build another eighty miles west to Jackson within three years. By 1849, after virtually no westward progress had been made, the Michigan legislature extended the time for completion.[2]

It was the following year that Jervis entered Michigan Southern employ. Upon returning from Europe, he was brought into the troubled company as its chief engineer. Apparently his prime sponsor was his long-time friend from Rome, board member John Stryker, although the railroad's board of directors included other New York acquaintances of Jervis as well. Most notable among them was Albany Regency politician and former New York governor William L. Marcy.

Jervis began immediately by assessing the condition of the road in order to move rapidly towards its completion. In brief, Jervis reported that the condition of the completed road was so antiquated and in such poor repair that he recommended rebuilding it. To support an adequate volume of business, Jervis wanted new track put down for the existing sixty-eight miles between Monroe and Hillsdale by September 1851. The track was scheduled to be placed while several trains continued to use the line each day. Jervis felt it was important that there be minimal interruption of service in order to maintain the line's income.

In his report, Jervis also included special reference to the Erie and Kalamazoo, a thirty-three-mile railroad running between the Michigan Southern at Adrian, Michigan, and Toledo, Ohio.[3] This dilapidated connecting line had recently been leased in perpetuity by Michigan Southern president George Bliss in partnership with Jervis's banking friend, Washington Hunt.[4] Bliss had become Michigan Southern's president in 1849 following nearly fifteen years in railroad management.[5]

The farsighted acquisition by Bliss and Hunt of the Erie and Kalamazoo gave the Michigan Southern a link to the line being built along the south shore of Lake Erie. The connection provided a route to the major roads leading to New York City. The importance of this acquisition became greater once it was known that the Michigan Southern was headed for Chicago. However, the acquisition also meant that Toledo would supplant Monroe as the principal eastern terminus of the Michigan Southern.[6] Jervis's report emphasized that the rebuilding of the Erie and Kalamazoo was "equally important" as the attention given to the main line to Monroe.[7]

The remainder of Jervis's report on the Michigan Southern involved cost estimates for refurbishing the existing lines, constructing new track from Hillsdale west to the Indiana state line, purchasing rolling stock, and building stations. The chief engineer concluded that everything could be accomplished for $2,750,000.

Jervis felt the investment was sound since the route of the railroad passed through land "favorable for the production of wheat and corn." Even though, at that time, the area was only "partially cultivated," the farms were "sending off a large surplus of agricultural produce." Jervis predicted that the Michigan Southern would "command the entire freight and passenger business for a large extent of country" and it

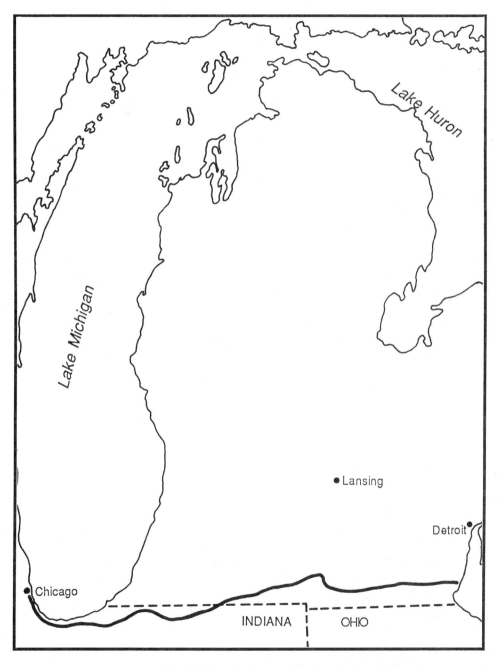

Fig. 9.1. Route of the Michigan Southern and Northern Indiana Railroad.

would "liberally pay on the investment of the capital required for its construction."[8]

The report that Jervis made on the current and future status of the Michigan Southern Railroad also included a section about a second railroad company. An offspring of the Michigan Southern, the new company was named after an earlier defunct company, the Northern Indiana Railroad. The new road was created as a logical extension of the Michigan Southern through Indiana to the Michigan railroad's goal of Chicago. George Bliss was president of both companies. Five of the New Yorkers, including Jervis, who were directors of the Michigan Southern were also among the directorate of the Northern Indiana, and Jervis served as chief engineer of the new Indiana railroad.[9]

Jervis laid out the route through Indiana, from the point where the proposed railroad entered from Michigan to the state line nearest Chicago. The distance was 100 miles, with another fourteen miles remaining from the Indiana line into the city itself. The route through Illinois called for the organization of yet one more company under the laws of that state. Jervis pointed that out to the Northern Indiana board. Then he called their attention to an infant enterprise in the western part of Indiana. A road modestly chartered as the Buffalo (N.Y.) and Mississippi Railroad Company controlled thirty-seven miles of convenient right-of-way in western Indiana approaching the Illinois line. A lease was arranged with Michigan Southern that allowed continual use of the Buffalo and Mississippi's roadway.[10]

Jervis's estimate for the cost of the Northern Indiana line, including equipment, was only $1,650,000. He seemed surprised at its relative paucity, but attributed the small figure to the level terrain and lack of any significant natural barriers. This sum, plus the total for the Michigan Southern line, amounted to less than $4,500,000 to build 252 miles of main line railroad together with 43 miles of branch line "all laid with iron rail of 58 lbs. to the yard."[11]

As was true when reporting on the Hudson River Railroad, Jervis presented population statistics for the region to substantiate his certainty for the success of the venture. He predicted that Chicago, "now containing a population of 28,000," would become one of the West's largest cities. It would be a railroad hub. Jervis was certain of Chicago's future, and he stressed that he should push through to the city by January 1, 1852.

The timetable Jervis set forth to the directors allowed him little more than thirteen months to complete the line. But he was so convinced of the economic success of the railroad as a link between Chicago and the major mid-Atlantic cities that he favored spending even more on construction of the line. He felt more money should be spent on the stations, engines, and railroad cars than approved by the directors. Jervis insisted that preparations be made for financing a second track to "accommodate the increasing traffic of the road."[12]

The directorate of the Michigan Southern and Northern Indiana Railroads reacted favorably to Jervis's report. They concurred with Jervis's urgency to reach Chicago by the beginning of 1852. Although the chief engineer's cost estimates differed from those of the directors', this did not prevent the directors from expressing confidence in Jervis. They supported his cost calculations as necessary to "cover the capital that will be wanted to put the whole road, from Lake Erie to Chicago, in complete operation."[13]

With this, the directors added, undoubtedly for the benefit of present and potential investors, that Jervis would give his complete attention to the construction of the entire line of both railroads. They emphasized that Jervis's "well known character and established reputation in connection with important existing public works" would serve as "an additional guarantee" of the Michigan Southern and Northern Indiana's "energetic prosecution, its steady progress, and its early and successful completion."[14]

Since Jervis was a member of both corporate boards and since he was the directors' choice for chief engineer, it was hardly noteworthy that they publicized support for his ability as an engineer. Also, the relatively level terrain of the Great Lakes plain and its environs posed none of the building challenges that Jervis had encountered during his most recent eastern work, the Hudson River Railroad. Jervis recognized this in his report. Nonetheless, he was a skilled engineer and proceeded with the road across southern Michigan and northern Indiana with the same vigor and perseverance that marked his eastern projects.

Perhaps the chief engineer compensated for the lack of impediments, which would have further honed his engineering skills, by attempting to break records for the speed of building track. He left no record of his intentions in this respect, but portions of the railroad line were pushed forward at a rate of nearly three-quarters of a mile per day.[15] Apparently, Jervis was intent on making good his claim that the road could enter Chicago by January 1, 1852. Yet a legal obstacle had to be surmounted before the fourteen miles from the Indiana line to Chicago could be finished: the builders had to acquire a right-of-way into the city.

The Michigan Southern was moving at a fever pitch towards Chicago and was being driven by the knowledge that a rival road, the Michigan Central, was hoping to reach that burgeoning boom town first. The

Central paralleled the line of the Southern, but ran across the middle portion of the state's lower peninsula. Two Central men, attorney James F. Joy and superintendent John W. Brooks, had attempted earlier to get into Chicago by way of the Northern Indiana Railroad. The Northern Indiana's first charter vaguely provided a way into the city, but when Joy and Brooks tried to convince the powerful Boston-based Forbes group, financial backers of the Michigan Central, to buy the Northern Indiana in 1848, they were unsuccessful. When Joy and Brooks insisted that the Northern Indiana's right-of-way could be used by the Michigan Central, they were ridiculed by the staid Bostonians. Joy and Brooks could not convince them of Chicago's future importance. The Michigan Central's inaction on the purchase of the early Northern Indiana charter left the way open for the Northern Indiana's eventual acquisition by the Michigan Southern.

However, the railroad charter that was ultimately purchased by the Michigan Southern did not specifically include passage through Illinois to Chicago. The Michigan Southern's board of directors was undaunted and sought an alternative route into the city. They soon found it by way of an infant line being pushed out of Chicago towards the Mississippi River. Chartered in February 1851 by the Illinois legislature as the Chicago and Rock Island, the railroad was projected to cross the mighty river into Iowa. The Rock Island's president, Judge James Grant of Davenport, Iowa, was anxious to see his line connect Iowa with Chicago.[16] Of course, the river would have to be bridged. At the time, no railroad bridges spanned the Mississippi. Construction of a bridge plus completion of the road into Iowa would consume more capital than the Rock Island had available. This provided an opening for the Michigan Southern and the active group of New York capitalists on its board.

The directors of the Michigan Southern promised eastern money to the Rock Island in return for permission to enter Chicago. A bargain was struck in the spring of 1851 that cleared the way for the Michigan Southern and Northern Indiana to reach Chicago.[17] It did so on May 21, 1852.[18] By then, the Rock Island's board of directors had been enlarged to include Michigan Southern board members. George Bliss, John Stryker, Elisha Litchfield, and Jervis joined the Rock Island's directorate. James Grant willingly stepped down from the road's presidency to make room for an experienced railroad builder John B. Jervis.[19]

Jervis's acceptance of the Rock Island presidency definitely marked his change in career emphasis. His responsibility was solely management, not management/engineering. As noted by Alfred D. Chandler, Jr., in *The Visible Hand,* Jervis was a management pioneer along with "George W. Whistler of the Western, Benjamin Latrobe of the Baltimore and Ohio, Daniel J. McCallum of the Erie, Herman Haupt and J. Edgar Thompson of the Pennsylvania, . . . and George B. McClellan of the Illinois Central [who] were all trained civil engineers . . . before they took over management" of railroads.[20] Chandler identified these men as "a new type of businessman" because they were "salaried employees with little or no financial interest in the companies they served." As such, they held positions "much closer to that of the modern manager than . . . the merchants and manufacturers who owned and operated business enterprises before the coming of railroads."[21]

Chandler felt that the managing of large railroads prompted operational innovation. "Unprecedented organizational efforts" were demanded since "no other business enterprise . . . had ever required the coordination and control of so many different types of units carrying out so great a variety of tasks that demanded such close scheduling." The variety of items carried plus the keeping of a number of different accounts added to the unique character of railroads as businesses and hastened the need for new management practices.[22]

Chandler referred to the influence of the military in providing a model for the creation of a management bureaucracy. He recognized the contribution of West Point in training civil engineers and noted that a number of the military academy graduates served in the Ordnance Department or the Corps of Engineers, "two of the very few professionally manned, hierarchical organizations in antebellum America."[23]

However, Chandler found evidence lacking to indicate that the managers of the first long distance railroads copied military organizational models. Chandler felt that the engineering training of the pioneer managers was more important than any military training they may have had. As engineers they were able to respond to complex operational problems "in much the same analytical way as they solved the mechanical problems of building a bridge or laying down a railroad." In support of this conclusion, Chandler pointed out that of the engineers on the cutting edge of the managerial revolution, only Whistler and McClellan "had any military experience, and they were the least innovative of the lot."[24]

Jervis could well have served as the pattern for Chandler's engineer-manager. He metamorphosed through several projects into the managerial role, as described. Jervis had no formal engineering education nor did he have military experience. In fact, as he expressed while building the Croton Aqueduct, he had little use for those who had been trained as engineers at the principal engineering school prior to the Civil War, West Point.

Many, if not all, of Jervis's projects prior to the western railroads were ones in which his role as chief engineer was confined to determining routes, structures, and kinds of rolling stock and coordinating the several contractors on the work. He did not become involved with operations after completion largely because of his movement from project to project, sometimes even before the completion of a particular job. Jervis might have become more involved with operations on the Croton Aqueduct after it was built into New York City, but the city water board hired another engineer to oversee the arrangements for the water to be piped from Jervis's distributing reservoir.

The Hudson River Railroad was another example of Jervis's not having the opportunity to manage what he had built, although there are indications that he desired to superintend the completed project. Jervis drove hard to open the railroad to Poughkeepsie, its original goal, from New York City. The overwork broke his health, forcing him to take his first genuine vacation since becoming a civil engineer. He travelled to Europe where, relieved of active involvement in engineering projects, his health rapidly improved. Upon his return from abroad in 1850, Jervis moved into positions that required combining engineering with managing.

Among the reasons that Jervis found managerial positions with the railroads of his post-1850 employment was the composition of the directorates. To no small extent, the board of directors of the Hudson River Railroad and those of Jervis's two earlier roads, the Mohawk and Hudson and the Saratoga and Schenectady, were composed of merchants, many of whom were ship owners. To them, railroads were simply another form of transportation, which they felt more competent to manage than a civil engineer. The boards of the western roads contained greater numbers of bankers, stock promoters, and railroad engineers than merchants. They felt differently 'about the engineer as manager. They were willing to accept this role as a logical outgrowth of civil engineering.

The engineer, while building the road, supervised the engineering and surveying parties and coordinated the efforts of the contractors. It stood to reason that the engineer should manage the completed road upon which the complexities of operation had increased considerably since the days of the small roads of the 1830s. The engineer-manager that Chandler and others described in their mid–twentieth century writings was evolving out of necessity in mid–nineteenth century railroad operations.

To Jervis, the engineer as manager was perfectly sensible and in keeping with his ideas about the total role of the engineer. In a book published ten years after he became president of the Rock Island, Jervis argued that engineers were most qualified to direct railway operations.[25]

In *Railway Property,* Jervis expressed the reasons he felt engineers should manage railroads, and he emphasized the need for training to better prepare them for their additional tasks.

Jervis practiced his beliefs by spending fifteen years in a supervisory capacity with railroads. He applied his rule that the "first business of operating a railway is to organize the conducting of traffic." This, wrote Jervis, "must be immediately followed by organization of a system of repairs and maintenance."[26]

While Jervis could handle this aspect of railway management, there is reason to believe he was not completely comfortable in his management positions. As president of the Rock Island line and, at various times, of the Michigan Southern and Northern Indiana, Jervis found himself involved in controversies that had little to do with traffic or repairs. In fact, these controversies were of the nature that Jervis warned against in advising engineers not to become "subservient to private interest or personal ambition."[27]

Jervis was no stranger to controversy, nor did he avoid the opportunity to engage in discussions involving engineering or, more particularly, his reputation and ability as an engineer. Yet, he was never at ease among the promoters and manipulators who had emerged in railroading by the 1850s and who recognized the financial rewards that could come just from the sale of stock. To Jervis, the successful completion and operation of a railroad was the primary goal of the company, its officers, its superintendents, and its engineers.

As early as his association with the Mohawk and Hudson, Jervis advocated constructing a railroad for durability and with future traffic increases in mind. Because of his foresightedness and his unwillingness to compromise solid building standards, Jervis was sometimes at odds with officers and directors who were unwilling to appreciate his thoroughness. Those who opposed him frequently did so on the basis of increased cost as a factor in reducing return on their investment. While this was not, in itself, objectionable, by the 1850s it had become apparent that railroads were often being used simply as a vehicle for personal gain on the part of some promoters. The Michigan Southern and Northern Indiana eventually fell among those so manipulated.

In the summer of 1852, President Bliss resigned and the Michigan Southern board of directors prevailed upon Jervis to succeed him. So began the tug-of-war between Jervis, who wanted to properly maintain the road as a profitable rail line, and a clique of directors, who were mainly interested in pushing up the value of the railroad's securities. Apparently Jervis retained the support of the majority of the directors insofar as his management policies were concerned, throughout the remainder of 1852.²⁸ However, Jervis soon discovered that there were officers and board members who did not share his ideas or ideals. The slender, balding builder who was always so devoted to engineering professionalism soon found himself in a situation unfamiliar to his high standards and moral values. While the first several months of his presidency were occupied almost solely with construction details (he also continued as chief engineer), Jervis eventually discovered that it was as necessary to read the railroad's financial statements as it was to be familiar with the reports of his subordinate engineers. In this regard, Jervis exhibited unusual naivete and a temporary hiatus of good sense.

During the year prior to his assuming the presidency of the railroad, Jervis jubilantly demonstrated talent as an engineer by pushing the railhead forward at almost unheard of speed. In one incredible flourish of building energy, thirty miles of track were put down in a mere forty-two days.²⁹ Although he could take pleasure in setting records, Jervis admitted he found little to interest him in crossing the relatively flat topography of the West. What little he said about midwestern railroads, other than the cryptic dryness of official reports, indicated that he missed the challenges to his building skills and the opportunities to innovate that he had experienced in New York and elsewhere in the East. For all his urgings and advice about the engineer as manager, Jervis discovered that, in practice, the role was much different than he had imagined.

Between the spring of 1852 and the spring of 1858, Jervis spent roughly three years as Michigan Southern and Northern Indiana president. Actually, most of his tenure in office was prior to April 1855, during which time Edwin C. Litchfield was corporate treasurer. Edwin C. was a brother of Elisha C., a member of the original New York directorate. During the period of Jervis's leadership, Edwin Litchfield emerged as spokesman for the anti-Jervis faction. This was the group of directors and stockholders who opposed Jervis's financially conservative policies. The final showdown between the two sides occurred after Jervis left the presidency for the last time in April 1858. The showdown was prompted by the disastrous impact that the Panic of 1857 had upon the Michigan Southern.

When Jervis had first assumed office in June 1852, the Michigan Southern had achieved its western goal of reaching Chicago. However, there was still sufficient work to be done along the entire main line and its branches to keep Jervis occupied in his capacity as chief engineer. This is why he spent his time reading engineering reports, not financial statements. Later he discovered that, as president, the road's balance sheets should have been scrutinized with greater diligence.

During the early years of Jervis's leadership, the Michigan Southern moved rapidly to consolidate its position of preeminence as a connecting link between Lake Erie and Chicago. Several smaller lines were brought under its influence. A fleet of steamboats was put in operation on Lake Erie to ensure domination of the passenger business from Buffalo.

It was true that the Michigan Southern would connect with the railroads being built between Buffalo and Toledo. However, Michigan Southern's arch-rival, the Michigan Central, was planning its own connection to New York's western metropolis. The Michigan Central, financed in part by the consortium that arranged for the creation of the New York Central Railroad, was acquiring a Canadian road across the Upper Canada (Ontario) peninsula to Detroit. Although in the end, the Canadian route did not prevail when the great trunk line between New York City and Chicago became a reality, it was a threat to the Michigan Southern in the 1850s.

As a company organized to carry passengers and freight, the Michigan Southern prospered during Jervis's presidency. However, a faction of the directors already favored more rapid acquisition of subsidiary holdings. Jervis, still simultaneously president of the Rock Island, began to feel that his policies of fiscal constraint no longer had majority support on the board. In a real sense, Jervis's sound management became a victim of its own success, especially in those heady days of pell-mell expansion in the mid-fifties. Jervis announced his intention to not seek reelection as company president, and in April 1855, he was succeeded by John Wilkinson.

Although there were those among the directors who wanted Jervis out of the Michigan Southern presidency, there remains little evidence of dissatisfaction with his management. Jervis tried to follow sound business principles as he envisioned them and was acclaimed by the directors for doing so.[30] Why should they not express "high regard" for Jervis's presidency? He put the company in an excellent financial position. In fact, its resources made possible the ill-advised spending that followed between 1855 and 1857.

A few months after he left the Michigan Southern presidency, Jervis was notified of an opportunity that could have resulted in abbreviating his career in railway management. In early September, he received word that the New York State Democratic convention had nominated him for the post of state engineer and surveyor.[31] Although he did not specifically say so, Jervis must have been delighted with the honor since he quickly accepted.[32]

Normally, the office of state engineer and surveyor would not generate much controversy in an election, but the enlargement of the Erie Canal, which had began in 1837, was still under construction. Although the Erie had proved a tremendous financial success, there were those, particularly among the Democrats, who were against the use of public money to widen and deepen it. That should be paid for by those who used the canal, they said. Democrats had succeeded in temporarily halting construction on the enlargement in the early 1840s; since that time the project had been a political football. In general, the Whigs supported continuation of the enlargement at public expense and the Democrats opposed it.

Had it been that simple an issue, Jervis probably would have won the election. Although a Democrat, he very likely would have attracted enough Whig votes to ensure victory. Jervis was more widely known than the Whig candidate, John Clark, and Whig voters could be confident of Jervis's commitment to complete the canal at state expense.[33] However, the election was complicated by divisions within the Democratic Party itself. The old Hunker-Barnburner schism was resurrected under different names.

This time it was an extreme group of Hunkers who felt ignored by the incumbent Pierce administration and refused to join with former Barnburners against the Whigs. Because of their stubbornness, they were called "Hardshell" Democrats or "Hards." The majority of Democrats backed Horatio Seymour, the New York governor then in office. They were known as "Softshell" Democrats or simply "Softs."[34] In 1855, Jervis, who was known to be a "Soft," was not supported by the "Hards," who threw their backing to Clark. Jervis's defeat in the fall 1855 elections ended his single attempt at seeking public office. It also marked the end of his long affiliation with the Democratic Party.

As noted earlier, Jervis refused to leave the party of Jackson and Van Buren even during the party's dark days of the late 1830s. Although his uncle favored the Whigs in 1840 and banker Washington Hunt and others of Jervis's business associates were Whigs, Jervis stuck with the Democrats. The Whigs were modernists who favored the kind of economic development that appealed to Jervis, yet they were unable to lure him into their party.[35] Prior to the mid-1850s, Jervis could have served as proof of the statement made by a historian of the period that in New York "to abandon one's party for a new political movement was an extraordinary, almost abnormal act from which most New Yorkers shrank."[36] In fact, Jervis simply had not found the cause that would move him to change parties.

Actually Jervis's apostasy from the Democratic Party had its origins at least twenty years before his leaving. In the 1830s, Jervis had fallen under the spell of the greatest revivalist of his time, Charles Grandison Finney. A Presbyterian like Jervis, Finney began his spellbinding oratory in 1825 in the town of Western, a few miles north of Rome. Western, incidentally, was the home of many of Jervis's in-laws, and his first wife, Cynthia, was a native of the town. In 1836 Jervis, captivated by Finney, wrote ecstatically to brother-in-law Henry Brayton that he had witnessed "the Rev. Mr. Finney" speak to an "overflowing church." Jervis was particularly attracted to what Charles Finney had to say about the evils of slavery.[37]

Sooner or later Jervis, with his love for individual enterprise and the dignity of labor, had to speak out against slavery. But Jervis, never a radical, would not go along with the abolitionists who were widely considered rabble-rousers in the 1830s and little better than that in the 1840s. It took Jervis nearly twenty years to reach the point of making a public statement on slavery, and then it was from a free-soiler's point of view, not an abolitionist's.

What Jervis said was first published under the pen name Hampden in a letter to the New York *Evening Post* in September 1855. When his first letter and two others written in September 1856 were printed in pamphlet form, it was explained in an introduction that the name Hampden was used because it was an election year. As a candidate of the Democratic Party, "he was unwilling to take any step which might appear disloyal" to that party. Yet the letter Jervis wrote while a Democratic candidate in 1855 clearly shows his disillusionment with the national Democratic Party, which he refers to as the "slave-holder's party." He lamented that many Democrats were slow to believe that their party could be used to subvert the principles the party name implies. Jervis warned that it was not the freedom of the "African race" that was at stake, but it was the "freedom of the whites that will be further encroached upon, if the slaveholder's party continue to hold the power of the government as they now do."[38]

Although Jervis did not mention the new Republican Party in his first letter, the fact that he defended sectional parties demonstrated his sentiment. In 1854 Congress passed the Kansas-Nebraska Act, which removed the final barriers against the expansion of slavery into the trans-Mississippi territories. One immediate result of the act was the formation of the Republican Party. It was a northern party and a free-soil party. As such, it drew Free Soil Party members and Barnburner Democrats into its ranks.

By fall 1856, Jervis openly called for support for Republicans in the upcoming presidential race. He blamed the Buchanan Democrats for supporting an undemocratic and unpopular government in "Bleeding" Kansas, where a prelude to the Civil War was taking place. Jervis dismissed the American or "Know Nothing" Party that nominated former president Millard Fillmore as not worthwhile to follow since it was "merely an ingenious device of the slave democracy to divide the free states."[39] Then Jervis defined and defended what he called the Democratic-Republican Party.

Jervis's "Democratic Republicans" favored democratic government, honored labor and the rights of man, and had no intention of interfering with any state in the exercise of its constitutional rights.[40] Thus Jervis in his September statement echoed the platform of the new Republican Party. For that matter, the Republican platform mirrored that of the Free Soil Party eight years earlier.

Although Jervis's call for support for the Republicans in 1856 was very typical of the stand taken by many Barnburner or Softshell Democrats, it served to confirm his change of parties. Not surprisingly, it took a moral issue, that of extending slavery beyond the states in which it existed, to do what other issues and arguments had been unable to accomplish. Jervis remained a Republican for the rest of his life.

John Wilkinson, Jervis's successor as Michigan Southern president, retained office until April 1857, when he was replaced by Edwin C. Litchfield. Although Wilkinson was not a member of the Litchfield group, he did allow the railroad to follow a course of expansion and acquisition that ultimately proved disastrous. The Michigan Southern committed itself to aid the new Detroit, Monroe, and Toledo Railroad, which it then leased in perpetuity. It made a large loan of rails to the Cleveland and Toledo, its connection to the east, but the benefactor railroad was never repaid. It guaranteed payment, including interest, on $200,000 of Cincinnati, Peru, and Chicago bonds. The Michigan Southern also purchased more than $900,000 in stocks, bonds, and notes in at least five other midwestern railroad companies.[41]

Although Litchfield succeeded Wilkinson as president, he claimed he did not do so directly from the office of treasurer; therefore, he could not be held responsible for the railroad's spending spree. In fact, between 1855 and 1857, Litchfield was in Europe, ostensibly to sell railroad securities. Although he resigned the treasurer's office before he left, the board of the Michigan Southern did not accept his resignation, and he was still regarded as treasurer when he came back to the United States. Shortly after returning, Litchfield assumed the presidency. This was preceded by his declarations of dissatisfaction with "conditions" regarding the railroad's financial affairs and his blaming them on his two predecessors.[42] Possibly, Litchfield was attempting to justify the upcoming statement that although the railroad's assets were nearly $2,300,000 with a debt of under $200,000, $1,500,000 of new stock was being requested.[43]

Unfortunately for the success of Litchfield's administration, the call for new securities came when the nation was falling into economic hard times. The calling of the railroad's debts revealed its inability to pay. Rising stockholder ire resulted in the resignation of the board and President Litchfield in August. Among those most irate was Jervis, who agreed to membership in the new board along with Bliss; Hiram Sibley, the telegraph mogul; and Schuyler Colfax, a future vice-president under Ulysses S. Grant. With the Litchfield crowd powerless and in disgrace, Jervis was asked in early October to resume the presidency.[44]

The task facing Jervis's second administration was formidable if not hopeless. In the words of Washington Hunt, the "Michigan Southern now appears like a vast wreck. Its endless expenditures and reckless mode of financing would destroy the best concern in the world."[45] Interest on the company's bonds had not been paid for some time, but neither had employees' wages. After six months of attempting to resurrect the failing railroad, Jervis gave up. Even his management skills could not prevail.

Jervis's failure to financially rebuild the Michigan Southern at a time when the effects of the Panic of 1857 were still being felt paved the way for the possible return of the Litchfield interests. In an effort to prevent what he and his supporters regarded as a totally undesirable alternative, Jervis spearheaded a campaign to prevent the revival of Litchfield domination. Still a board member, Jervis attempted to garner enough stockholder proxies to halt Litchfield. He publicly explained his actions in the New York *Evening Post* when he claimed that he and his supporters were acting to warn the stockholders. While he recognized that it was the right of the stockholders to exercise their choice, Jervis added that it was also his prerogative "to keep myself out of a Board not constituted to act harmoniously for the efficient and faithful promotion of the interest of the Company."[46]

Jervis's opening attack brought a rapid reply from Litchfield. He faulted Jervis for publicly besmirching his name in "an undignified and personal attack upon myself and my friends."[47] Litchfield indignantly asserted that "the sole reason assigned by these gentlemen" (Jervis, Robert M. Olyphant, and Joseph K. Riggs) in attempting to get proxy support "is their fear that the parties spoken of by Mr. Jervis as the Litchfield influences are making an effort to reinstate their former control." With this, Litchfield emphatically denied that he, his family, "or personal friends" had any interest in a company office.[48]

Litchfield then began his own offensive by citing Jervis as responsible for the ill-advised purchases and expenditures that brought down the company by 1857. He included references to the steamboats and charged that Jervis voted in favor of their purchase. In support of his "evidence" of Jervis's mismanagement, Litchfield included earnings figures on the boats from the 1857 directors' report. But this was more than two years after Jervis left the presidency of the Michigan Southern. Statements for 1855 would have been more convincing. In any case, the newspaper battle continued.[49]

Jervis, no stranger to editorial wars, fired back with his rebuttal ten days later. Writing from Toledo, he systematically reacted to each of Litchfield's allegations. In brief, Jervis's lengthy reply was an assertion that he managed the railroad properly, and that what he spent was for improvements to the Michigan Southern and Northern Indiana. Jervis noted that when he ended his first term as president, "the total liabilities of the company . . . were about eleven millions [of dollars]." By the time he returned to office in October 1857, the corporate debt stood at $18,000,000 "though not over two and a half million was expended in construction during that time."[50] Jervis wondered how Litchfield, although in Europe during the period when liabilities rose more than sixty percent, could claim ignorance of the situation, especially since the treasury had reverted "to the care of a committee composed essentially of Mr. Elisha [Litchfield] and company."[51]

Of the Jervis–Edwin Litchfield public correspondence in 1858, Jervis's letters were more methodically organized and contained more supporting data than did Litchfield's. There is little question that the railroad's financial distress in 1857 and after would seem to support Jervis's assertion of poor management and improper practices. Jervis quite naturally did not include himself as culpable for the railroad's problems. The company's annual reports support his contentions,[52] as do the number of proxies entrusted to him by stockholders in 1858.[53] Curiously, the Litchfields also marshalled much support in 1858, even though Edwin Litchfield had been chased from office in August of the preceding year.

In the end, George Bliss resumed the presidency of a beleaguered and reorganized Lake Shore and Michigan Southern Railroad,[54] which represented a victory for the Jervis faction. At least in 1858, the majority of voting shareholders preferred Jervis's more conservative management practices to those of his opponents.

Jervis's managerial role in the Michigan Southern was far more interesting and exciting than his engineering duties. However, if any impressions can be gained about Jervis as a manager from his Michigan Southern experience, they are that as much as he found little to stimulate his interest in the railroad's relatively mundane engineering tasks, he discovered that management was far more complicated than he may have envisioned.

In *Railroad Leaders,* Thomas C. Cochran concludes that the early railroad managers were "practical men" who felt that problems they encountered in running a railroad could be "solved by experience rather than by reading or theory."[55] This idea was part of Cochran's summary of his discussions of the foundations of railroad management. It should be understood that he preceded the above conclusion with an explanation of the problems that led to formal corporate administrative practice. Jervis's experience supports Cochran's findings on the locus of power in the ante-bellum railroad corporations. That is, the directors held the top position in the line of authority because they were the direct representatives of the stockholders.[56]

Jervis felt overly constrained and frustrated by this. He complained that "there was so much interference from the directors that I found my duty very unsatisfactory." He realized he was not at liberty to solve problems and make decisions according to his reason and experience. However, he noted "in the duties of engineering" he had "mostly" his own way.[57] Perhaps this was why Jervis felt more comfortable as a chief engineer or perhaps even as a general superintendent—his position on the Pittsburgh, Fort Wayne, and Chicago—than as a president. It was not that he could not handle controversy, but that many railroad directors by the 1850s were men whose ideas on management and on morality, in relation to their delegated trust, were in sharp conflict with those of the sixty-year-old professional engineer.

One reason for Jervis's dissatisfaction with the Michigan Southern presidency might have been his having occupied several positions simultaneously. There is no question that his serving as president of two railroad companies and chief engineer of one, all at the same time, placed severe demands on his time and ability. The increasing complexity of a railroad president's job probably was more perplexing to Jervis than he was willing to admit. He was a perfectionist in thought as well as deed. As he strongly felt engineers to be the best and most logical railroad managers, it is no wonder that he never admitted to inability to cope with administrative positions. Yet, as the complexity of railroad operations increased, so did the work load of their chief executives. Had Jervis been a decade or so younger and less optimistic in terms of his imagined energy and work capacity, he might have been equal to the demands of the several jobs.

If the Michigan Southern and Northern Indiana presidency was somewhat perplexing and uncomfortable to Jervis, the Rock Island position was less so. One advantage was that he did not also serve as chief engineer. That position went to his younger brother William. Another point in favor of ease of management, although this turned out to be more trouble than it should have been, was the fact that the railroad had only one contractor charged with construction. Henry Farnam, in partnership with Joseph Sheffield, was the prime contractor for the Rock Island.

Jervis had come into contact with Farnam, the senior partner of Farnam and Sheffield, when the firm contracted to build the Michigan Southern from Hillsdale, Michigan, to Chicago. Farnam was a likeness of Jervis in that he began his career on the Erie Canal in 1821. Starting as a cook in an engineering party, he graduated as a civil engineer from the same "school" that produced Jervis. Prior to his arrival in Michigan and Illinois, Farnam had been chief engineer of the New Haven and Northampton Railroad. As a testimony to his industriousness, integrity, and engineering ability, the stockholders of that railroad passed a resolution in 1850 in which they extended to him the "highest consideration."[58]

Although Farnam refused Jervis's offer to make him superintendent of the Michigan Southern, he and his partner did agree to build the Chicago and Rock Island. As a builder, Farnam was indeed acceptable to Jervis. He built the road to the Mississippi at Rock Island by January 1854. Farnam then organized the Mississippi Bridge Company and, after completing the structure, became the first to push rails across the great river. The bridge was put into use on April 22, 1856,[59] and provided a connection with the sixty-odd miles of railway that Farnam had constructed in Iowa under the auspices of a corporation called the Mississippi and Missouri Railroad. It became the Rock Island's trans-Mississippi link.

Farnam's drive and ambition brought him into confrontation with the Rock Island's chief engineer, William Jervis. Of course, Rock Island president John B. Jervis was drawn into the dispute, and in the interest of road progress it was necessary for him to mend the rift between Farnam and William Jervis. Again, Jervis found that managing a railroad could be more stressful than building one.

As has been stated previously, the Chicago and Rock Island was charted in 1851 with James Grant as president. However, its acquisition later that year by investors from the Michigan Southern resulted in Grant's replacement by Jervis. Grant, however, agreed to stay on as vice president. Within a year of Jervis's taking the company reigns, the Rock Island had been built to Joliet, some 40 miles west of Chicago.[60]

About two months later, in response to a concerned Grant, Jervis optimistically predicted that the Rock Island Railroad would be *"the*

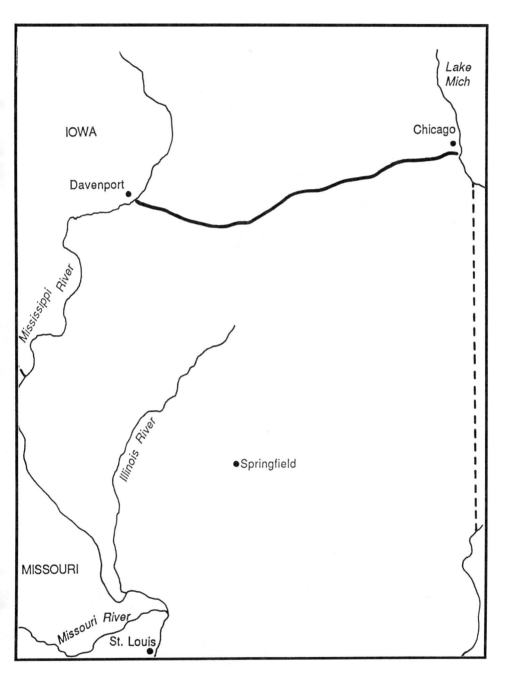

Fig. 9.2. Route of the Chicago and Rock Island Railroad.

line" west of Chicago. He pointed out to the worried Iowan that the Rock Island "has the geographical position and the connections that cannot be materially affected by any other" and added that the line should cross the Mississippi and "go directly on to Council Bluffs [Iowa]."[61] The president's predictions were supported even before the end of that year. Chief Engineer William Jervis reported on December 15 that the road had been completed to Geneseo, Illinois, 158 miles west of Chicago. Even though the track was still twenty-three miles short of the Mississippi at Rock Island, "traffic on the road [was] so large that it has been difficult to provide machinery fast enough to do the business."[62] The railroad reached its river goal by July, 1854.[63]

Although the laying of Rock Island track progressed as scheduled and without mentionable problems, relations between the railroad's chief engineer and its leading contractor were less than smooth. Jervis became aware of his brother's dissatisfaction while on a trip to New York City. William wrote to him routinely informing the railroad president of progress made on the line. William then requested his brother to formally define the duties and authority of the chief engineer. William did so because of a developing struggle with Farnam over supervision of the engineering department. According to William, "Farnam tries too much to influence the engineers because Farnam is a stockholder."[64]

Whether or not Jervis replied to William's concern is unknown. However, apparently the situation did not improve since William again corresponded with his brother about the matter on February 14. It was obvious by then that William attributed additional motivation to Farnam's interest in extending his influence over the engineers. William charged that Farnam's interference prevented the engineers from acting "according to their own judgments." William believed that Farnam was using his position as a stockholder and principal contractor to intimidate the engineers and cause them to "quarrel" with the chief engineer because it was in Farnam's interest.[65]

Additional indication of Farnam's "interest" and motivation behind the dispute with Jervis can be found in an undated letter from Farnam to his partner, Joseph Sheffield. Farnam alerted his partner that the "Chief Engineer is working more industriously than Hubbard [the previous chief engineer] did to find out our profits."[66]

Exactly what Farnam meant by his cautioning message to Sheffield remains a mystery. Apparently, though, Farnam had had some trouble with Hubbard over cost estimates and the supervision of resident engineers.[67] In any case, Sheffield was anxious for President Jervis to intervene. He reminded Jervis that it was his "duty to put a stop to the bad spirit between the two men." Sheffield felt that Farnam was entitled to different treatment from the "average contractor of a mile or two."[68] According to Sheffield, Farnam complained that William Jervis deliberately avoided him, making it difficult for the contractor to complete the railroad. Farnam felt that this was a power play on the part of the chief engineer.[69]

John B. Jervis's reply to Sheffield was brief and vague. He told Sheffield that by the time Sheffield arrived in New York City (from New Haven), Jervis "might" have more information about the dispute.[70] However, with this short message of February 21, the affair, as far as remaining evidence indicates, came to a close.

The real reasons for the Farnam–William Jervis argument remain obscure, as does Jervis's adjudication of the affair. The one assumption that can reasonably be made is that the event must have proved painful to Jervis. As president of the railroad, he was placed in the position of having to decide between the road's chief engineer and its chief contractor. Jervis was as attached to members of his own family as he was protective of them. However, he also felt strongly about the need to maintain the impartiality that his position demanded. Perhaps most important in tempering his actions or lack of same was his ever-present regard for the welfare of the company. Jervis always thought of his various positions as a trust and, above all, he believed that the interests of the project or concern must take precedence over personal feelings. If nothing else, the Farnam-Jervis controversy served as further evidence of the difficult decisions that burdened Jervis as a railroad administrator.

Soon after the road was completed to Rock Island, Jervis resigned as president. He was succeeded by contractor Farnam. Farnam was already president of the Mississippi Bridge Company and of the Missouri and Mississippi Railroad, which was being built across Iowa and eventually became part of the Rock Island. Jervis continued to serve the Rock Island and its associated companies as a consultant.

Jervis's first major assignment was in relation to a case involving the railroad bridge across the Mississippi River. Two weeks after the bridge was opened, the steamboat *Effie Afton* crashed into the bridge and partially destroyed the structure. The owners of the steamboat sued the bridge company. The boat owners claimed the bridge was a hazardous and unnatural obstruction of river traffic. The bridge company hired Abraham Lincoln as its lawyer and retained Jervis as its engineering expert.

Jervis examined the bridge on September 26, 1856, approximately five months after the incident occurred. By then, the bridge had been repaired and reopened. Jervis called the bridge a "substantial and beautiful" structure and deemed it stable even under a thirty-car train pulled by a twenty-five-ton locomotive. After measuring the east and west draws, Jervis determined them to be of sufficient width to allow free passage of the "class of vessels that usually navigate the river at this location."[71]

Jervis concluded his report with a lengthy statement supporting the logic that increased railroad construction would increase the number of bridges across many western rivers. Eventually, railroad traffic would increase much beyond the river trade. Jervis provided statistics for four months of river and railroad traffic at Rock Island to prove his point. To the experienced engineer-manager, the "practicability of the bridge and its great economy and convenience to the public interests can no longer be questioned."[72]

Attorney Lincoln undoubtedly found the report of the respected engineer valuable as he successfully defended the Mississippi River Bridge Company against the owners of the *Effie Afton*. The outcome of the case cleared the way for future railroad bridges across the Mississippi and other western rivers.

After resigning from the Chicago and Rock Island presidency, Jervis briefly returned to the leadership position of the Michigan Southern and Northern Indiana from October 1857 to March 1858. When the sixty-three-year-old Jervis left the Michigan Southern, he went to his home in Rome for a long overdue rest. However, still driven by a desire to see others benefit from his experience and to help engineering develop into a recognized profession, he soon produced his pioneer study *Railway Property*. The book was published in 1861, the year that Jervis's "retirement" ended. That year, he was called back into railroading.

When Jervis went west in 1850 to build railroads that would eventually become part of Commodore Vanderbilt's great rail system from New York City, other lines were being built to connect the Pennsylvania Railroad at Pittsburgh with Chicago. A company was chartered to build across Ohio, another was organized to connect the first with Fort Wayne, Indiana, and a third was created to extend from Fort Wayne to Chicago. Soon, the three roads were brought under a single board of directors as the Pittsburgh, Fort Wayne, and Chicago.

Although completed through to Chicago, the new railroad was not a success. Plagued by mismanagement, lack of capital, and finally lack of business due to the hard times of the late 1850s, the road went into receivership. Instead of disposing of the forlorn line with its worn rails and rolling stock in disrepair, the receivers reorganized the railroad in late 1861. The new directorate was composed of bankers and lawyers from New York City, including future New York governor and presidential candidate Samuel J. Tilden. Because the outbreak of the Civil War in April 1861 was beginning to stimulate Northern agriculture and business, the new board undoubtedly felt that a rejuvenated Pittsburgh, Fort Wayne, and Chicago could be a success. To help ensure that it would be, they prevailed upon Jervis to come out of retirement as the road's general superintendent.

Jervis began by refurbishing the track, rebuilding the roadbed, and ordering new equipment.[73] This, plus the increase of traffic due to the war, which Jervis estimated at fifty percent,[74] had an almost unbelievable impact on the road's financial position. In late 1861, when Jervis began his new assignment, the company was $18,000,000 in debt. In two years, sufficient bonds were sold to secure the debt, and the directors were able to declare a ten percent stock dividend.[75]

Actually, Jervis's tenure as general superintendent ended in 1863. During that year, the Pittsburgh, Fort Wayne, and Chicago acquired the Cleveland and Pittsburgh Railroad by merger. Jervis resigned as general superintendent to become chief engineer. His superintendent's position was taken by J. N. McCullough, former president of the Cleveland and Pittsburgh.[76]

Jervis remained chief engineer for one year, then served as a consulting engineer until 1866. His service to the Pittsburgh, Fort Wayne, and Chicago was largely administrative. His contribution involved improving management and increasing traffic. His only significant engineering duty was as consulting engineer in the construction of a novel forked iron trestle at Allegheny.[77]

Then, at age seventy, the man who had devoted nearly fifty years to civil engineering finally retired from full-time participation in his profession.

JERVIS'S RESIGNATION from the superintendency of the Pittsburgh, Fort Wayne, and Chicago coincided with the final year of the Civil War. About to turn seventy, Jervis came back to his home in Rome where he spent the last two decades of his life. For a time, he remained a consultant to the Pittsburgh, Fort Wayne, and Chicago and did other consulting work was well.[1]

Perhaps the most interesting and significant of his consulting work was his review of a survey for an inter-oceanic canal across the Isthmus of Darien (Panama). Between 1870 and 1874, Commander Thomas O. Selfridge, Jr., of the United States Navy was assigned to survey the isthmus and report on the feasibility of constructing a canal to connect the Atlantic and Pacific oceans. Selfridge sent a draft of the survey to Jervis for his review.

The senior engineer enthusiastically commented on the naval officer's work and offered advice on general construction, railroad building, and the digging of tunnels. He specifically referred Selfridge to an article on hydrodynamics in the *Edinburgh Encyclopedia,* American edition. In all, Jervis praised the work as having been done in a "scientific and satisfactory manner." He felt the project was worthy of support and accurately predicted that within the commander's lifetime there would be such a canal. Ever mindful of the importance of a professional approach, Jervis advised that the "main point will be to put it [the canal construction] in the hands of a reliable and intelligent commission."[2] That is exactly what President Theodore Roosevelt did nearly thirty years later when the Panama Canal was constructed.

The Rome that Jervis returned to in the middle 1860s was a village of some 6,000 inhabitants. It was a market town with a few industries, including some wagon works, a soap factory, a planing mill, a small foundry, and a railroad repair shop. However, the small community was about to leap into its century of industrialization. Jervis, with his managerial skills and accumulated capital, was among those who built Rome's iron factories, the forerunners of the metal works for which Rome later became famous.

The end of the Civil War brought a return to railroad construction, notable among which was the completion of the transcontinental link in 1869 and the reconstruction of transportation and industry in the shattered South. Capital that had gone into the effort to save the Union and to abolish slavery was available once again for civilian production. The great armies were rapidly disbanded, and both Union and Confederate veterans led the reinvigorated westward expansion. Immigrants continued to pour into eastern ports, and many joined the trek to fill in the trans-Mississippi territory. America's hunger for manufactured goods seemed insatiable, particularly for products of the iron mills. Entrepreneurs across the Northeast were investing in factories, and those in the village of Rome were no exception. As the railroads drove the need for iron products nationally, so they did in Rome.

Rome, New York was at the junction of the New York Central Railroad's main line and the shorter Rome and Watertown line. In 1866, the superintendent of the Watertown line convinced a group of Rome merchants, bankers, and physicians to put up $100,000 in capital for a mill to re-roll the railroad rails. For the railroad superintendent, it was a matter of necessity. The iron rails of the Watertown line were being beaten out of shape by the pounding trains. As a result, Rome's first heavy industry was incorporated as the Rome Iron Works.[3]

Soon this rolling mill was reprocessing rails from many railroads. Although the iron and coal for fuel had to be shipped into the community, Rome was well situated to receive and send bulk commodities. It had direct access to the New York Central, soon to be joined with the Hudson River Railroad and others to form a single line from New York City to Chicago. It was also on the Erie Canal. As the Watertown Railroad to northern New York joined the Central at Rome, so did the Black River Canal connect Watertown with the Erie at Rome. It is no wonder that by 1868 a second iron mill was incorporated in Rome. It was called the Merchant Iron Mill, and Jervis was secretary-treasurer of the corporation.

The early history of the Merchant Iron Mill remains obscure. Apparently its products included commercial iron rods and bars of the kind frequently sold to blacksmiths. The mill may have also straightened iron railroad rails.[4] Jervis was a member of the first board of trustees of the Merchant Iron Mill, and his nephew Bloomfield Jervis Beach was the company's vice-president. Beach was also a director in the Rome Iron Works, and he sat on the board of trustees of three of Rome's banks.

Five years after the Merchant Iron Mill was organized, the Panic of

Fig. E.1. Jervis (seated in second chair from left) with managers and laborers of the Rome Merchant Iron Mill. Photo (probably taken in the 1870s) courtesy Jervis Public Library.

1873 hit, bringing on the boom-and-bust cycles of the seventies. The Merchant Iron Mill survived, and by the late seventies it had expanded its labor force to about seventy-five workers. Jervis had a major role in guiding the company through the hard times, and in 1878 he was still listed as corporate secretary,[5] a post he held until his death nearly seven years later.[6]

One reason for the Merchant Iron Mill's prosperity was its product diversity. The Rome Iron Works, with its single product, was not as fortunate. Railroads were beginning to change to steel rails, which, coupled with the depression, reduced the demand for rerolled iron rails. In order to survive, by the late 1870s, the Rome Iron Works switched from rerolling iron rails to manufacturing brass and German silver products. In so doing, the company led Rome into the era when it became known as "The Copper City" because of the large quantity of brass and copper products produced by its mills.[7] Although the Merchant Iron Mill reorganized the year after Jervis's death as the Rome Iron Mill, it continued to produce merchant iron and, by then, structural steel.

Even though in the late 1860s, Jervis was committed to the launching of a new industry, he still found time for other pursuits as well. During the presidential campaign of 1868, Jervis argued against repudiation of the national debt from the recent Civil War and in favor of the gradual retirement of legal tender notes (greenbacks) from circulation. The $300,000,000 worth of government "greenbacks" that were issued by a federal government seeking ways to finance the war effort were not backed by gold or silver. As such, they differed from paper money issued by banks.

After the war's end, the Democrats and those who favored an increase in the amount of money in circulation argued in favor of keeping the legal tender notes in circulation. Jervis's stand against the notes was typical of those who opposed them. The "greenbacks" posed a threat to sound money and price stability. Jervis was not troubled by banks issuing currency redeemable in coin, but he thought the "greenbacks" were unsound and bad precedent. He felt that repudiation of the national debt was bad precedent also.

Jervis never mentioned that he held United States government bonds issued during the Civil War nor is there evidence to show him as a bondholder. However, given his outspoken loyalty to the Union and his personal wealth, there is reason to believe he bought bonds. As a bondholder, his argument against repudiation or even reduction in interest payable on the bonds would make sense.[8]

In any case, Jervis's *Currency and the Public Debt* was standard fare for those who held the debt. They wanted the bonds honored and the "greenbacks" withdrawn from circulation by redeeming them in coin. Also, Jervis's views on money and the national debt were perfectly consistent with those he had held before the war, particularly in regard to debt and the responsibility for paying what was owed.

In addition to giving advice on the nation's debt and money supply, Jervis seldom demurred from an opportunity to speak on the importance of civil engineers' developing standards for the profession. He had long been in the forefront of the movement to inculcate professionalism in engineering. As early as 1839, Jervis and sixteen others, including Benjamin Wright, Benjamin Latrobe, Jr., J. Edgar Thompson, and George Whistler, called a meeting at the Franklin Institute to form an association known as the American Society of Civil Engineers.

On February 11, forty engineers convened and elected Benjamin Latrobe, Jr., president of the convention. Jervis was named to a committee of five to draft a statement of purpose to be circulated to engineers throughout the country. Although his actual input into this draft is not known, Jervis's influence is apparent in the statement that the society would serve to "bring the experience of [engineers throughout] the whole country within reach of each member." This idea prevailed throughout the circular, that is, that the chief purpose of the society was to gather and disseminate information about the "facts and experience of its membership" pertaining to new developments in engineering.[9] Jervis should have enthusiastically supported the society's proposed purpose since he frequently practiced his belief that engineering innovations should be "freely given" to the profession by the innovator.

About three weeks after the committee of five met, a meeting of a larger committee of seventeen was scheduled to write a constitution. Jervis was appointed to the constitutional committee, but was not among the four members who actually attended.

The proposed constitution reiterated the earlier recommendation that the society be "instituted for the collection and diffusion of professional knowledge, the advancement of mechanical philosophy, and the elevation of the character and standing of the civil engineers of the United States."[10] To help ensure the dissemination of "professional knowledge," a ten dollar fine was to be levied "against any member who failed to produce to the Society at least one unpublished communication in each year, or present a scientific book, map, plan or model, not already in the possession of the Society. . . . "[11] Membership was to be limited to civil engineers, but architects, machinists, and others "whose pursuits constitute branches of Engineering" were to be eligible for associate membership.[12]

The proposed document was defeated. Only five of the seventeen committee members voted approval. Jervis was not one of them. According to committee secretary Edward Miller, the constitution was voted down because "most of these appointed [to the committee] were ignorant of their appointment, several absolutely indifferent or hostile to the formation of any institution; and . . . many were unknown to each other and so scattered as to render a meeting difficult."[13]

Jervis was almost alone among the committee members who voted against the proposed constitution in explaining his negative vote. He replied to Miller's inquiry of July 30, 1839, that not only did he vote against the document but he declined to "become a member of a society formed on the principals of the proposed constitution." He did not elaborate specifically on his objections.[14]

At any rate, this attempt to organize a national engineering society failed. Some of the potential members felt the construction of railroads would help bring the membership together from distant parts of the nation. However, because of the nature of their profession, civil engineers were spread throughout the United States and would have found it difficult to use the society's hall or attend meetings. Whatever their reasons, most civil engineers were not willing to commit themselves at that time to a national society and its proposed rules of membership.

In 1852, the moribund society was resurrected. The important difference between the 1852 effort and its predecessor was that the membership was small and located in New York City and its environs. Even at that, the average attendance among its forty-seven regular members was six.[15] Jervis was not among the members of the renewed society. At the time, his duties demanded his presence in the Midwest.

Small attendance continued to be the rule at the society's meetings. Finally, between 1855 and 1867, the society was dormant, with the Civil War contributing to its inactivity.

In November 1867, when the society's annual meeting was held, a new era of stability began, marked by regular meetings and increased membership.[16] Two years later, a convention of the society's full membership was held. By that time William J. McAlpine, one of several engineers trained by Jervis, was society president. Jervis was made an honorary member of the society and was chosen as the main speaker for the convention. Jervis must have considered one of the greatest moments of his life when he was included among the six charter honorary members of the civil engineering society.[17]

Jervis's address to the convention could be cited as a creed for the modern engineering profession. In it he urged, with McAlpine's support, that the American Society of Civil Engineers (ASCE) encourage a combination of formal study with apprenticeship. This would help make possible the transition of engineering from a craft to a profession. Jervis suggested the need for future engineers to learn mathematics, mechanical philosophy, hydraulics, and structural architecture. After academic training, the emerging engineer should enter the field under the guidance of an experienced civil engineer.

Jervis also stressed the need for the engineer to become familiar with business methods. He particularly referred to the management of railroads and reiterated his belief that the "education of an engineer gives him superiority over the lay manager in all that concerns the maintaining, improvement and operating business of a railway."

Finally, the 74-year-old professional interjected his personal morality into his recipe for the creation of an engineer. Since the interests of others, "in various ways," were dependent upon the engineer, he must possess integrity and be of high moral character. Above all, the engineer must "guard against committing himself until he is fully prepared to set forth his views clearly and decidedly."[18]

Five years later in a similar address to the ASCE, Thomas C. Clarke

Fig. E.2. Mr. and Mrs. John B. Jervis at their home in Rome, New York, c. 1878. The Jervis home is now part of the Jervis Public Library. Photo courtesy Jervis Public Library.

supported Jervis's views on the education of civil engineers. Clarke stressed the study of mathematics, but added natural science to Jervis's mechanical philosophy, hydraulics, and structural architecture. In his engineering curriculum, Clarke also included a reading knowledge of ancient and modern languages. Clarke agreed with Jervis that, after study, the engineering student should go into the field. Clarke's proposal for an engineer's "motto" — "accuracy in measurement; truth in statement; justice in action" — also put him in harmony with Jervis.[19]

Both Clarke and Jervis were concerned with young engineers having to come to terms with, as a modern writer on the subject expressed, "the contradiction inherent in engineering professionalism." That contradiction involved the struggle "to attain professional autonomy and define standards of ethics and social responsibility within a context of professional practice that demanded subservience to corporate authority."[20]

Even more recently another engineer making a similar point about the engineering profession cited Jervis himself as an example of the possible conflict that could occur between engineers and businessmen. He noted that Jervis "threatened to withdraw as chief engineer of the Croton Aqueduct when its sponsors sought to use a mortar he considered inferior."[21] Again, this was simply in keeping with his character both as an individual and a civil engineer.

To many people, Jervis might have seemed unbending and self-righteous. But if he failed to see more than one side to a question, it was because he felt he had thoroughly examined the situation before arriving at his own conclusions. In fact, Jervis became impatient with those who questioned his thoroughness. If he frequently preached about morals, it is because he lived according to a strict moral code and felt others should also.

Perhaps Jervis was so persistent in his preachings because of his continued belief in the ability of mankind to improve, a notion common to the early nineteenth century. People of intellect and vision had faith in "man's ability to alter his environment."[22] Knowledge was seen as a key to universal improvement.[23]

In a final expression of his commitment to this manner of thinking, Jervis's will provided for contributions to two colleges and the placing of his home in a trust to be used as a library and Christian meeting place for all "liberal minded citizens of Rome."[24] Jervis felt he was providing for the improvement of man in his legacy, just as he had done in his numerous engineering works. Also, in his many projects Jervis had constantly worked towards his own improvement as an engineer and, if his letters to his family are any indication, as a person. In many ways, Jervis was his own severest critic.

Jervis also desired some acclaim for his achievements. A reserved individual who avoided direct public contact and felt uncomfortable making speeches, Jervis nonetheless was disturbed when he did not get recognition he felt was due. The incident in the Croton celebration and Vanderbilt's neglect to provide Jervis with a railway pass are two good examples of his disappointment when his contributions went unrecognized. Jervis considered acknowledgement of his achievements part of his professional compensation.

A reticent man, Jervis tended to be conservative in his personal habits. This did not mean he was unwilling to accept change. Jervis had the ability to recognize the benefits of innovation, and he had been in the vanguard of those engineers who sought improvement and modification of existing methods and works. The end of the pre-1850 projects signaled the completion of one phase of Jervis's life. It did not mean the end of his search for improvement. As Jervis's career itself changed, he continued to work for the advancement of mankind and to seek the simple solution. Late twentieth-century reflections on the life and times of John B. Jervis cannot help but reveal the irony that the very person who searched for simplicity in life was instrumental, through his engineering and entrepreneurial activities, in creating a more complex society.

NOTES

PROLOGUE

1. There was considerable similarity between the careers of Jervis and Allen. Both were important engineers of the nineteenth century. Both men were pioneers in building railroads; they both served as railway presidents and worked on the Croton Aqueduct. Allen later became involved in the management of the Novelty Iron Works in New York City and Jervis in the Rome Merchant Iron Works.

2. Jervis, *Croton Aqueduct,* 27.

3. Ellis et al., *A History of New York State,* 252.

CHAPTER 1

1. William Bullus to Timothy Jarvis [Jervis] by Warranty Deed, November 1, 1796, Oneida County Clerk's Office, Deed Book 8, 18; John and Ann Bloomfield to Timothy Jervis by Warranty Deed, June 15, 1797, Oneida County Clerk's Office, Deed Book 10, 89. John Bloomfield was the brother of Phebe Jervis.

2. FitzSimons, *Reminiscences,* 21.

3. George Clinton to Timothy Jarvis [Jervis] by Warranty Deed, June 28, 1805, Oneida County Clerk's Office, Deed Book 19, 260; FitzSimons, *Reminiscences,* 21–22.

4. FitzSimons, *Reminiscences,* 23.

5. Between 1796 and 1805, Timothy Jervis purchased more than 500 acres of land at a total cost that exceeded $2,800. Approximately one-third of the total cost was secured through mortgages. By 1810, the amount outstanding on the mortgages plus the accrued interest was $1,504.10. Timothy and Phebe Jarvis [Jervis] to George Clinton, mortgage dated June 29, 1805, Oneida County Clerk's Office, Mortgage Book 5, 62; Calculations of Interest on $950 from June 29, 1805, Jervis MSS, Box 29; Timothy Jervis to Abraham Culver, mortgage dated June 10, 1809, Oneida County Clerk's Office, Mortgage Book 5, 319.

6. FitzSimons, *Reminiscences,* 22.

7. Among the textbooks probably in use in Rome during the early nineteenth century were *The New England Primer;* Daboll's *Schoolmaster's Assistant;* Murray's *English Reader;* and Dilworth's *Schoolmaster's Assistant.* All contain examples of the character as well as the content of education.

8. Jervis, *Labour and Capital,* 192.

9. Ibid., 13, 54, 130–132, 135, 196–206, 216.

10. Jervis, *Railway Property,* 61, 68, 340.

11. Jervis, *Labour and Capital,* 206.

12. FitzSimons, *Reminiscences,* 25.

13. Shaw, *Erie Water West,* pp. 90–91.

14. Calhoun, *The American Civil Engineer,* 27.

15. Ibid., 28.

16. Ibid., 29.

17. FitzSimons, *Reminiscences,* 25; Friends of W. C. Young, *Biography of William C. Young,* 50–51. An extensive search of manuscript collections revealed little of what Jervis's mentors and other contemporaries thought about him. Sources relating to Jervis are generally abundant for the post-1825 years, but sparse for the era of the building of "Clinton's Ditch."

18. Ibid., 26.

19. Ibid.

20. Jervis, "Memoir," 2.

21. FitzSimons, *Reminiscences,* 27.

22. Ibid.

23. Jervis, "Memoir," 3. The amount Jervis received as a targetman was only a slight increase over his pay as an axeman. However, engineers received a monthly salary beginning at $100.

24. Jervis, *Labour and Capital,* 192.

25. FitzSimons, *Reminiscences,* 29.

26. Ibid., 30.

27. Ibid., 30–31.

28. Jervis, "Memoir," 4.

29. Ibid.

30. FitzSimons, *Reminiscences,* 32–33.

31. Ibid., 34.

32. Jervis, "Memoir," 4.

33. FitzSimons, *Reminiscences,* 37.

34. Ibid.

35. Jervis, "Memoir," 7.

36. FitzSimons, *Reminiscences,* 38.

37. Ibid., 38–40.

38. Ibid., 40–41.

39. Ibid., 45.

40. Jervis, "Memoir," 8.

41. FitzSimons, *Reminiscences,* 45.

42. Ibid., 47.

43. Ibid., 47–48.

44. Ibid., 48.

45. Ibid., 50.

46. Ibid.

47. Bill of Particulars, July–September 1822, Jervis MSS, Box 49. The case cost Jervis twenty-five dollars in lawyer's fees.

48. FitzSimons, *Reminiscences,* 50. Examples of Jervis's records and receipts can be found in the New York State Archives in the extensive Canal Commissioners Contracts and Accounts for Construction and Repair (1817–1828) MSS, Boxes 3, 7, 8, and 9.

49. Ibid.

50. Ibid., 51.

51. Ibid. See also Jervis, Workbook containing calculations on the stress on arches, 1822, Jervis MSS.

52. Jervis, "Memoir," 8.

53. FitzSimons, *Reminiscences,* 54. Dr. Martineau was involved to a limited extent in the planning stages of the Croton Aqueduct project.

54. Ibid., 55–58.

55. Ibid., 62.

56. State of New York, *Laws of the State of New York,* 208.

57. FitzSimons, *Reminiscences,* 63.

58. Ibid., 63–64.

59. Ibid.

60. McKelvey, "The Erie Canal," 55–71.

61. Calhoun, *The American Civil Engineer,* 30.

CHAPTER 2

1. FitzSimons, *Reminiscences,* 65.

2. Delaware and Hudson Company, *A Century of Progress,* 9–16.

3. FitzSimons, *Reminiscences,* 66.

4. Ibid., 62. At the time of Jervis's appointment, Benjamin Wright was a member of the engineering board of the Chesapeake and Delaware Canal and was a consulting engineer on the James River and Kanawha Canal (Va.). Between 1825 and 1827, Wright spent very little time on the Delaware and Hudson project, hence he relied on Jervis a great deal.

5. Delaware and Hudson Company, *A Century of Progress,* 15, 22.

6. FitzSimons, *Reminiscences,* 67, 68.

7. Ibid., 69. Slack-water navigation is achieved by constructing dams in rivers to flood out rapids, increase the water depth, and decrease the velocity of the flow. In this manner, the rivers may be used in place of canals.

8. Ibid.

9. Wakefield, *Coal Boats to Tidewater,* 3. One of the chief occupations of the upper Delaware region was the rafting of timber down the Delaware River to Philadelphia. The construction of dams in the river would hinder the passage of rafts.

10. FitzSimons, *Reminiscences,* 69–70.

11. Ibid., 70–71.

12. Delaware and Hudson Company, *A Century of Progress,* 30–31.

13. FitzSimons, *Reminiscences,* 73.

14. *Report of Benjamin Wright and J. T. Sullivan,* 12.

15. Benjamin Wright to the president and board of managers, Delaware and Hudson Canal Company, September 30, 1826, Unnumbered box, Jervis MSS.

16. Ibid. Wright advised the construction of a road from Carbondale to the summit level between that place and Honesdale. It was the steepest portion of the route, with an inclination of approximately 900 feet in four miles.

17. Benjamin Wright to J. B. J., November 13, 1826, Box 35, Jervis MSS.

18. J. B. J. to Benjamin Wright, November 23, 1826, Box 35, Jervis MSS.

19. Ibid.

20. Ibid.

21. Benjamin Wright to J. B. J., December 14, 1826, Box 35, Jervis MSS.

22. Ibid.

23. Ibid.

24. J. B. J. to Benjamin Wright, December 16, 1826, Box 35, Jervis MSS.

25. Ibid.

26. Ibid.

27. Ibid.

28. Delaware and Hudson Company, *A Century of Progress,* 43.

29. Philip Hone to Harrison Gray Otis, July 19, 1827, Box 20, Jervis MSS.

30. Jervis, "Report of the Projected Carbondale Railroad. The pages of the report are not numbered. Page numbers appearing in subsequent footnotes that refer to the report are those of a typewritten copy also contained in Box 44.

31. Delaware and Hudson Company, *A Century of Progress,* 43.

32. J. B. J., "Report of the Projected Carbondale Railroad," 1–3.

33. Ibid., 4–5.

34. Ibid., 8–15.

35. Wakefield, *Coal Boats to Tidewater,* 15.

36. J. B. J., "Report of the Projected Carbondale Railroad," 15.

37. Ibid., 6.

38. Ibid., 23.

39. Ibid., 16–18.

40. Wood, *A Practical Treatise on Railroads,* 245.

41. Long, *Railroad Manual,* 61–62.

42. Ibid., 62.

43. J. B. J, "Report on the Projected Carbondale Railroad," 28.

44. Ibid., 30–33.

45. Ibid., 47.

46. Ibid., 48.

47. Ibid.

48. Ibid., 49.

49. Ibid., 50–51.

50. James Renwick was a professor of science at Columbia. He often served as an engineering consultant and at times took an active part in projects such as the Mohawk and Hudson Railroad. He and Jervis became friends and had great respect for each other's ability. For example, in 1830 Renwick asked for Jervis's opinion on the wisdom of offering a course on civil engineering at Columbia. Renwick's son, James Jr., worked under Jervis on the Croton project. The younger Renwick later became a leading architect.

51. FitzSimons, *Reminiscences,* 79.

52. James Renwick to John Bolton, November 17, 1827, Jervis MSS; J. B. J. to president and board of managers, Delaware and Hudson Company, November 23, 1827, Box 29, Jervis MSS. Jervis's "autobiography," written more than a quarter century after the event, indicates that Jervis did not discover his error until the Renwick report mentioned it. The Renwick report of November 17, which was followed closely by the Jervis letter of November 23 to the board of managers clearly indicates that Jervis saw the error before Renwick submitted his report.

53. Benjamin Wright to John Bolton, December 6, 1827, Jervis MSS.

54. FitzSimons, *Reminiscences,* 80.

55. *New York Times,* August 9, 1877, 3.

56. Ibid.

57. Ibid.

58. FitzSimons, *Reminiscences,* 85.

59. Horatio Allen to J. B. J., February 24, 1828, Box 37, Jervis MSS.

60. Ibid.

61. Ibid., Horatio Allen to J. B. J., March 1828, Box 37, Jervis MSS.

62. J. B. J. to Horatio Allen, March 1828, Box 37, Jervis MSS.

63. Wakefield, *Coal Boats to Tidewater,* 9.

64. LeRoy, *The Delaware and Hudson Canal,* 28.

65. Sanderson, *The Delaware and Hudson Canalway,* 37.

66. Ibid., 37–38.

67. Horatio Allen to J. B. J., June 22, 1829, Box 37, Jervis MSS.

68. Wakefield, *Coal Boats to Tidewater,* 9–10.

69. Ibid., 10. Neither the Delaware nor the Hudson arrived in New York until after the trial run of the Lion. They never arrived in Pennsylvania.

70. J. B. J., "Report of the Projected Carbondale Railroad," 33.

71. Ibid., 6, 32.

72. Ibid.

73. FitzSimons, *Reminiscences,* 86, 88.

74. Ibid., 86.

75. Ibid., 87.

76. J. B. J. to John Bolton, August 6, 1829, Box 45, Jervis MSS.

77. Ibid.

78. J. B. J. to John Bolton, August 8, 1829, Box 45, Jervis MSS.

79. Wakefield, *Coal Boats to Tidewater,* 10.

80. FitzSimons, *Reminiscences,* 89.

81. Ibid., 88. The monetary loss to the company was $2,914, the cost of the Lion. The three other locomotives were purchased by the company for between $2,900 and $3,300 each.

82. Ibid.

83. Ibid., 88–89.

84. Ibid., 90.

85. Ibid.

86. Wakefield, *Coal Boats to Tidewater,* 15.

87. Rufus L. Lord to J.B.J., November 19, 1829, Box 29, Jervis MSS.

88. Ibid.

89. J. B. J. to Horatio Allen, January 14, 1830, Box 37, Jervis MSS.

90. Ibid.

91. Ibid.

92. S. Flewelling to J. B. J., April 15, 1830, Box 46, Jervis MSS.

93. J. B. J., "Memoir," 28.

94. FitzSimons, *Reminiscences,* 81.

95. J. B. J., "Report to the Board of Managers, Delaware and Hudson Company," February 16, 1831, Box 44, Jervis MSS.

96. Spann, *The New Metropolis,* 118.

97. White, *A History of the American Locomotive,* 7.

98. Ibid., 8.

99. Ibid., 3.

100. Ibid.

101. Ibid., 3–4.

CHAPTER 3

1. Stover, *American Railroads,* 19.
2. Ibid., 146, 159. The first locomotive, the Best Friend of Charleston, exploded after six months of service on the road. The second, the West Point, was placed in service shortly before the destruction of the Best Friend.
3. James Renwick to John B. Jervis, March 8, 1830, Box 61, Jervis MSS.
4. J. B. J. to James Renwick, March 10, 1830, Box 61, Jervis MSS.
5. Stevens, *New York Central,* 8, 21. Two months after he accepted employment, Jervis received a letter from Lynde Catlin that opened with the query, "would [you] like to have 40 or 50 shares of Mohawk and Hudson Co. stock?" Catlin apparently felt Jervis might wish to become a stockholder.

The brief note ends with Catlin's request that should Jervis "want a few shares," he should inform Catlin. No mention is made of the price per share or if, in fact, the company expected Jervis to pay for the stock. It is doubtful, however, that the stock was to have been a gift, since the asking price at the time of its initial offering on the New York Stock Exchange in October 1830 was $110. Lynde Catlin to J. B. J., May 26, 1830, Box 61, Jervis MSS.
6. Stevens, *New York Central,* 21.
7. Stover, *Baltimore and Ohio Railroad,* 33–36.
8. Stover, *American Railroads,* 14.
9. Kanarek, *The Mid-Atlantic Engineers,* 20–22.
10. J. B. J. to John Clark, March 15, 1830, Box 61, Jervis MSS.
11. Ibid.
12. Ibid.
13. J. B. J. to James Renwick, March 20 and March 31, 1830, Box 61, Jervis MSS.
14. Stevens, *New York Central,* 30.
15. Bloodgood, "Hudson and Mohawk Rail Road," 142.
16. Stevens, *New York Central,* 31.
17. Jervis, "Report to the President and Board of Managers of the Mohawk and Hudson Rail Road," July 20, 1830, Letter Book dated 1827, Jervis MSS.
18. Ibid., 1–3. The white pine was obtained from the vicinity of Seneca Lake, according to Bloodgood.
19. Jervis, "Report . . . Mohawk and Hudson," 1–2, 7.
20. Ibid., 7. Bloodgood gives the actual weight of the iron straps or plates at twenty-one tons per mile. They were manufactured at Wolverhampton, England.
21. Jervis, "Report . . . Mohawk and Hudson," 11.
22. FitzSimons, *Reminiscences,* 105.
23. Bloodgood, "Hudson and Mohawk Railroad," 142–143.
24. FitzSimons, *Reminiscences,* 106.
25. Jervis, "Historical Sketch," 1.
26. Ibid., 2.
27. J. B. J. to James Renwick, September 22, 1830, Letter Book dated 1827, Jervis MSS.
28. James Renwick to J. B. J., September 23, 1830, Box 61, Jervis MSS.
29. J. B. J. to President and Board of Managers of the Mohawk and Hudson Railroad, November 9, 1830, Letter Book dated 1827, Jervis MSS.
30. Ibid. The letter even contained a proposal for the daily schedule of trains. It was suggested that locomotives leave the end of the track at two-hour intervals, "Commencing at 5 or 6 A.M." and making "seven trips per long day – 6 per short."

31. J. B. J. to C. C. Cambreling, September 22, 1831, Letter Book dated 1827, Jervis MSS.

32. J. B. J. to C. C. Cambreling, October 1, 1831, Letter Book dated 1827, Jervis MSS.

33. Ibid.

34. C. C. Cambreling to J. B. J., October 2, 1831, Box 62, Jervis MSS.

35. Bloodgood, "Hudson and Mohawk Railroad," 147. A more detailed description of the DeWitt Clinton has been provided by David Matthew. Matthew delivered it and drove it in some of its early runs in July and August 1831. See Brown, *First Locomotives,* 178.

36. Ibid., 185.

37. Bloodgood, "Hudson and Mohawk Railroad," 148.

38. Apparently some confusion exists about the name of the Mohawk and Hudson's first English locomotive. Brown stated that the engine was called Robert Fulton, while Stevens says it was the John Bull. The usually exact Jervis is confusing in his own references to the English machine. In a letter to William Brown written in April 1869, Jervis mentioned the John Bull as arriving in late 1831. In a second letter to Brown sent one year later, Jervis was "certain the English engine John Bull did not arrive until the spring of 1832." Yet approximately five years later, he named the John Bull as the second locomotive on the railroad. In this instance, Jervis might have been referring to the John Bull as the second English locomotive. In any case, the issue of the engine names has remained a subject of some controversy for the past century and a half. Brown, *First Locomotives,* 182–183, 196–200; FitzSimons, *Reminiscences,* 107; Stevens, *New York Central,* 45.

39. Bloodgood, "Hudson and Mohawk Railroad," 147.

40. Ibid.

41. Warner, "Anthracite-Burning Locomotive," 11–13; Earle, *Treatise on Rail-Roads,* 119–120.

42. James Renwick to J. B. J., December 28, 1831, Box 62, Jervis MSS.

43. Bloodgood, "Hudson and Mohawk Railroad," 141.

44. Stevens, *New York Central,* 43.

45. Ibid.

46. J. B. J. to Adam Hall, April 25, 1832, Box 63, Jervis MSS.

47. Ibid. Jervis's comment on workmanship and the "beauty of the thing" was prompted by Hall's prior correspondence about the quality of the DeWitt Clinton.

48. Adam Hall to J. B. J., April 30, 1832, Box 63, Jervis MSS.

49. Stevens, *New York Central,* 43–44.

50. Jervis, "Historical Sketch," 1.

51. FitzSimons, *Reminiscences,* 85–108. Jervis's omission of unfortunate experiences is not unusual in his autobiography.

52. J. B. J. to William Kemble, December 26, 1831, Box 62, Jervis MSS.

53. Jervis, "Improved Wheel for Railroad Wagons," 452–453.

54. Brown, *First Locomotives,* 213–214.

55. Ibid.

56. Kirby, *Engineering in History,* 285.

57. Those showing signs of special use are Grey, *General Iron Rail-way;* Tredgold, *Treatise on Railroads;* Walker, *Liverpool and Manchester Railroad Reports;* and Wood, *A Practical Treatise on Rail-Roads.*

58. Tredgold, *Treatise on Railroads,* 94, 179.

59. J. B. J., *Railway Property,* 170.

60. Brown, *First Locomotives,* 215.

61. FitzSimons, *Reminiscences,* 100–101.
62. Ibid.
63. FitzSimons, *Reminiscences,* 97.
64. Ibid., 98.
65. Ibid. See also Brown, *First Locomotives,* 168–170.
66. Ibid.
67. Brown, *First Locomotives,* 170; FitzSimons, *Reminiscences,* 92. FitzSimons notes that Allen's engine was eventually modified following "five months of vexatious break-downs." He does not specify the kinds of changes made on the machine.
68. FitzSimons, *Reminiscences,* 98.
69. J. B. J. to editor of the *Rail Road Gazette,* December 13, 1871, Box 28, Jervis MSS. The letter was written in reply to a review of Brown's book on locomotives, in which Allen's claim to the truck engine is recognized. Jervis's remarks in his autobiography (FitzSimons, *Reminiscences,* 92) seem to support his belief that Allen may have written the review.
70. FitzSimons, *Reminiscences,* 98.
71. J. B. J. to *Rail Road Gazette,* December 13, 1871.
72. FitzSimons, *Reminiscences,* 108.
73. Brown, *First Locomotives,* 213–215.
74. Thurston, *Growth of the Steam Engine,* 213–214.
75. Hollingsworth, *World's Steam Passenger Locomotives,* 21. Mr. Hollingsworth, however, incorrectly stated that the idea for the bogie truck was suggested to Jervis by Robert Stephenson when the American engineer visited England. Jervis did not travel to England until 1850, eighteen years after the introduction of the bogie truck. There is also no evidence that Jervis and Stephenson corresponded on the subject.
76. White, *The American Locomotive,* 33.
77. Ibid., 34.
78. Ibid. See also Jervis, "Historical Sketch," 3.
79. Ibid.
80. Ibid.
81. Delaware and Hudson Company, *A Century of Progress,* 83–85.
82. J. B. J. to C. C. Cambreling et al., March 21, 1831, Box 64, Jervis MSS.
83. Ibid.
84. Friends of W. C. Young, *Biography of William C. Young,* 25–26. Based on material found in many English and American works on railroad construction techniques written during the 1825–1830 period, it appears that the "proposed and practically introduced" cross ties claim written by Young's friends on his behalf has greater validity in terms of the ties having been "practically introduced" by Young. Even this is questionable.
85. *American Railroad Journal,* July 27, 1833, 469.
86. Ibid.
87. White, *The American Locomotive,* 34.
88. *American Railroad Journal,* July 27, 1833, 469.
89. Ibid.
90. FitzSimons, *Reminiscences,* 107–108.
91. Ibid., 101.

CHAPTER 4

1. Soule, *Chenango Canal,* 11–13.
2. Ibid., 15.

3. Ibid., 13.

4. FitzSimons, *Reminiscences,* 109; Soule, *Chenango Canal,* 13.

5. Jervis, "Facts and Circumstances." Only 2½ handwritten pages out of approximately 200 are given to the Chenango. However, although Jervis regarded the project as being of little import, it did bring him back to central New York and the Rome area for three years. It was during this period that he found time to court and marry his first wife, Cynthia Brayton.

6. J. B. J., Instructions to Resident and Assistant Engineer on the Chenango Canal, Untitled Letter Book (Chenango Canal), Jervis MSS.

7. Soule, *Chenango Canal,* 13.

8. J. B. J., Report to the Canal Commissioners, October 2, 1833, Untitled Journal, Jervis MSS.

9. S. Newton Dexter to J. B. J., April 22, 1833, Box 48, Jervis, MSS.

10. Sands Higinbottom to J.B.J., April 30, 1833, Box 48, Jervis MSS.

11. Soule, *Chenango Canal,* 17.

12. Ibid., 31.

13. J. B. J., Report to the Canal Commissioners, October 2, 1833, Untitled Journal, Jervis MSS.

14. J. B. J., "Memoir," 34.

15. J. B. J., Report to the Canal Commissioners, December 29, 1834, Box 50, Jervis MSS. This document contains figures from gauge readings from Eaton and Madison Brooks taken between January and June 1834. Six different measurements were taken from the gauges. The gauges consisted of flumes ten feet wide and from twenty-four to thirty-three feet long. A wooden ball filled with lead was used to measure velocity. Depth and capacity were measured by a ruler.

16. Ibid.

17. FitzSimons, *Reminiscences,* 109n. FitzSimons noted that the major early nineteenth century work by an American on engineering, D. H. Mahan's *An Elementary Course of Civil Engineering,* mentions only stream gauging and not the measurement of rainfall.

18. Soule, *Chenango Canal,* 36.

19. J. B. J., "Memoir," 34. McAlpine's distinguished career began under Jervis on the Delaware and Hudson Canal project. In addition to serving under Jervis on the Chenango, McAlpine worked with him in 1836 on the Erie enlargement. McAlpine later became chief engineer of the Erie enlargement, state engineer of New York, and chief engineer of the Erie Railroad; he also supervised the construction of many domestic and foreign projects. In 1868 McAlpine became president of the American Society of Civil Engineers. See Merritt, *Engineering in American Society,* 27, 55.

20. Soule, *Chenango Canal,* 39.

21. Ibid., 37.

22. State of New York, *Assembly Document #65,* 7.

23. The techniques Jervis developed to measure rainfall and runoff were later used in his report to the Boston Water Commission about the Cochituate Aqueduct. J. B. J., "Facts and Circumstances," 73.

24. J. B. J. to William Bouck, January 10, 1834, Box 1, William Bouck MSS, Cornell University Library. The letter to Bouck contained a printed report on a proposed hydraulic canal in Herkimer, New York. The report, dated October 26, 1833, contained calculations about power derived from West Canada Creek. Jervis, the author of the report, felt that if improvements were made in the creek, it would furnish enough power for a "large manufacturing town." Between February and June 1834, Jervis received several letters from individuals connected with the proposed hydraulic canal. They requested Jervis to visit

Herkimer with a view towards directing construction of the project. There exists no evidence to show that Jervis did any more than supply calculations for the work. William Small to J. B. J., February 15, March 2, March 10, and June 25, 1834, Box 59, Jervis MSS. In October 1835, Jervis received correspondence from Erastus Corning of Albany seeking Jervis's opinion and perhaps skill in regard to the construction of a direct route canal between Albany and Schenectady. Erastus Corning to J. B. J., October 28, 1835, Box 59, Jervis MSS.

25. In May 1834, Jervis received a letter from John Suydam, an acquaintance from Jervis's Delaware and Hudson service. Suydam informed Jervis that the post of chief engineer on the New York and Erie Railroad was about to be offered to him. Suydam added a request for Jervis to appoint one of his friends as principal assistant. John Suydam to J. B. J., May 6, 1834, Box 59, Jervis MSS.

26. J. B. J. to George Miller, May 16, 1834, Box 59, Jervis MSS. One can only speculate as to the reasons for Jervis rejecting the opportunity to head the engineering department of the New York and Erie Railroad. His recommendation was that the position be offered to James Archbald, Jervis's assistant on the Delaware and Hudson. James Archbald to J. B. J., July 6, 1834, Box 59, Jervis MSS.

27. [Signature Illegible] to J. B. J., February 9, 1835, Box 59, Jervis MSS. A reply to Jervis's inquiry informed him that the position of chief engineer of the Champlain and St. Lawrence Railroad had been filled.

28. Jonas Earll, Jr., to J. B. J., June 26, 1833, Box 48, Jervis MSS.

29. Whitford, *Canal System,* vol. 1, 133.

30. J. B. J. to William Bouck, February 22, 1834, Box 50, Jervis MSS. Untitled Letter Book (Chenango Canal), Jervis MSS.

31. J. B. J. to William Bouck, January 26, 1835, Untitled Letter Book (Chenango Canal), Jervis MSS.

32. J. B. J. to the Canal Commissioners, February 17, 1835. Untitled Letter Book (Chenango Canal), Jervis MSS. Jervis was most concerned with the potential of an ice barrier being created by the dam. He felt it might cause flooding and destroy the canal structures. His report was buttressed with references to English works on hydraulics. Specific page citations were from Tredgold, *Tracts on Hydraulics.*

33. Whitford, *Canal System,* vol. 1, 145.

34. Ibid., 146.

35. Ibid.

36. FitzSimons, *Reminiscences,* 111.

37. State of New York, *Assembly Document #99A,* 9–16. A recent tragic testimony to the violence of the Schoharie in flood season occurred in April 1987. Several lives were lost when a New York State Thruway bridge collapsed. The bridge was located only a few hundred yards upstream from Jervis's Schoharie Aqueduct. Apparently scouring under the piers caused the collapse. The new bridge, which opened in 1988, avoids the problem since it was built without piers in the creek. About half of the Jervis Aqueduct still stands, but not the portion across the Schoharie's main channel.

38. Ibid., 1–9.

39. Ibid. Both Jervis and Frederick C. Mills had refrained from giving their opinion about the size they felt most suitable for the canal. When they discovered that the other engineers had made specific recommendations on size, they submitted an additional document recommending a depth of eight feet and a width of eighty feet. State of New York, *Assembly Document #99E.*

40. J. B. J. to the Canal Commissioners, November 24, 1835, Scrapbook titled "Erie Canal Reports and Estimates," Jervis MSS.

41. Ibid.

42. Whitford, *Canal System*, vol. 1, 149–50, 105–106.

43. J. B. J. to the Canal Commissioners, June 20, 1836, Scrapbook titled "Erie Canal Reports and Estimates," Jervis MSS.

44. Ibid.

45. Whitford, *Canal System*, vol. 1, 150.

46. The commissioners not only disagreed with Jervis's recommendations for the canal dimensions but also changed his specifications for the construction of locks. FitzSimons, *Reminiscences*, 114–115. Also, a Jervis proposal to construct a Steamboat Canal from the Hudson River to Lake Ontario was rejected by the Canal Commission. J. B. J. to William Bouck, April 2, 1835, #2206, Box 5, William Bouck MSS.

47. FitzSimons, *Reminiscences*, 119.

CHAPTER 5

1. Blake, *Water for the Cities*, 100–133. Blake's work is the best account of New York's early struggle to obtain an adequate supply of pure water.

2. State of New York, *Assembly Document #61*, 420–430; *Assembly Document #5*, 53–60.

3. State of New York, *Assembly Document #4*, 41–44; *Assembly Document #36*, 235.

4. The best way to move Croton water across the Harlem River was a subject of much discussion. DeWitt Clinton's report of 1832 recommended an aqueduct bridge 138 feet high and 1,000 feet long. Douglass also recommended an open aqueduct bridge across the Harlem at a grade uniform with the rest of the aqueduct. Martineau favored the use of wrought iron pipes in the form of an inverted siphon. The pipes could rest on an embankment, and the embankment could be provided with an arch to permit navigation of the river. The use of the inverted siphon would eliminate the need to maintain a uniform grade level and would therefore eliminate the necessity of an expensive high bridge. State of New York, *Assembly Document #36*, 235; *Report of the Commissioners;* State of New York, *Assembly Document #44*, 496.

5. Blake, *Water for the Cities*, 139.

6. Ibid., 140–142.

7. Ibid., 313n.

8. Jervis, *Croton Aqueduct*, 7.

9. Ibid., 10–11.

10. Ibid., 12–14.

11. Ibid., 24.

12. J. B. J., Croton Reports, vol. 3, April 28, 1840, Jervis MSS.

13. J. B. J., *Croton Aqueduct*, 27.

14. Blake, *Water for the Cities*, 129.

15. Condit, *American Building Art*, 257.

16. J. B. J., *Croton Aqueduct*, 14.

17. Ibid., 17.

18. FitzSimons, *Reminiscences*, 10.

19. J. B. J., *Croton Aqueduct*, 16.

20. Ibid., 17.

21. FitzSimons, *Reminiscences*, 11. FitzSimons traced the advent of modern dams to the Zola Dam, begun in France in 1843. He terms the Croton Dam a transition structure because of its unconventional construction and novel design. *Reminiscences*, 10.

22. J. B. J., *Croton Aqueduct,* 18–24. The three other crossings were the eighty-eight-foot bridge across the Sing Sing Kill, the iron pipeline across the 4,180-foot-wide Manhattan Valley, and the 1,900-foot-long masonry wall across the Clendinning Valley. Archways were constructed in this wall to accommodate the planned streets of northern Manhattan.

23. Condit, *American Building Art,* 243.

24. J. B. J., *Croton Aqueduct,* 20.

25. Ibid.

26. FitzSimons, *Reminiscences,* 11.

27. Ibid.

28. King, *Croton Aqueduct,* 169.

29. Schramke, *New York Croton Aqueduct,* 20. The profusely illustrated edition was published in German, French, and English.

30. Blake, *Water for the Cities,* 147. The most recent work on the water supply system of the city of New York also praises the choice of Jervis as chief engineer and briefly describes his contribution to the project. However, since the focus of the book is on the water system after 1850, only one of the twenty-seven chapters is given to the construction of the "Old Croton." The author relies on three secondary sources for his information. Weidner, *Water for a City,* 38–47.

31. J. B. J. to Stephen Allen, September 27, 1836, Reports of J. B. J. on New York Water Works (hereafter N. Y. W. W.), vol. 2, Jervis MSS. The terms also provided Jervis with an annual salary of $5,000 plus travel expenses.

32. J. B. J. to E. French, November 10, 1836, Reports of J. B. J. on N. Y. W. W., vol. 2, Jervis MSS.

33. J. B. J. to H. J. Anthony, November 10, 1836, Reports of J. B. J. on N. Y. W. W., vol. 2, Jervis MSS.

34. FitzSimons, *Reminiscences,* 122.

35. J. B. J. to the Board of Water Commissioners, November 12, 1836, Reports of J. B. J. on N. Y. W. W., vol. 2, Jervis MSS. Both French and Anthony were included among the five. The following spring, both men were appointed resident engineers in charge of a section of the line.

36. J. B. J. to Resident Engineers, April 1, 1837, Reports of J. B. J. on N. Y. W. W., vol. 2, Jervis MSS.

37. J. B. J. to E. French, February 5, 1837, Reports of J. B. J. on N. Y. W. W., vol. 2, Jervis MSS.

38. J. B. J. to Resident Engineers, May 30, 1837, Reports of J. B. J. on N. Y. W. W., vol. 2, Jervis MSS.

39. J. B. J. to Resident Engineers, June 5, 1837, Reports of J. B. J. on N. Y. W. W., vol. 2, Jervis MSS.

40. J. B. J. to Water Commissioners, December 23, 1836, Reports of J. B. J. on N. Y. W. W., vol. 1, Jervis MSS.

41. J. B. J. to Water Commissioners, August 12, 1837, Reports of J. B. J. on N. Y. W. W., vol. 1, Jervis MSS.

42. FitzSimons, *Reminiscences,* 126. Allen did not start work on the project for nearly a year after Jervis recommended his appointment. Jervis's high regard for Allen's abilities was expressed when he notified the commissioners that "Mr. Horatio Allen . . . has entered upon his duty and it is hardly necessary for me to say I consider him an able auxiliary in the department. He will attend immediately to the setting of the flow lines around the Croton Reservoir. . . . " J. B. J. to Water Commissioners, April 9, 1838, J. B. J., Croton Reports, vol. 1., 78.

43. Ibid. The appointment of William was an obvious example of John B. Jervis using his influence on behalf of a member of his family. Timothy B. Jervis, also younger than John, was an engineer on the Erie enlargement prior to his entering the Presbyterian ministry. Timothy was not employed within his older brother's district, and there is no evidence to indicate that John interceded on Timothy's part to obtain the position. In any case, of the many projects under the direction of John Jervis, the employment of members of the Jervis family on the project was not automatically the rule.

44. J. B. J. to James Renwick, Jr., February 7, 1837, Reports of J. B. J. on N. Y. W. W., vol. 2, 15.

45. James Renwick, Jr., to J. B. J., September 3, 1842, Box 33, Jervis MSS. Renwick's resignation resulted from Hastie's accusing him of not paying proper attention to his work. Renwick held no ill feelings toward Jervis and stated this in his letter. Following his resignation as an engineer, Renwick experienced a meteoric career rise to become one of the leading American architects of the nineteenth century.

46. The four resident engineers, the division under their supervision, and their annual salaries were as follows: Edward French, First Division, $1,800; Henry T. Anthony, Second Division, $1,500; William Jervis, Third Division, $1,500; Peter Hastie, Fourth Division, $1,800. Horatio Allen's annual salary was $3,500.

47. FitzSimons, *Reminiscences,* 123–124.

48. J. B. J., Letter Book on Croton Water Works, vol. 3, Jervis MSS, 19–21, 56–57.

49. J. B. J. to Colonel J. J. Abert, December 29, 1838, Reports of J. B. J. on N. Y. W. W., vol. 2, Jervis MSS.

50. J. B. J. to the New York City Water Commissioners, February 13, 1837, Reports of J. B. J. on N. Y. W. W., vol. 1. Construction of the dam did not begin until January 1838.

51. Ibid.

52. Ibid.

53. J. B. J., *Croton Aqueduct,* 15.

54. King, *Croton Aqueduct,* 179.

55. Blake, *Water for the Cities,* 163.

56. King, *Croton Aqueduct,* 179.

57. FitzSimons, *Reminiscences,* 133.

58. J. B. J., *Croton Aqueduct,* 15.

59. Ibid., 15–16.

60. FitzSimons, *Reminiscences,* 133.

61. Ibid.

62. Ibid.

63. J. B. J. to J. Stevens, President of the Water Commission, January 9, 1841, Reports of J. B. J. on N. Y. W. W., vol. 2, Jervis MSS.

64. Ibid.

65. Ibid.

66. Blake, *Water for the Cities,* 164.

67. Ibid.

68. King, *Croton Aqueduct,* 191.

69. FitzSimons, *Reminiscences,* 134.

70. Ibid., 135.

71. King, *Croton Aqueduct,* 191, 197.

72. Weidner, *Water for a City,* 116.

73. J. B. J. to Water Commissioners, December 12, 1837, J. B. J., Croton Reports, vol. 2.

74. King, *Croton Aqueduct,* 150.

75. Ibid., 150–151.

76. Ibid., 151.

77. Ibid.

78. Ibid., 151–152.

79. Ibid., 152.

80. Ibid.

81. *New York American,* March 7, 1838.

82. *New York Journal of Commerce,* March 12, 1838.

83. Ibid.

84. Ibid.

85. *New York American,* March 15, 1838.

86. *New York Evening Star,* March 12, 1838; *New York Times and Commercial Intelligencer,* March 16, 1838; *New York Evening Post,* March 12 and 13, 1838.

87. J. B. J., Memorandum, April 2, 1838, Reports of J. B. J. on N. Y. W. W., vol. 3, Jervis MSS.

88. Ibid.

89. Ibid.

90. King, *Croton Aqueduct,* 156.

91. Ibid., 160–163.

92. J. B. J. to Colonel J. J. Abert, December 29, 1838, Reports of J. B. J. on N. Y. W. W., vol. 2, Jervis MSS.

93. J. B. J., Report on Plans for Crossing Harlem River, J. B. J., Croton Reports, Vol. 2.

94. Ibid.

95. Ibid. Jervis pointed out to the commissioners that the Thames Tunnel, began in 1825, was estimated to cost 160,000 pounds sterling. By 1837, 264,000 pounds had already been spent, and it was figured that an additional 350,000 pounds would be needed to complete the tunnel.

96. Ibid.

97. Ibid.

98. Ibid.

99. FitzSimons, *Reminiscences,* 143–144.

100. Ibid.

101. Ibid., 144–145.

102. Ibid., 144n.

103. Ibid., 145n.

104. For a complete description of the High Bridge, see J. B. J., *Croton Aqueduct.*

105. Nevins and Thomas, *George Templeton Strong,* 305.

106. Tanner, *Internal Improvements,* 49–60.

107. Ibid., 68.

108. J. B. J., *Croton Aqueduct,* 31.

109. King, *Croton Aqueduct,* 221. The $9,500,000 expenditure did not include the amount needed for the distribution pipes beyond the distributing reservoir.

110. Nevins, *Philip Hone,* 624.

111. Tanner, *Internal Improvements,* 59–60.

112. Spann, *The New Metropolis,* 118.

113. Reports of J. B. J. on N. Y. W. W., vol. 3. An article appeared in the *American* about the debate in the Common Council over the naming of the chief engineer. Alderman Leonard praised Jervis's skill and ability in directing the construction of the aqueduct.

Leonard felt Jervis was entitled to the honor that belonged to him as project chief and that Jervis "felt sensitive on this subject." Alderman Davis seconded Leonard's statement, but Davis was under the impression that Jervis intended to leave the city by the end of 1842 and was not interested in the appointment. *New York American,* September 14, 1842.

CHAPTER 6

1. Blake, *Water for the Cities,* 142.
2. Ibid., 136.
3. State of New York, *Assembly Document #4,* 41–44.
4. Blake, *Water for the Cities,* 133–136.
5. Ibid., 136.
6. Ibid.
7. Ibid. Other members of the water commission were William Fox, Charles Dusenberry, Saul Alley, and Benjamin Brown. Brown resigned in 1836 and was replaced by Thomas Woodruff.
8. *Report of the Commissioners Relative to Supplying the City of New York with Pure and Wholesome Water.*
9. State of New York, *Assembly Document #4,* 192–196.
10. Blake, *Water for the Cities,* 146.
11. Ibid.
12. Ibid., 147. Commissioner William Fox had switched his allegiance to the Whig Party. The events surrounding Jervis's appointment were discussed in a Ph.D. dissertation done on the Croton project and Jervis's contributions to its completion. The author concluded that Jervis's engineering skills, not his political affiliation, were the reason for his selection. Lankton, "Manhattan Life Line."
13. Benson, *Jacksonian Democracy,* 3.
14. Booraem, *Republican Party,* 17–18.
15. FitzSimons, *Reminiscences,* 154. Because of the circumstances, Fox declined to remain on the board. The new Board of Water Commissioners, including Fox's successor, consisted of Samuel Stevens, John Ward, Zebedee Ring, R. Birdsall, and Samuel Childs. Stevens was named chairman.
16. King, *Croton Aqueduct,* 177.
17. *New York American,* July 18, 1840.
18. Douglass, an army lieutenant during the War of 1812, was cited for heroism for his role in the defense of Fort Erie in August 1814.
19. *New York Times,* October 30, 1840.
20. *New York American,* November 10, 1840. During and after the Van Buren presidency, Whigs frequently used the term Loco-Foco to apply to Democrats in general, as opposed to simply the leftwing splinter group of the mid-1830s.
21. *New York Courier and Enquirer,* November 3, 1840.
22. Ibid.
23. FitzSimons, *Reminiscences,* 155–156. Jervis chose Horatio Allen, a Whig, as his principal assistant. Two of the four resident engineers were reappointed from the Douglass staff.
24. *New York Courier and Enquirer,* November 12, 1840. Each time a project was begun, Jervis was deluged with requests for positions. If the person in question was qualified, Jervis often gave him a job. There is little evidence to show that politics, position, or personal relationship with Jervis caused him to make unwarranted appointments.
25. John Bloomfield to J. B. J., December 11, 1840, Box 34, Jervis MSS.

26. Ibid.

27. *New York Commercial Advertiser,* March 18, 1845. This would seem to lend credence to Major Douglass's claim that his replacement by Jervis was decided at Baltimore in 1835. However, it is doubtful that Bouck suggested Jervis's appointment to the Croton project, since he was reluctant to have Jervis leave the Erie enlargement.

28. Ibid.

29. *New York Evening Post,* May 13, 1845.

30. *New York Evening Post,* May 19, 1845.

31. *New York Evening Post,* May 27, 1845.

32. FitzSimons, *Reminiscences,* 156. Stephen Allen's recollection of the Douglass firing and Jervis hiring can be found in his memoirs edited by his great-grandson. Travis, "Memoirs of Stephen Allen," 157–161.

33. See Jervis MSS, Box 33.

34. Ibid.

35. King, *Croton Aqueduct,* 189–190.

36. FitzSimons, *Reminiscences,* 157.

37. *New York Plebian,* October 15, 1842.

38. J. B. J. to Philip Hone, June 30, 1849, Reports of J. B. J. on N. Y. W. W., Jervis MSS.

39. *New York Evening Post,* September 15, 1874.

40. *New York Evening Post,* October 7, 1874. The editor of the Jervis autobiography attributes the letter to Douglass's youngest son, Major Henry Douglass. FitzSimons, *Reminiscences,* 165n. It is more probable that the author of the letter was Malcolm Douglass, D.D., a brother of Henry Douglass. Malcolm Douglass had possession of his father's papers.

41. *New York Evening Post,* November 20, 1874.

42. Ibid.

43. Cullum, *War of 1812–15,* 261. Cullum, a brevet major-general of engineers during the Civil War, personally knew Douglass. The biographical account lauded Douglass but did point out that Douglass had a history of disagreements with his superiors. After serving three years as president of Kenyon College, Douglass was asked to resign by the Board of Trustees. He declined and was removed by the board. In terms of the actual removal, the affair was reminiscent of the Croton situation.

44. Ibid., 262.

45. Lankton, "Manhattan Life Line," 68–69. Lankton wrote that Stephen Allen interceded with Douglass on behalf of F. B. Jervis to get Jervis's younger brother a position in the Croton engineering department. Jervis also wrote Douglass on his brother Timothy's behalf in April 1835. However, since T. B. (not F. B.) Jervis resigned on May 9, 1836, to study for the ministry, it is unlikely he was much real help, as Lankton suggests, in providing information to his brother John regarding Douglass's progress on the Croton. David Bates Douglass MSS, Hobart and William Smith Colleges, Geneva, NY.

46. Ibid.

CHAPTER 7

1. Jervis's personal book collection is housed in the original portion of the Jervis Library in Rome.

2. A more detailed list of the subjects in Jervis's library would include biographies, botany, classical studies, economics, education, finance, government, history, literature, mathematics, philosophy, and travel and description.

3. Jervis's appointment in 1827 as head of the Delaware and Hudson Canal works brought him a salary of $4,000 annually. Within a decade, his income had increased to $5,000 a year as a result of his appointment to the Croton project. The pay Jervis received was high compared to the salary of his assistant engineers. Their income ranged from approximately one-fourth to three-fourths of his annual earnings. If Jervis's income is compared with those of skilled building trade workers, the difference is even more striking. His earnings were, depending on the project, from five to ten times greater than those of the skilled workers in the building trades.

4. FitzSimons, *Reminiscences,* 186.

5. Ibid., 187.

6. The banks in which Jervis held stock during the 1830s were, with one exception, in cities along the line of the Erie Canal. They were the Watervliet Bank, the Bank of Utica, the Bank of Rome, a bank in Lyons, the Lockport Bank and Trust Company, and the City Bank of Buffalo. Jervis also held stock in an Illinois bank.

7. John Bloomfield to J. B. J., May 27, 1840, Box 26, Jervis MSS. The Whigs successfully courted the voters in 1840 with slogans and banners conveying the idea that their presidential candidate, General Harrison, was a plain person who had been born in a log cabin and who drank hard cider.

8. J. B. J. to John Wood, April 25, 1837, Box 31, Jervis MSS.

9. A. C. Flagg to J. B. J., April 3, 1838, Box 23, Jervis MSS.

10. In 1868, Jervis wrote a series of letters for the *Roman Citizen* that were published in pamphlet form and titled *Currency and Public Debt of the United States.*

11. J. B. J. to John Bloomfield, June 22, 1827, Box 20, Jervis MSS.

12. John Bloomfield to J. B. J., May 7, 1830, Box 30, Jervis MSS.

13. John Bloomfield to J. B. J., May 29, 1830, Jervis MSS, Box 30. Jervis received more than $400 in annual interest from these loans. If relatively modest interest of only 5 percent had been charged, this would mean that Jervis had loaned over $8,000 between 1827 and 1830.

14. S. N. Dexter to J. B. J., June 21, 1838, Box 63, Jervis MSS.

15. Ibid.

16. John Bloomfield to J. B. J., July 23, 1838; John Bloomfield to J. B. J., October 29, 1838, Box 24, Jervis MSS.

17. R. F. Lord to J. B. J., April 2, 1838, Box 23, Jervis MSS; R. F. Lord to J. B. J., October 15, 1839, Box 32, Jervis MSS; R. F. Lord to J. B. J., June 3, 1842, Box 33, Jervis MSS. See also Russell F. Lord, MSS, Public Library, Port Jervis, NY.

18. John Bloomfield to J. B. J., April 27, 1837, Box 31, Jervis MSS.

19. John Bloomfield to J. B. J., August 16, 1842, Box 33, Jervis MSS.

20. Information on Jervis's land purchases in Oneida County between 1829 and 1840 can be found in the Oneida County Clerk's Office, Deed Books 48, 155; 63, 570; 66, 189; 89:127; and 96:37, 38.

21. John Bloomfield to J. B. J., April 26, 1837, Box 31, Jervis MSS.

22. Benjamin was nearly twenty-one years younger than John and five years younger than William Jervis.

23. B. F. Jervis to J. B. J., January 13, 1836, Box 31, Jervis MSS; B. F. Jervis to J. B. J., January 3, 1838, Box 32, Jervis MSS; B. F. Jervis to J. B. J., August 13, 1838, Box 24, Jervis MSS; John Bloomfield to J. B. J., February 10, 1840, Box 26, Jervis MSS.

24. B. F. Jervis to J. B. J., January 9, 1838, Box 23, Jervis MSS.

25. B. F. Jervis to J. B. J., January 22, 1838, Box 23, Jervis MSS.

26. J. B. J. to H. Huntington, April 10, 1837, Jervis MSS (letter located in a file in the library director's office).

27. Ibid.

28. Henry Brayton to J. B. J., January 31, 1838, Box 23, Jervis MSS.

29. B. F. Jervis to J. B. J., January 22, 1838; B. F. Jervis to J. B. J., October 13, 1838, Box 24, Jervis MSS.

30. B. F. Jervis to J. B. J., July 3, 1839, Box 32, Jervis MSS.

31. Henry Brayton to J. B. J., December 26, 1839, Box 32, Jervis MSS.

32. Ibid.

33. B. F. Jervis to J. B. J., August 13, 1839, Box 24, Jervis MSS.

34. William Jervis to J. B. J., March 9, 1842, Box 33, Jervis MSS.

35. Benjamin and William Jervis to J. B. J., April 1, 1842, Box 33, Jervis MSS.

36. From the time he was able to write, Benjamin corresponded with his older brother. Benjamin seemed eager to show Jervis that he too could be a success. Benjamin thought enough of his brother to name a son after him. The boy lived only eighteen years.

37. J. B. J. to Mrs. S. Norris, April 1822, Box 19, Jervis MSS.

38. J. B. J. to E. B., March 28, 1822, Box 19, Jervis MSS.

39. J. B. J. to Mrs. S. Norris, April 1822.

40. J. B. J. to Ann Jervis, May 13, 1822, Box 19, Jervis MSS.

41. J. B. J. to Ann Jervis, May 4, 1825, Box 20, Jervis MSS.

42. Cynthia Jervis to J. B. J., August 1, 1838, Box 24, Jervis MSS.

43. Cynthia Jervis to J. B. J., August 1838, Box 24, Jervis MSS.

44. John Bloomfield to J. B. J., April 8, 1840, Box 26, Jervis MSS.

45. During the months of June and July 1840, Jervis received congratulatory messages from several members of the Brayton family. Box 26, Jervis MSS.

46. Jervis's second wife was fifteen years younger than her husband. His first wife had been twelve years his junior.

47. Eliza Jervis to J. B. J., October 25, 1845, Box 27, Jervis MSS.

48. Timothy Jervis to J. B. J., May 25, 1828, Box 27, Jervis MSS. Susannah Maria was the mother of Bloomfield Jervis Beach, a favorite nephew of Jervis's. Beach, while in his mid-twenties, became Jervis's financial agent in Rome after the death of John Bloomfield.

49. John Bloomfield to J. B. J., March 1, 1830, Box 30, Jervis MSS.

50. Timothy B. Jervis to J. B. J., October 2, 1838, Box 24, Jervis MSS.

51. Ibid.

52. Timothy Jervis to J. B. J., May 25, 1828, Box 35, Jervis MSS.

53. FitzSimons, *Reminiscences,* 15. According to FitzSimons, all evidence indicates that Jervis was "a very tolerant man." There is reason to believe that his tolerance extended to other Protestants, but not Roman Catholics. Jervis's library contained many volumes on the Papacy and Roman Catholics. Not all were complimentary. How Jervis interpreted or reacted to these is difficult to determine, but one fact is certain: Jervis was not at all tolerant towards Irish Catholics. This was very apparent from references Jervis made about Irish Catholics while involved in his many projects, especially the Croton works. Probably Jervis's unfriendly attitude toward the Irish was due more to their living and working habits than to their religion. The Irish workers did not maintain the strict work regimen that Jervis did, but then neither did many others.

54. *New York Evening Post,* September 15, 1874.

CHAPTER 8

1. E. Cunard to J. B. J., June 24, 1845, Box 27, Jervis MSS.

2. L. S. Brown to J. B. J., September 30, 1845, Box 27, Jervis MSS.

3. Blake, *Water for the Cities,* 199–206; S. Norcross to J. B. J., July 11, 1845, Box 27, Jervis MSS.

4. FitzSimons, *Reminiscences,* 174.

5. Ibid., 175.

6. Ibid.

7. Henry Tracy to J. B. J., August 5, August 28, September 3, September 10, and October 2, 1845, Box 27, Jervis MSS.

8. FitzSimons, *Reminiscences,* 175.

9. Ibid.

10. Ibid.

11. Blake, *Water for the Cities,* 208.

12. FitzSimons, *Reminiscences,* 175.

13. Blake, *Water for the Cities,* 211. Jervis's salary was equal to that of each of the two chief engineers at the waterworks.

14. Kirby, *The Early Years,* 199.

15. *Amended Act of Incorporation of the Hudson River Rail-Road Company,* 5.

16. The New York and Harlem, chartered in 1831, was slowly being constructed north to East Greenbush. Its route was close to the New York–New England border, and therefore it posed no great threat to the Hudson River Railroad in terms of competition.

17. FitzSimons, *Reminiscences,* 176.

18. Jervis, *Report on the Hudson River Railroad,* 20.

19. Ibid., 25.

20. Ibid., 34.

21. Ibid., 21–34.

22. Ibid., 37. Following Jervis's reading of his report, a resolution was adopted by the assembly that expressed "full confidence in the ability, judgement, and fidelity" of Jervis. Ibid., 42.

23. *New York Commercial Advertiser,* January 4, 1846, Box 60, Jervis MSS.

24. Ibid.

25. Hungerford, *Men and Iron,* 138. Also see Matthew Vassar MSS.

26. *Memorial to the Legislature,* 1–10.

27. One of the People, *An Answer to the Minority Report,* 4–14.

28. Ibid.

29. Among those listed in addition to Jervis were Horatio Allen, Saul Alley, Stephen Allen, William Fox, James Boorman, Myndert Van Schaick, James Tallmadge, and Benjamin F. Butler.

30. *The Commissioners and Directors,* 9–18.

31. Ibid.

32. Jervis, "New York: And the Railroad Enterprise," 461.

33. Ibid.

34. FitzSimons, *Reminiscences,* 177.

35. *Amended Act of Incorporation of the Hudson River Rail-Road Company,* 4.

36. J. B. J. to Board of Directors, Hudson River Railroad, June 1, 1847, Hudson River Railroad Letter Book, Jervis MSS.

37. FitzSimons, *Reminiscences,* 178.

38. Condit, *The Port of New York,* 33. In a conversation with the special collections librarian at the U.S. Military Academy at West Point, the author was reminded that the railroad line along the river bank also had the effect of preventing camps from being built there, which has preserved the esthetics of the river.

39. Ibid.

40. Ibid.

41. J. B. J. to Board of Directors, Hudson River Railroad, June 1, 1847, Hudson River Railroad Letter Book, Jervis MSS.

42. J. B. J. to Board of Directors, Hudson River Railroad, July 3, 1847, Hudson River Railroad Letter Book, Jervis MSS.

43. J. B. J. to Board of Directors, Hudson River Railroad, September 6, 1847, Hudson River Railroad Letter Book, Jervis MSS.

44. J. B. J. to Board of Directors, Hudson River Railroad, September 13, 1847, Hudson River Railroad Letter Book, Jervis MSS.

45. Jervis, "The Hudson River Railroad," 282.

46. Ibid.

47. J. B. J. to Board of Directors, Hudson River Railroad, April 5, 1847; J. B. J. to Board of Directors, Hudson River Railroad, July 1, 1847, Hudson River Railroad Letter Book, Jervis MSS.

48. J. B. J., "The Hudson River Railroad," 283. The inland route followed the line that had been proposed by R. P. Morgan in 1842. Morgan was the civil engineer hired by the citizens of Poughkeepsie in their attempt to obtain a railroad charter. Hungerford, *Men and Iron,* 136–137.

49. Jervis, *Hudson River Rail Road Report,* 1–31.

50. J. B. J., "The Hudson River Railroad," 283.

51. Letter to the Board of Directors of the Hudson River Railroad Company; Memorial to the Board of Directors of the Hudson River Railroad Company, Jervis MSS.

52. J. B. J. to Board of Directors, Hudson River Railroad, July 1, 1847, Hudson River Railroad Letter Book, Jervis MSS.

53. J. B. J., "The Hudson River Railroad," 283.

54. J. B. J. to Board of Directors, Hudson River Railroad, December 6, 1847, Hudson River Railroad Letter Book, Jervis MSS.

55. J. B. J. to Board of Directors, Hudson River Railroad, January 31, 1848; J. B. J. to Board of Directors, Hudson River Railroad, June 5, 1848, Hudson River Railroad Letter Book, Jervis MSS.

56. J. B. J., "The Hudson River Railroad," 283–284.

57. Ibid. In the seventy-five miles of railroad between New York and Poughkeepsie, more than 1,100,000 cubic feet of stone was removed by excavation, more than half of which was used in the construction of river walls.

58. J. B. J. to Board of Directors, Hudson River Railroad, March 4, 1848; J. B. J. to Board of Directors, Hudson River Railroad, April 3, 1848; J. B. J. to Board of Directors, Hudson River Railroad, June 5, 1848, Hudson River Railroad Letter Book, Jervis MSS.

59. J. B. J. to Board of Directors, Hudson River Railroad, July 20, 1849, Hudson River Railroad Letter Book, Jervis MSS.

60. Ibid.

61. *Second Annual Report of the Directors,* 9.

62. Ibid., 10.

63. Albion, *The Rise of New York Port,* 417.

64. *Second Annual Report of the Directors,* 12.

65. FitzSimons, *Reminiscences,* 178. Jervis resigned as consulting engineer in the spring of 1850 as a result of a dispute with railroad president Boorman.

66. *Second Annual Report of the Directors,* 25.

67. Hungerford, *Men and Iron,* 149.

68. Condit, *Port of New York,* 34.

69. Spann, *The New Metropolis,* 14.

70. FitzSimons, *Reminiscences,* 179–180. The bridge, known as the Britannia Railroad Bridge, was an engineering marvel of the mid-nineteenth century. Its opening in 1850 was accompanied by celebration dinners to which Jervis was invited. Jervis was surprised at the manner in which the English engineers "excelled in making speeches." Obviously he felt uncomfortable when called upon to do so and found it curious that engineers were so adept in the art of speech-making as well as the art of engineering.

CHAPTER 9

1. Parks, *Democracy's Railroads,* 126–132.
2. Dunbar, *All Aboard!,* 68–69.
3. Jervis, *Report of the Michigan Southern,* 9–10.
4. Harlow, *The Road of the Century,* 252.
5. Cochran, *Railroad Leaders,* 263. Between 1842 and 1846, Bliss was president of the Western Railroad in Massachusetts.
6. Harlow, *Road of the Century,* 253.
7. Jervis, *Report of the Michigan Southern,* 10.
8. Ibid., 11–14.
9. Michigan Southern and Northern Indiana Railroads, *Director's Statement,* 2.
10. Jervis, *Report of the Michigan Southern,* 14–15.
11. Ibid., 16–17.
12. Ibid., 18–20.
13. Michigan Southern and Northern Indiana Railroad, *Director's Statement,* 4–6.
14. Ibid., 7.
15. Harlow, *Road of the Century,* 255.
16. Stover, *Iron Roads to the West,* 146.
17. Johnson and Supple, *Boston Capitalists and Western Railroads,* 111.
18. Ibid., 114.
19. Ibid., 111.
20. Chandler, *The Visible Hand,* 95.
21. Ibid.
22. Ibid., 94.
23. Ibid., 95.
24. Ibid.
25. Jervis, *Railway Property,* 247–248.
26. Ibid., 204.
27. Merritt, *Engineering in American Society,* 86.
28. E. C. Litchfield, Michigan Southern Railroad Secretary's Statement, November 23, 1852, Jervis MSS, Box 57.
29. Harlow, *Road of the Century,* 255.
30. J. Hofburn, Michigan Southern Railroad Secretary's Statement, May 3, 1855, Box 57, Jervis MSS.
31. John B. Miller, William Cassidy, and Thomas Alvord to J. B. J., September 3, 1855, Box 57, Jervis MSS.
32. J. B. J. to Miller, Cassidy, and Alvord, September 5, 1855, Box 57, Jervis MSS.
33. Typical of Whig support for Jervis was the letter from a Whig voter in Waterloo, New York who promised to vote for Jervis because he felt that Jervis would be a stronger voice than Clark in pushing for completion of the enlargement. William Wright to J. B. J., October 3, 1855, Jervis MSS, Box 57.

34. At least one northern New York "Soft" blamed the Democrats' defeat on the *New York Evening Post* and, curiously, on Horatio Seymour. Apparently Seymour made a speech in Watertown, Jefferson County, that the "Hards" found acceptable to their cause. As a result, the Soft observer thought Seymour's speech injurious to the Democratic Party to the point that he did not "want him to ever come in to our county again for he just divided our party this time right square in two and if he divides it again we won't have any party at all." Henry D. Rich to John Van Buren, November 21, 1855, Samuel J. Tilden MSS, New York Public Library.

35. For a succinct description of ante-bellum modernization, see McPherson, *Ordeal by Fire,* 5–22.

36. Booraem, *Republican Party,* 16.

37. J. B. J. to Henry Brayton, August 12, 1836, Box 31, Jervis MSS.

38. J. B. J., *Letters Addressed to the Friends,* 3–10.

39. Ibid, 11–20.

40. Ibid.

41. Harlow, *Road of the Century,* 259. See also Michigan Southern and Northern Indiana Railroads, *Director's Statements,* 1852–56.

42. Ibid.

43. Michigan Southern and Northern Indiana Railroads, *Director's Statement.*

44. Harlow, *Road of the Century,* 261.

45. Ibid.

46. *New York Evening Post,* March 29, 1858.

47. *New York Daily Tribune,* April 3, 1858.

48. Ibid.

49. There are many of examples of Jervis's editorializing on behalf of himself and others. He did not shrink from using newspapers to explain his actions or question those of others.

50. *New York Evening Post,* April 13, 1858.

51. Ibid.

52. Michigan Southern and Northern Indiana Railroads, *Director's Statements.*

53. Proxy statements from stockholders in several eastern and midwestern states were sent to Jervis during the fight to elect a board of directors in 1858. Box 75, Jervis MSS.

54. Cochran, *Railroad Leaders,* 263.

55. Ibid., 93.

56. Ibid., 79–93.

57. *New York Evening Post,* April 13, 1858.

58. American Society of Civil Engineers, *Proceedings,* vol. 22, No. 9, November 1896.

59. Stover, *Iron Roads to the West,* 114.

60. Ibid., 146.

61. J. B. J. to James Grant, January 4, 1853.

62. Chicago and Rock Island Railroad, *Director's Report,* 1854.

63. Chicago and Rock Island Railroad, *Director's Report,* 1855. See also Hayes, *Iron Road to Empire.*

64. William Jervis to J. B. J., January 24, 1853, Jervis MSS.

65. William Jervis to J. B. J., February 14, 1853, Jervis MSS.

66. Henry Farnam to Joseph Sheffield, n.d., Jervis MSS.

67. Joseph Sheffield to J. B. J., February 16, 1853, Jervis MSS.

68. Ibid.

69. Ibid.

70. J. B. J. to Joseph Sheffield, February 21, 1853, Jervis MSS.

71. J. B. J., *Report in Relation to the Railroad Bridge.*

72. Ibid.

73. Pittsburgh, Fort Wayne, and Chicago Railroad, *1st Annual Report of the Directors.*

74. Pittsburgh, Fort Wayne, and Chicago Railroad, *2nd Annual Report of the Directors.*

75. Pittsburgh, Fort Wayne, and Chicago Railroad, *3rd Annual Report of the Directors.*

76. Pittsburgh, Fort Wayne, and Chicago Railroad, *2nd Annual Report.*

77. Pittsburgh, Fort Wayne, and Chicago Railroad, *4th and 5th Annual Reports of the Directors.*

EPILOGUE

1. Two notable examples of the demand for Jervis's skills as a consultant were both Canadian projects. The first involved the construction of a canal from the St. Lawrence River to Lake Champlain, and the second was a water supply for the city of Hamilton, Ontario. For more complete details, see *Report of John B. Jervis* and *Report of Messrs. John B. Jervis and Alfred Craven.*

2. J. B. J. to Thomas O. Selfridge, Jr., undated; J. B. J. to Thomas O. Selfridge, Jr., January 30, 1875. Thomas O. Selfridge, Jr., MSS.

3. Marcosson, *Industrial Main Street,* 43–45.

4. Ibid., 46–47. Marcosson does not list his sources, which raises a doubt about the accuracy of his information. In addition, he credits Jervis with the construction of the South Carolina, the Utica and Schenectady, and the Utica and Syracuse railroads. Jervis, of course, built none of them. See also Wager, *A Descriptive Work,* 532.

5. Durant, *Oneida County,* 390.

6. Marcosson, *Industrial Main Street,* 45.

7. Ibid., 45–47. Curiously, the Rome newspapers are relatively silent on the fortunes of the city's industries in the 1870s. The arrival of a locomotive works in 1881 created interest, but the focus on the copper and brass industries and the accompanying wire mills did not come until after the beginning of the twentieth century when these industries formed the city's chief economic base.

8. J. B. J., *Currency and Public Debt,* 3–32.

9. Wisely, *American Civil Engineer,* 6–8.

10 *American Railroad Journal and Mechanics Magazine,* April 15, 1839, 225–232; Wisely, *American Civil Engineer,* 10–11.

11. Wisely, *American Civil Engineer,* 10–11.

12. Ibid.

13. *American Railroad Journal and Mechanics Magazine,* February 1, 1840, 81–83.

14. Ibid.

15. Wisely, *American Civil Engineer,* 19–22.

16. Ibid., 24–27. Jervis was in the company of his old friend and pupil Horatio Allen, along with General A. A. Humphreys, John Barnard, Moncure Robinson, and Squire Whipple, the bridge builder.

17. ASCE, *Transactions, 1875.*

18. ASCE, *Transactions, 1867–1872,* 137–151.

19. ASCE, *Transactions, 1874,* 255–266.

20. Noble, *America by Design,* 35.

21. Florman, *The Civilized Engineer,* 119. Not to detract from Florman's point, Jervis did not exactly threaten to quit the Croton project. According to Jervis, "if the Board insisted on the use [of quicklime], they must assume the responsibility of the measure." This was a strong statement for the board's engineer, but he did not mention resignation. FitzSimons, *Reminiscences,* 123.

22. Sinclair, *Philadelphia Philosopher Mechanics,* 2.

23. Ibid., 10.

24. FitzSimons, *Reminiscences,* 22.

BIBLIOGRAPHY

MANUSCRIPT COLLECTIONS

Bouck, William C., MSS. Cornell University Library, Ithaca, N.Y.
Canal Commissioners Contracts and Accounts for Construction and Repair
(1817–1828) MSS. New York State Archives, Albany, N.Y.
Corning, Erastus, MSS. Albany Institute of History and Art, Albany, N.Y.
Douglass, David Bates, MSS. Hobart and William Smith College, Geneva, N.Y.
Flagg, Azariah C., MSS. New York Public Library, New York City.
Jervis, John B., MSS. Jervis Public Library, Rome, N.Y.
Lord, Russell F., MSS. Public Library, Port Jervis, N.Y.
Marcy, William, MSS. Library of Congress, Washington, D.C.
Selfridge, Thomas O., Jr., MSS. Naval History Foundation Collection. Library
of Congress, Washington, D.C.
Tilden, Samuel J., MSS. New York Public Library, New York City.
Vassar, Matthew, MSS. Vassar College Library, Poughkeepsie, N.Y.

PUBLIC DOCUMENTS

*Amended Act of Incorporation of the Hudson River Rail-Road Company, By-
Laws and Extracts from Revised Statutes, etc.* New York: Thomas Snow-
den, 1847.
Chicago and Rock Island Railroad. *Director's Report.* New York: William C.
Bryant, 1854.
_____. *Director's Report.* New York: William C. Bryant, 1855.
*Memorial to the Legislature of the State of New York, in answer to objections
against the passage of an act to incorporate the Hudson River Railroad
Company.* New York: Leavitt, Trow and Company, 1846.
Michigan Southern and Northern Indiana Railroad. *Director's Statement.* New
York: Van Norden and Amerman, 1850.
_____. *Director's Statement.* New York: Van Norden and Amerman, 1852.
_____. *Director's Statement.* New York: Van Norden and Amerman, 1853.
_____. *Director's Statement.* New York: Van Norden and Amerman, 1854.
_____. *Director's Statement.* New York: Van Norden and Amerman, 1855.

_____. *Director's Statement.* New York: Van Norden and Amerman, 1856.

_____. *Director's Statement.* New York: Van Norden and Amerman, 1857.

_____. *Director's Statement.* New York: Van Norden and Amerman, 1858.

One of the People. *An Answer to the Minority Report of a Member of the Rail-Road Committee.* New York: William Osborn, 1846.

Pittsburgh, Fort Wayne, and Chicago Railroad. *1st & 3rd Annual Report of the Directors.* Pittsburgh: W. S. Haven, 1863, 1865.

_____. *2nd, 4th & 5th Annual Report of the Directors.* Pittsburgh: Barr and Myers, 1864, 1866, 1867.

Report of Benjamin Wright and J. L. Sullivan, Engineers engaged in the survey of the route of The Proposed Canal from the Hudson to the headwaters of the Lackawaxen River. Philadelphia: John Young, 1824.

Report of John B. Jervis, Civil Engineer, in relation to the Railroad Bridge over the Mississippi River, at Rock Island. New York: Wm. C. Bryant, 1857.

Report of John B. Jervis relative to the Survey of the Proposed Caughnawaga Canal. Quebec: Lovell and Lamoureau, 1855.

Report of Messrs. John B. Jervis and Alfred Craven, Esquires, New York on A Supply of Water for the City of Hamilton. Hamilton, Ont.: *Morning Banner,* 1857.

Report of the Commissioners Relative to Supplying the City of New York with Pure and Wholesome Water. New York: P. Van Pelt, 1833.

Second Annual Report of the Directors of the Hudson River Rail-Road Co. August 29, 1849. New York: Wm. C. Bryant, 1849.

State of New York. *Assembly Document #4.* "Report of Benjamin Wright to the Mayor and Aldermen of New York City, January 28, 1834."

_____. *Assembly Document #5.* "Report of Canvass White to the Directors of the New York Water Works Company, January 9, 1826."

_____. *Assembly Document #36.* "Report of Colonel DeWitt Clinton to the Committee on Fire and Water, December 22, 1832."

_____. *Assembly Document #44.* "Report of J. Martineau to the New York Water Commission, January 25, 1835."

_____. *Assembly Document #61.* "Report of William Weston to the Common Council, March 16, 1799."

_____. *Assembly Document #65.* "Report of John B. Jervis to the Canal Commissioners, January 14, 1836."

_____. *Assembly Document #99A.* "Report and Estimate of John B. Jervis, Eng., from Albany to Fultonville, October 17, 1835."

_____. *Assembly Document #99E.* "Report of John B. Jervis and Frederick C. Mills, October 23, 1835."

_____. *Laws of the State of New York in relation to the Erie and Champlain Canals.* Albany: 1825.

The Commissioners and Directors appointed by the Act Incorporating the Hudson River Rail Road Company submit to the Considerations of the Public the Following Statement, Showing Prospects of Business and the Importance of the Proposed Railroad. New York: E. B. Clayton and Son, 1846.

NEWSPAPERS AND JOURNALS

American Railroad Journal. 1833.
American Railroad Journal and Mechanics Magazine. 1839–1840.
New York American. 1838–1842.
New York Commercial Advertiser. 1845–1846.
New York Courier and Enquirer. 1840.
New York Daily Tribune. 1858.
New York Evening Post. 1838–1845, 1858, 1874.
New York Evening Star. 1838.
New York Journal of Commerce. 1838.
New York Plebian. 1842.
New York Times. 1840, 1877.
New York Times and Commercial Intelligencer. 1838.

BOOKS, PAMPHLETS, ARTICLES, AND UNPUBLISHED WORKS

Albion, Robert G. *The Rise of New York Port.* New York: Charles Scribner's Sons, 1939.
American Society of Civil Engineers. *Transactions, 1867–1872.* New York: ASCE, 1872.
————. *Transactions, 1875.* New York: ASCE, 1875.
————. *Proceedings, 1896.* New York: ASCE, 1896.
Benson, Lee. *The Concept of Jacksonian Democracy.* New York: Atheneum, 1965.
Blake, Nelson M. *Water for the Cities: A History of the Urban Water Supply Problem in the United States.* Syracuse, N.Y.: Syracuse University Press, 1956.
Bloodgood, S. DeWitt. "Some Account of the Hudson and Mohawk Rail Road," *The American Journal of Science and Arts,* vol. 21 (January 1832), 141–149.
Booraem, Hendrik, V. *The Formation of the Republican Party in New York.* New York: New York University Press, 1983.
Brown, William H. *The History of the First Locomotives in America.* New York: D. Appleton and Company, 1871.
Calhoun, Daniel H. *The American Civil Engineer.* Boston, Mass.: The Technology Press (Massachusetts Institute of Technology), 1960.
Chandler, Alfred D. *The Visible Hand: The Managerial Revolution in American Business.* Cambridge, Mass.: Harvard University Press, 1977.
Cochran, Thomas C. "Did the Civil War Retard Industrialization?" *The Mississippi Valley Historical Review,* vol. 48 (September 1961), 197–210.
————. *Railroad Leaders, 1845–1890.* New York: Russell and Russell, 1965.

Condit, Carl W. *American Building Art: The Nineteenth Century.* New York: Oxford University Press, 1960.

_____. *The Port of New York.* Chicago: University of Chicago Press, 1980.

Cullum, George W. *Campaigns of the War of 1812–15, against Great Britain, Sketched and Criticized; with Brief Biographies of the American Engineers.* New York: James Miller, 1879.

Daboll, Nathan. *Schoolmaster's Assistant: Improved and Enlarged Being a Plain Practical System of Arithmetic Adopted to the United States.* New London: Samuel Green, 1813.

Delaware and Hudson Company. *A Century of Progress: History of the Delaware and Hudson Company, 1823–1923.* Albany, N.Y.: J. B. Lyon, 1925.

Dilworth, Thomas. *The Schoolmaster's Assistant.* New York: G. and R. White, 1800.

Dunbar, Willis Frederick. *All Aboard! A History of Railroads in Michigan.* Grand Rapids, Mich.: William B. Eardmans, 1969.

Durant, Samuel. *History of Oneida County.* Philadelphia: Everts and Fariss, 1878.

Earle, Thomas. *Treatise on Rail-Roads.* Philadelphia: Mifflin and Perry, 1830.

Ellis, David M., et al. *A History of New York State.* Ithaca, N.Y.: Cornell University Press, 1967.

Finch, J. K. "John Bloomfield Jervis, Civil Engineer," *Transactions of the Newcomen Society,* vol. 11 (1931), 109–120.

FitzSimons, Neal, ed. *The Reminiscences of John B. Jervis: Engineer of the Old Croton.* Syracuse, N.Y.: Syracuse University Press, 1971.

Florman, Samuel C. *The Civilized Engineer.* New York: St. Martin's Press, 1987.

Friends of W. C. Young. *Biography of William C. Young.* New York: Styles and Cash, 1889.

Grey, Thomas. *Observations on A General Iron Rail-way or Land Steam Conveyance, etc.* 5th ed. London: Baldwin, Cradock, and Jay, 1825.

Harlow, Alvin F. *The Road of the Century.* New York: Creative Age Press, 1947.

Hawke, David. *Nuts and Bolts of the Past: A History of American Technology, 1776–1860.* New York: Harper & Row, 1988.

Hayes, William E. *Iron Road to Empire.* New York: Simmons-Boardman, 1953.

Hollingsworth, Brian. *The Illustrated Encyclopedia of the World's Steam Passenger Locomotives.* London: Salamander Books, 1982.

Hungerford, Edward. *Men and Iron: The History of New York Central.* New York: Thomas Y. Crowell, 1938.

Jervis, John B. *Currency and Public Debt of the United States.* Rome, N.Y.: Sanford and Carr, 1868.

_____. *Description of the Croton Aqueduct.* New York: Slamm and Guion, 1842.

_____. "Facts and Circumstances in the Life of John B. Jervis," Jervis MSS.

_____. "Historical Sketch of the Mohawk and Hudson Rail Road," 1867, Jervis MSS.

_____. *Hudson River Rail-Road Report on the Location of the Line between*

Fishkill and Albany; with General Remarks on the Prospects of the Road. New York: Wm. C. Bryant and Company, 1848.

_____. "Improved Wheel for Railroad Wagons," *American Railroad Journal,* (July 1833), 452–453.

_____. *Letters addressed to the Friends of Freedom and the Union.* New York: William C. Bryant and Company, 1856.

_____. "Memoir of American Engineering," March 1876, Jervis MSS.

_____. "New York: And the Railroad Enterprise," *The Merchant's Magazine,* vol. 15 (November 1846), 456–463.

_____. *Railway Property: A Treatise on the Construction and Management of Railways.* New York: Phinney, Blakeman, and Mason, 1861.

_____. "The Hudson River Railroad," *The Merchant's Magazine,* vol. 22 (March, 1850), 278–289.

_____. *Report on the Hudson River Railroad.* New York: J. F. Trow and Company, 1846.

_____. *Report of the Michigan Southern and Northern Indiana Railroads.* New York: Van Norden and Amerman, 1850.

_____. "Report on the Projected Carbondale Railroad to the Delaware and Hudson Canal Co.," 1827, Jervis MSS.

_____. *The Question of Labour and Capital.* New York: G. P. Putnam's Sons, 1877.

Johnson, Arthur M. and Supple, Barry E. *Boston Capitalists and Western Railroads: A Study in the Nineteenth-Century Railroad Investment Process.* Cambridge, Mass.: Harvard University Press, 1967.

Kanarek, Harold. *The Mid-Atlantic Engineers: A History of the Baltimore District U.S. Army Corps of Engineers, 1774–1974.* Washington, D.C.: U.S. Government Printing Office, 1978.

King, Charles. *A Memoir of the Construction, Cost, and Capacity of the Croton Aqueduct.* New York: Charles King, 1843.

Kirby, Richard, et al. *Engineering in History.* New York: McGraw-Hill, 1956.

Kirby, Richard S. *The Early Years of Modern Civil Engineering.* New Haven: Yale, 1932.

Lankton, Larry D. "Manhattan Life Line: Engineering the Old Croton Aqueduct 1833–1842." Unpublished Ph.D. dissertation, University of Pennsylvania, 1977.

LeRoy, Edwin D. *The Delaware and Hudson Canal.* Wayne County, Pa.: Wayne County Historical Society, 1950.

Long, S. H. *Railroad Manual.* Baltimore: Wm. Woody, 1829.

Mahan, D. H. *An Elementary Course of Civil Engineering.* New York: Wiley and Putnam, 1837.

Marcosson, Isaac F. *Industrial Main Street.* New York: Dodd, Mead and Company, 1953.

McKelvey, Blake. "The Erie Canal: Mother of Cities," *The New York Historical Society Quarterly,* vol. 25 (January 1951), 55–71.

McPherson, James M. *Ordeal by Fire.* New York: Knopf, 1982.

Merritt, Raymond H. *Engineering in American Society 1850–75*. Lexington, Ky.: University Press of Kentucky, 1969.

Morison, Elting E. *From Know-How to Nowhere: The Development of American Technology*. New York: Basic Books, 1974.

Murray, Lindley. *The English Reader*. Cooperstown, N.Y.: H. and E. Phinney, 1827.

Nevins, Allan, ed. *The Diary of Philip Hone, 1828–1851*. New York: Arno Press, 1970.

Nevins, Allan and Halsey, Milton, eds. *The Diary of George Templeton Strong*, vol. 1. New York: Macmillan Company, 1952.

Noble, David F. *America by Design: Science, Technology, and the Rise of Corporate Capitalism*. New York: Knopf, 1977.

Parks, Robert J. *Democracy's Railroads: Public Enterprise in Jacksonian Michigan*. Port Washington, N.Y.: Kennikat Press, 1972.

Sanderson, Dorothy H. *The Delaware and Hudson Canalway: Carrying Coals to Rondout*. Ellenville, N.Y.: Rondout Valley Publishing Company, 1974.

Schramke, T. *Description of the New York Croton Aqueduct*. Berlin: T. Schramke, 1846.

Shaw, Ronald E. *Erie Water West: A History of the Erie Canal*. Lexington, Ky.: University Press of Kentucky, 1966.

Sinclair, Bruce. *Philadelphia Philosopher Mechanics: A History of the Franklin Institute 1824–1865*. Baltimore: Johns Hopkins University Press, 1974.

Soule, F. C. *The Chenango Canal*. Syracuse, N.Y.: Canal Society of New York State, 1970.

Spann, Edward K. *The New Metropolis: New York City 1840–1857*. New York: Columbia University Press, 1981.

Stevens, Frank W. *The Beginnings of the New York Central Railroad: A History*. New York: G. P. Putnam's Sons, 1926.

Stover, John F. *American Railroads*. Chicago: University of Chicago Press, 1961.

_____. *History of the Baltimore and Ohio Railroad*. West Lafayette, Indiana: Purdue University Press, 1987.

_____. *Iron Road to the West: American Railroads in the 1850s*. New York: Columbia University Press, 1978.

Tanner, Henry S. *A Description of the Canals and Railroads of the United States Comprehending Notices of all the Works of Internal Improvements throughout the Several States (1840)*. New York: Augustus M. Kelly, 1970.

The New England Primer improved for the more easy attaining the true reading of English to which is added The Assembly of Divines and Mr. Cotton's Catechism. Boston: Edward Draper, 1777.

Thurston, Robert H. *A History of the Growth of the Steam Engine (1878)*. Port Washington, N.Y.: Kennikat Press, 1972.

Travis, John C., ed. "The memoirs of Stephen Allen (1767–1852)." New York City, 1927. Unpublished Allen autobiography located in the New York Public Library, New York, N.Y.

Tredgold, Thomas. *A Practical Treatise on Railroads and Carriages etc.* London: Josiah Taylor, 1825.

_____. *Tracts on Hydraulics.* London: F. Taylor, 1826.

Wager, Daniel E. *A Descriptive Work on Oneida County, New York.* Boston: Boston History Company, 1896.

Wakefield, Manville B. *Coal Boats to Tidewater: The Story of the Delaware and Hudson Canal.* South Fallsburg, N.Y.: Steingart Associates, 1965.

Walker, J., Stephenson, R., et al. *Liverpool and Manchester Railroad Reports.* Philadelphia: Carey and Lea, 1831.

Warner, Paul T. "The Development of the Anthracite-Burning Locomotive." *Bulletin of the Railway and Locomotive Historical Society.* May 1940, 11–13.

Weidner, Charles H. *Water for a City: A History of New York City's Problem from the Beginning to the Delaware River System.* New Brunswick, N.J.: Rutgers University Press, 1974.

White, John H., Jr. *A History of the American Locomotive.* New York: Dover, 1979.

_____. *American Locomotives: An Engineering History, 1830–1880.* Baltimore: Johns Hopkins University Press, 1968.

Whitford, Noble E. *History of the Canal System of the State of New York.* Albany, N.Y.: Brandow Printing Company, 1906.

Wisely, William H. *The American Civil Engineer, 1852–1874.* New York: American Society of Civil Engineers, 1974.

Wood, Nicholas. *A Practical Treatise on Railroads etc.* 1st American edition. Philadelphia: Carey and Lea, 1832.

OTHER SOURCES

Deed Books 48, 63, 66, 89, 96. Oneida County Clerk's Office, Utica, N.Y.

George Clinton to Timothy Jarvis [Jervis] by Warranty Deed, June 28, 1805. Oneida County Clerk's Office. Deed Book 19.

John and Ann Bloomfield to Timothy Jervis by Warranty Deed, June 15, 1797. Oneida County Clerk's Office. Deed Book 10.

Timothy and Phebe Jarvis [Jervis] to George Clinton, Mortgage, June 29, 1805. Oneida County Clerk's Office. Mortgage Book 5.

Timothy Jervis to Abraham Culver, Mortgage, June 10, 1809. Oneida County Clerk's Office. Mortgage Book 5.

William Bullus to Timothy Jarvis [Jervis] by Warranty Deed, November 1, 1796. Oneida County Clerk's Office. Deed Book 8.

INDEX

Abeel and Dunscomb Foundry, 29
Abert, J. J., 69, 75
Adrian, Mich., 122
Albany, N.Y., 6, 16, 17, 35, 37–39, 46, 58, 59, 110, 112, 115, 117, 118
Albany Regency, 81, 83–88, 92, 94, 122
Allen, Horatio, 28–30, 33, 46–48, 68, 74, 77–80, 86, 87, 166n.42
Allen, Stephen, 82, 83, 89–92, 110, 170n.45
Alley, Saul, 110
American [Know-Nothing] Party, 133
American Railroad Journal, 43, 49, 50
American Society of Civil Engineers (ASCE), 148, 150
Amsterdam, N.Y., 11, 14, 102, 103
Anthony, Henry T., 67
Anti-Rent War, 106
Archbald, James, 31, 32
Astor, John Jacob, 38

Baldwin, Matthias, 49
Baltimore, 16, 37
Baltimore and Ohio Railroad, 27, 37, 38, 41, 42, 126, 127
Bank charters, 85
Bank of Rome, 97, 100
Barnburner Democrats, 107, 108, 132–34
Bates, David S., 9, 10
Beach, Bloomfield Jervis, 146
Binghamton, N.Y., 52
Blake, Nelson, 62
Bliss, George, 122, 124, 126, 129, 135, 136
Bloodgood, DeWitt, 42
Bloomfield, John, xvii, 11, 89, 90, 97–99

Bolton, John, 30, 31
Boorman, James, 110, 112
Boston, Mass., 16, 109, 110, 126
Bouck, William, 54, 56, 57, 89, 91, 92, 106
Brayton, Henry, 100, 101, 133
Brayton, William, 100, 101
British railroads, 33
Bronx River, 62, 82
Brooks, John W., 126
Brown, William H., 48
Buffalo, N.Y., 58, 118, 131
Buffalo and Mississippi Railroad, 124

Calhoun, Daniel, 7
Cambreling, Churchill C., 40, 41, 49
Canal commissioners, 7, 52, 54, 55–60, 99
Carbondale, Pa., 19, 21, 24
Catlin, Lynde, 38
Cazenovia, N.Y., 100, 121
Chandler, Alfred D., 126–28
Chapman, William, 45
Charleston and Hamburg Railroad, 31, 35, 36, 46
Chenango Canal, xviii, 52, 54–56, 59, 103, 163n.5
Chenango River, 54
Chesapeake and Ohio Canal, 35
Chicago, 122, 124–26, 130, 131, 138, 140, 142, 146
Chief Engineer (canal boat), 11
Cincinnati, Peru, and Chicago Railroad, 134
Civil War, 97, 106, 121, 127, 142, 145, 146, 148
Clarke, John, 38, 115, 132
Clarke, Thomas C., 150–52

Cleveland and Pittsburgh Railroad, 143
Clinton, DeWitt
 civil engineer, 82
 governor, 6, 85
Coal, 17–19, 24, 27, 42
Cochituate Aqueduct, 110
Cochran, Thomas C., 137
Coffer dam, 75
Colfax, Schuyler, 135
Compromise of 1850, 120
Conservative Democrats, 106
Croton Aqueduct, 62–69, 75, 77–79, 81,
 83, 90, 93, 96, 103, 108, 110, 115,
 127, 128, 152, 167n.46
Croton Dam, xix, 63, 65, 68–71, 79,
 165n.21
Cullum, George W., 94
Currency and the Public Debt, 148

Darien, Isthmus of, 145
Davenport, Iowa, 126
Delaware and Hudson Canal, xvii, xviii,
 14, 16, 19, 33, 35, 38, 52, 54, 58,
 99, 115
Delaware and Hudson Company, 17, 19,
 20, 22, 27, 28, 33, 34, 40
Delaware River, 18
Democratic Party, 85–87, 89, 90, 97,
 106–8, 132, 133, 176n.34
Depression of 1837, 35, 87, 97, 102
*Description . . . of Internal
 Improvements,* 77
Description of the Croton Aqueduct, 62
Detroit, 121, 131
Detroit, Monroe, and Toledo Railroad,
 134
Dexter, Simon Newton, 54, 98
Disbrow, Levi, 61
Distributing reservoir, xix, 62, 63, 79, 80
Douglass, David Bates, 62, 67, 68, 71,
 72, 74, 79–83, 87–89, 93, 94

Earle, Thomas, 42
Earll, Jonas, Jr., 56
Edinburgh Encyclopedia, 11, 145
Effie Afton, 141, 142
Engineers
 Erie Canal "school," 8

as managers, 126–29
Erie and Kalamazoo Railroad, 122
Erie Canal, xviii, 5–7, 8, 11–16, 21, 35,
 37, 38, 52, 54, 56–59, 77, 90, 91,
 96, 99, 102, 106, 131, 146, 163n.24,
 164n.40
Erie Railroad, 108, 127, 164n.25

Farnum, Henry, 138, 140, 141
Fillmore, Millard, 134
Finney, Charles G., 132
Fishkill, N.Y., 115, 116
FitzSimons, Neal, 104, 162n.67, 165n.21
Flagg, Azariah C., 97
Fleming, Peter, 36, 38
Forbes group, 126
Fort Stanwix, N.Y., 3
Fort Wayne, Ind., 142
Foster, Rastrick, and Company, 29
Fox, William W., 88
Franklin Institute, 148
Free-Soil Party, 108, 133, 134
French, Edmund, 66, 67, 68, 115

Genesee Aqueduct, 56
Geneseo, Ill., 140
Graff, Frederick, 74
Grant, James, 126, 138
Gravity Railroad, xvii, 16, 20, 21, 25,
 26, 27, 30, 32
Greenbacks, 148

Halifax, 108
Hall, Adam, 42, 43
Hardshell Democrats, 132
Harlem River, xix, 61, 62, 65, 69, 71,
 72, 75, 79, 82, 83
Hastie, Peter, 68
Haupt, Herman, 127
Havemeyer, William F., 112
High Bridge, xix, 61, 62, 65, 69, 72, 74–
 77, 79, 81, 83, 93, 165n.4
Hillsdale, Mich., 121, 122, 138
Hollingsworth, Brian, 48, 162n.75
Hone, Philip, 19, 77
Honesdale, Pa., 19, 21, 24, 26, 28, 30,
 99

Hudson River, 6, 18, 38, 46, 62, 66, 113–16
Hudson River Railroad, xviii, 17, 110, 111 (map), 112, 113, 117, 118, 121, 124, 125, 128, 146, 173n.16
Hunker Democrats, 107, 132
Hunt, Washington, 96, 122, 132, 135
Hunt's Merchants Magazine, 112
Hutchinson, Holmes, 58
Hydraulic engineering, 12

Inter-oceanic canal, 145
Inverted siphons, 72–75, 83, 92, 165n.4
Irish workers, 117, 172n.53
Iron rails, 40, 41, 115, 147

Jackson, Mich., 121
Jervis, Benjamin, 100–102
Jervis, Cynthia (Brayton), 103, 104, 133, 165n.5
Jervis, Eliza R. (Coates), 104
Jervis, John B.
    arch stresses, calculations on, 157n.51
    Boston water supply, 109, 110
    Chicago and Rock Island Railroad, 138
    chief engineer
        Chenango Canal, 52
        Croton Aqueduct, 60, 89–91, 169n.12, 170n.27
        Delaware and Hudson Canal, 24, 32
        Erie Canal enlargement, eastern section, 58
        Hudson River Railroad, 114
        Mohawk and Hudson Railroad, 36
    Croton Aqueduct
        cost estimate, 77
        quicklime, 177n.1
    Croton Dam, description, 63
    daughter's death, 104
    Democratic Party, 87
    description of Croton Dam, 63
    designs
        improved railroad wheel, 43, 44
        iron trestle, 143
        method for Erie Canal to cross small streams, 12
        pneumatic convoy, 26

    rainfall and run-off gauge, 55, 56
    education
        early, 4
        of engineers, 151
    Effie Afton case, 141, 142
    engineering society, early, 148, 149
    Erie Canal
        engineering party, 8, 9
        enlargement, 58
        record keeping, 13
        resident engineering, 11
        salary, 14
        Schoharie Crossing, 58, 164n.37
        superintendent, 13, 14
    Erie Railroad commission, 108
    "Facts and Circumstances" (autobiography), 94
    family, 102–4, 167n.43
    Gravity Railroad, use of chains on, 32
    Halifax water supply, 108
    Hamilton (Ontario) water supply, 177n.1
    Hampden (pseud.), 133
    Harlem River tunnel, cost estimate, 75, 76
    High Bridge
        cost estimate, 75
        description, 65
    "Historical Sketch of the Mohawk and Hudson Railroad," 43
    Hudson River, 114, 115
    Hudson River Railroad
        cost estimate, 117
        estimates for speed of travel, 112
        report on, 112–13
        routes, 116
    hydraulic canal plans, 163n.24
    investments
        banks, 96, 97
        businesses, 100–102
        loans, 98
        property, 99
    marriage, 103, 104
    Michigan Southern and Northern Indiana Railroad
        cost estimate, 124
        named president, 129, 130
        proxy fight, 135
    Michigan Southern Railroad, 122

Jervis, John B. (*continued*)
  New York State Engineer and
      Surveyor, candidacy, 131, 132,
      175n.33, 176n.34
  personal library, 95
  pile load bearing experiments, 76, 77
  Pittsburgh, Ft. Wayne, and Chicago
      Railroad, 143
  pseudonym (Hampden), 133
  railroad travel passes, 46
  regulations for Croton engineering
      office, 67–68
  religion, 4, 104–5
  report on the Croton flood damage,
      70
  Republican Party, 133
  resigns as principal engineer of the
      Mohawk and Hudson and
      Saratoga and Schenectady
      Railroad, 51
  Rome Merchant Iron Mill, 146, 147
  salary as an engineer, 171n.3
  Saratoga and Schenectady Railroad,
      survey for, 49
  specifications for Mohawk and
      Hudson locomotive, 40
  stockholder in the Hudson River
      Railroad Company, 113
  Stourbridge Lion, 30, 31
  trip to the British Isles, 108, 118, 119,
      162n.75
  wife's death, 104
  will, provisions of, 152
  Wright, Benjamin, dispute with, 22,
      23
Jervis, Timothy (brother), 38
Jervis, Timothy (father), 3, 4, 6, 155n.5
Jervis, William, 101, 115, 138, 140, 141
Johnson, Walter, 109
Joy, James F., 129

Kansas-Nebraska Act, 133
Kemble, Governeur, 44
Kemble, William, 43
Kingston, N.Y., 18, 19, 22

Lackawaxen River, 18, 19
Lake Cochituate (Long Pond), 109, 110
Lake Erie, 6, 122, 125, 131

Lake Michigan, 121
Lake Shore and Michigan Southern
      Railroad, 136
Latrobe, Benjamin, Jr., 126, 148
Lincoln, Abraham, 141, 142
Litchfield, Edwin C., 130, 134–36
Litchfield, Elisha, 121, 126, 130, 136
Little Falls, N.Y., 57
Liverpool and Manchester Railroad, 29,
      41
Locomotive engines, 26–29, 31, 33, 36,
      40–43, 47, 50
Locomotives
  Best Friend of Charleston, 35, 160n.2
  Davy Crockett, 50, 51
  DeWitt Clinton, 35–37, 41–43
  Experiment, 45, 50
  Jervis-type, 48, 49
  John Bull, 161n.38
  Robert Fulton, 41–43, 50, 161n.38
  South Carolina, 46, 47, 162n.67
  Stourbridge Lion, xviii, 28–33, 36, 40,
      42
  Tom Thumb, 42
  York, 42
Long, S. H., 26
Long Pond (Lake Cochituate), 109, 110
Lord, Russell F., 32, 99

McAlpine, William, J., 55, 58, 59, 150,
      163n.19
McCallum, Daniel J., 127
McClellan, George B., 127
McCullough, J. N., 143
Manhattan Company, 61
Marcy, William, 52, 84, 87, 107, 122
Martineau, John, 14, 62, 71, 72, 83,
      157n.53
Matthew, David, 45
Mauch Chunk Railroad, 24
Menai Straits, 118, 175n.70
Merchants as railway owners, 128
Michigan Central Railroad, 125, 126,
      131
Michigan Southern and Northern
      Indiana Railroad, 123 (map), 126,
      129–31, 134–38, 142
Michigan Southern Railroad, 121, 122,
      124–26

Miller, Edward, 149
Mills, Frederick C., 58
Mills, John B., 18
Mississippi and Missouri Railroad, 138, 141
Mississippi Bridge Company, 138, 141, 142
Mississippi River, 118, 120, 126, 138, 140–42
Mohawk and Hudson Railroad, 17, 32, 35–39, 40, 42, 43, 45, 46, 128
Mohawk River, 6, 12
Monroe, Mich., 121, 122

New England Primer, 4, 5
New Haven and Northhampton Railroad, 138
New York American, 73, 74, 88, 89
New York and Harlem Railroad, 112, 113, 173n.16
New York Central Railroad, 118, 131
New York City, 3, 16, 17, 22, 30, 33, 61, 62, 67, 72, 74, 97, 108, 110, 112, 113, 116, 118, 122, 128, 140, 141, 146, 150
New York Common Council, 62, 72, 74, 80, 82, 92
New York Evening Post, 74, 80, 93, 133, 135, 176n.34
New York Journal of Commerce, 73, 74
New York Times, 28, 31
New York University, 112
Northern Indiana Railroad, 124–26

Olyphant, Robert M., 135

Panama Canal, 145
Panic of 1857, 130, 135
Panic of 1873, 146–47
Peekskill, N.Y., 117
Philadelphia, 16–18, 35, 61, 62, 69, 109
Philadelphia Water Works, 74
Pittsburgh, 142
Pittsburgh, Fort Wayne, and Chicago Railroad, 137, 142, 145
Polk, James K., 107
Port Jervis, N.Y., 19, 108

Potomac Aqueduct, 69
Poughkeepsie, N.Y., 17, 112, 113, 116, 128

Question of Labor and Capital, The (Jervis), 4, 5
Quincy Railroad, 24

Radical Democrats, 106
Railroad cars, 25
Railroad expansion, 120
Railroad Gazette, 48
Railroad Manual, 26
Railway Property, 129, 142
Rainfall and run-off gauge, 55, 163n.15
Receiving reservoir, 63
Reminiscences of John B. Jervis, 104
Renwick, James, 27, 36, 38, 40, 42, 44, 158n.50
Renwick, James, Jr., 68, 167n.45
Republican Party, 86, 133, 134
Reservoir supply system for the Chenango Canal, 56
Riggs, Joseph K., 135
River embankments, construction of, 115, 174n.57
Roberts, Nathan, 8, 9, 58
Rock Island Railroad (Chicago and Rock Island Railroad), 126, 128, 129, 131, 137–39 (map), 140–42
Rolling mill, 146
Rome, N.Y., 3, 6, 9, 11, 15, 17, 54, 93, 98–100, 102, 108, 122, 123, 145, 146, 152
Rome and Watertown Railroad, 146
Rome Iron Works, 146, 147
Rome Merchant Iron Mill, 146, 147
Roosevelt, Theodore, 145
Root, William Stanton, 118

Saratoga and Schenectady Railroad, 8, 38, 49, 51, 128
Schenectady, N.Y., 14, 58, 59
Schoharie Aqueduct, 58, 59
Schoharie Creek, 58
Selfridge, Thomas O., Jr., 145
Seward, William, 87, 88, 92, 106

Seymour, Henry, 13, 56
Seymour, Horatio, 132, 176n.34
Sheave (cog) wheels, 25
Sheffield, Joseph, 138, 140, 141
Sibley, Hiram, 135
Single-rail railroad, 24, 25
Slavery, 85, 86, 107
Softshell Democrats, 132, 134
Spann, Edward K., 118
Stationary engines, 25, 32
Steamboats, 112, 131, 165n.46
Steel rails, 147
Stephenson, Robert, 28, 29, 41, 118,
    162n.75
Stevens, Frank W., 42
Stevens, Samuel, 92
Stilling basin, 65, 71
Stockton and Darlington Railroad, 29
Stop and tax bill, 102
Strong, George Templeton, 77
Stryker, John, 122, 126
Sullivan, John T., 18, 61
Swivel (bogie) truck, 45, 48, 162n.75
Syracuse, N.Y., 9, 10

Taberg, N.Y., 100, 101
Tanner, Henry, 77, 78
Targetman, 8, 9
Texas annexation, 107
Thames Tunnel, 76, 168n.95
Thompson, J. Edgar, 127, 148
Thurston, Robert, 48
Tilden, Samuel, 142
Toledo, Ohio, 122, 131, 136
Track gauge, 40, 49
Traction, 25, 26, 30, 39
Tracy, Henry, 109, 112
Tracy, John, 52
Treatise on Railroads (Earle), 42
Tredgold, Thomas, 27, 45

Upper Canada peninsula, 131
U.S. Corps of Engineers, 38, 94, 112,
    127
Utica, N.Y., 54, 55, 57
Utica and Schenectady Railroad, 117

Van Brunt, Teunis, 121
Van Buren, Martin, 84, 85, 87, 108
Vanderbilt, Cornelius, 46, 142
Van Schaick, Myndert, 82, 90, 91
Visible Hand, The (Chandler), 126

Ward, John D., 92
War of 1812, 5
Washington, D.C., 69
Water commissioners, 62, 68, 69, 71–74,
    80–83, 86, 88, 92
Weed, Thurlow, 85, 86
Westchester County, 62, 82, 83
Western (Town of), N.Y., 133
Westminister Review, 112
Weston, William, 82
West Point (U.S. Military Academy), 36,
    66, 127, 173n.38
West Point Foundry, 29, 36, 42–44, 48
Whig Party, 86, 88, 90, 92, 97, 107, 132
Whistler, George W., 126, 127, 148
White, Canvass, 11–14, 71, 72, 82
White, John, Jr., 48
Wilkinson, John, 131, 134
Wilmot Proviso, 107
Wood, Nicholas, 25–27
Wright, Benjamin, xvii, 3, 4, 6, 10, 11,
    13, 14, 16–24, 27, 82, 87, 148
Wright, Silas, 106, 107
Wurts, Maurice, 18
Wurts, William, 18

Yankee Invasion, 3
Young, William C., 8, 49, 117, 118